ACTUAL PRAISE FOR THE INDIE CRED TEST
(AND HENRY OWINGS)

"[Owings is] the Renaissance Man lurking in the shadows of the underground rock Renaissance."

—LA TIMES

"Highly recommended as superior toilet reading for masochists who like music too much."

—MOJO

"Pointlessly insular and gut-bustingly hilarious, sacred-cow slaughterhouse Chunklet magazine compiled thousands of takedowns into this 192-page opus of pure passion and bile. None of your friends – or their record collections – are safe from editor Henry Owings."

—SPIN (NAMED ONE OF THE 10 BEST MUSIC BOOKS OF 2011)

"The book is super packed with yuks...the book is mostly very funny and worth buying."

—VICE.COM

"You don't get extra credit for owning more than one copy of Radiohead's latest humcore opus. How do we know? By testing ourselves with this encyclopedic, tongue-in-Will-Oldham's-bearded-cheek series of indie rock quizzes."

—ENTERTAINMENT WEEKLY

"Every time you flip through the book you'll find some new piece of minutiae that will have you laughing out loud."

—THE AGIT READER

"The truth is, there are not very many people writing this style of satirical culture book anymore."

—SLUG MAGAZINE

"Something laugh-out-loud funny pops up nearly every four or five sentences."

—BLURT ONLINE

"*The Indie Cred Test* is the most dense expression of an unnecessarily self-obsessed culture you may ever see."

—THE DAILY SWARM

"Henry Owings has been fearlessly and amusingly taking the piss out of rock'n'roll for nearly 20 years."

—PITCHFORK

A PERIGEE BOOK
PUBLISHED BY THE PENGUIN GROUP
PENGUIN GROUP (USA) INC.
375 HUDSON STREET, NEW YORK, NEW YORK 10014, USA

Penguin Group (Canada), 90 Eglinton Avenue East, Suite 700, Toronto,
Ontario M4P 2Y3, Canada (a division of Pearson Penguin Canada Inc.)
Penguin Books Ltd., 80 Strand, London WC2R 0RL, England
Penguin Group Ireland, 25 St. Stephen's Green, Dublin 2, Ireland
(a division of Penguin Books Ltd.)
Penguin Group (Australia), 250 Camberwell Road, Camberwell,
Victoria 3124, Australia (a division of Pearson Australia Group Pty. Ltd.)
Penguin Books India Pvt. Ltd., 11 Community Centre,
Panchsheel Park, New Delhi—110 017, India
Penguin Group (NZ), 67 Apollo Drive, Rosedale, Auckland 0632,
New Zealand (a division of Pearson New Zealand Ltd.)
Penguin Books (South Africa) (Pty.) Ltd., 24 Sturdee Avenue, Rosebank,
Johannesburg 2196, South Africa

Penguin Books Ltd., Registered Offices:
80 Strand, London WC2R 0RL, England

While the author has made every effort to provide accurate telephone
numbers, Internet addresses, and other contact information at the time of
publication, neither the publisher nor the author assumes any responsibility
for errors, or for changes that occur after publication. Further, the publisher
does not have any control over and does not assume any responsibility for
author or third-party websites or their content.

PUBLISHING HISTORY
Chunklet Industries first trade paperback edition / Spring 2011
Perigee second trade paperback edition / September 2012

ISBN: 978-0-399-15980-0

PRINTED IN THE UNITED STATES OF AMERICA

10 9 8 7 6 5 4 3 2 1

Most Perigee books are available at special quantity discounts
for bulk purchases for sales promotions, premiums, fund-raising,
or educational use. Special books, or book excerpts, can also
be created to fit specific needs.
For details, write: Special Markets, Penguin Group (USA) Inc.,
375 Hudson Street, New York, New York 10014.

ALWAYS LEARNING   PEARSON

WARRANTY AND DISCLAIMER

PLEASE READ THE FOLLOWING CLOSELY

The entities described herein as comprising the first party (also referred to hereafter, interchangeably as "You," "Reader," "User," "Initiate," "Cred-Seeker," "Flagrant Ass-Kisser," or "Julian") agree that the entities described herein as comprising the second party (also referred to hereafter as "Publisher," "Sugar Daddy," "Baby-Killer," "Captain Money-Pants," or "Amorphous Cabal") have entered into a non-binding (and ultimately completely fictional) agreement. This agreement is subject to cancellation, suppression, modification and/or molestation without notification, at which time your physical assets, including your biological form as well as those of your parents, pets and children, shall be liquidated and sold to the Chinese in order to cover the judge's Camaro payments. The first party certifies that you are an individual (i.e., not a corporation, agent, band manager, Scientologist or Freegan). Approved use of the publication is to determine a rough approximation of your Credentials (hereafter referred to as "Cred") only. The first party is responsible for any and all charges (e.g., ridicule, banishment, excessive mocking, judgment, stern talking-tos, beatings about the face and chest) associated with reading and absorbing information disseminated via the publication into your psyche. You are also responsible for obtaining and conforming to all necessary content-related suggestions designed to improve, negate, enhance or deplete your standing within a respective scene, clique, 'hood, schoolyard, food court, practice warehouse, radio station transmission shanty or other means of adaptation necessary to glean Cred. In purchasing, borrowing, reading, trying to get laid at a party by talking about, positing a review of (whether true or simply an attempt to make one's self feel better about their own real lack of Cred and/or ability to score with attractive members of the opposite/same sex without the promise of money, goods, and/or services being exchanged), or otherwise using this publication, the first party agrees not to restrict or inhibit any other user from using, enjoying, or grossly misapplying the principles espoused within this publication as that is station only allowed to the second party. Don't get too big for your Cred-britches, Cred-Seeker. The first party also agrees not to: overuse, wrongly attribute, or erroneously distort any hilarious quips from this publication (which applies to any and all sexual references, nicknames, hateful-but-remarkably accurate generalizations, scenester propaganda, "text speak," Pig Latin, or any deliciously offensive comments pertaining to Cred); solicit other readers to become members of or contribute money to any rival credibility-defining service or competing social organization, as Captain Money-Pants didn't get that name through charity work; impersonate any person, entity, musician, poet, bartender, writer/director of any one-man show, participant in any after-party gang bang, or management-level employee of a food co-op, or otherwise falsely state their affiliation with any applicable Cred-bearing person or entity; disguise yourself to thwart the second party's detection processes; and/or attempt to gain unauthorized access to the master Cred data set, which you could totally never find because it's hidden so well, but if you could find it would *totally* make you the cock-of-the-walk and a king among losers. For the purposes of this Agreement, "losers" shall include, without limitation, persons you wouldn't be caught dead with at a Lightning Bolt concert, major asswads, and/or subscribers to *Paste* magazine. You agree that you will not use the publication, including any information provided therein and all related miscellany, for any "uncool" purpose (defined as "any purpose used for the level of self-promotion that befits a fallen-from-grace child actor"). The second party, at its sole and absolute discretion, shall determine whether any information transmitted or heard around town violates this provision. You may not use any material from this publication in connection with any other book, magazine, e-zine, blog, vlog, Tweet, video, wax-cylinder, vinyl b-side etching, or pamphlet that contains or is associated with information or content prohibited by this section. Use of this publication constitutes consent by the first party to any monitoring measures (whether manual, electronic, or old-fashioned "peein'-in-a-cup"-style) that the second party deems necessary to determine Cred levels or compliance with any of the conditions outlined in this section. Should the second party choose to provide reader-based services (such as in-house Cred assessment, categorization, pointing-and-laughing, etc.), you will be required to provide certain information about yourself. You agree to provide true, accurate and complete information about yourself. Misrepresentation, deliberate or otherwise, will result in the nullification of all Cred and the immediate confiscation of any second-hand denim jackets, Lomo™-brand cameras, Converse™-brand footwear, Criterion Collection™ DVDs, original copies of the *Touch and Go* or *Ulysses Speaks!* zine(s), silkscreen materials, limited-release cassettes, books about architecture, first-pressing funk or garage rock 45s, and musical instruments other than the flute or autoharp. Additionally, male transgressors will be forcibly shaven clean. Dem's the brakes. The first party acknowledges and agrees that the second party (and all parties that the second party has over for dinner or otherwise deems worthy to be "in on the action") reserves the right to, and may from time to time, laugh its bound-and-numbered ass off at any and all examples explained or revealed by others which make you look worse than you did before use of the publication. There's nothing funnier than hazing a would-be scenester — it's so funny to watch the tears smear their eyeliner. During monitoring, behaviors may be examined, recorded, copied, and used for authorized purposes in accordance with the Privacy Policy that we just made up and don't have to show you. It changes to fit the situation. Further, the second party has no obligation to monitor the effectiveness of stated credibility algorithms, which are probably right anyway and yes, your Cred probably is that weak. Don't be a crybaby. You can't win 'em all, and it was only a matter of time before you found out that your parents, significant others, friends, employers, grade school teachers and clergy were only making you feel better when they said they liked you. If they just can't stop whining about it, the first party is entitled to a review (appeal) of any determination of their cred. To obtain a review, you or your authorized representative should call our Member Services Department (which can be accessed using the telephone number for any US governing agency, including the Franklin Mint) and ask for either "the head cheese" or "the Honky in charge." Verbal or written requests for review of the adverse determination must be communicated, mailed or delivered within one-hundred eighty (180) days following receipt of the adverse determination. Notice of a determination will be sent within three-thousand (3,000) days following receipt of your request or such longer period as may be required if you live in a location that is not within walking distance of the publisher. If you do not agree with such determination, you have the right to file a second request for review. That request will be subsequently thrown in bottom cage of a parrot named Chumley. Furthermore, the second party reserves the right at all times to parlay any observed embarrassing travails and/or deplorable anecdotes inspired by the misinterpretation of this publication's content into a series of low-budget comedy sketches entitled Kip Hipster: Dapper in Denim, in whole or in part, while laughing all the way to the Bank (of Cred). The first party understands that by using this publication, you may be exposed to Copy, Instructions, Comparisons, Illustrations, Marginalia, Saturnalia, and/or Genitalia that are offensive, indecent, objectionable, brutally true, biased, sobering, slanted, enchanted, and/or possibly surgically-enhanced. Insofar as the first party and the Amorphous Cabal have agreed that the content of this book does not dictate a course of action, Amorphous Cabal is legally insulated from all liability resulting from said publication's actionable passages and/or poorly-rendered illustrations. At no time is the Initiate bound to follow any of the publication's rules except as they explicitly relate to the acquisition of Cred (also referred to as The Ability to Hang Out With Your Favorite Band After Its Show Without Lapsing Into Awkward, Grinning Silences), unless commanded to by The Band (the one you're trying to do drugs with after the show, or the Robbie Robertson vehicle) or Friends of the Amorphous Cabal (hereafter referred to as unpaid contributors and/or people the Publisher once booked on a tour). This contract is neither implied nor stated. You probably just dreamed it. Either way, you can't sue us. The publication is authored by the Sugar Daddy and its conspiring network of like-minded denizens and contains material that is derived in whole or in part from material supplied and owned the Amorphous Cabal and other sources. Such material is protected by copyright, trademark, David Lee Roth, Bun E. Carlos, and applicable laws, but you would probably way rather not cross a pair of angry Labradoodles, 'cuz that shit can get nasty. Seriously. All of the affection can get a little cloying. You may not modify, copy, reproduce, republish, upload, post, transmit, publicly display, prepare derivative works based on, mimic, make PowerPoint presentations based on, parody, misinterpret or otherwise discuss in any way any material from the publication, including but not limited to supplemental special-edition re-releases such as *The Big Book of Cred: Coloring Book Edition* or *The Big Book of Cred for Dummies* (English or Spanish editions.) You may, however, utilize material from the service for your personal, non-commercial use only, provided you keep intact all copyright and other proprietary notices and provide "hella props" in instances where advice from this book totally hooks you up and shit. Information in this publication is provided "AS IS" without warranty of any kind, either express or implied, including, but not limited to, the implied warranties of merchantability, fitness for a particular purpose, or non-infringement. We do not guarantee that you will be satisfied, nor satiated by said book, but that is because you probably grew up in a household that only listened to classic rock and you are slow on the latest trends. Some jurisdictions do not allow the exclusion of implied warranties, so the above exclusion may not apply to you although a sound beating is still not entirely out of the question. The data set forth herein is for informational purposes only, and no warranty is made that the information is error-free. Please note that once you have read this publication, either by looking over the shoulder of the guy on the bus or because it was in the bathroom at a party you went to or by your convenience or by actually purchasing it, you may have influenced your Cred. We accept no responsibility for the content, products and/or services provided and the influence on your life unless the result is favorable, in which case you owe it all to us. Information may be changed or updated without notice. Someone might come into your room when you are sleeping and write something in it when you are not looking which totally changes the meaning and intention of the publisher, or someone might rip out a page or get pizza stains on it, but that is not our fucking problem. We have no obligation to update information presented in the publication (unless funds are running low in Captain Money-Pants' off-shore accounts, in which case subsequent volumes may be deemed necessary and entirely appropriate, not that we're justifying that to you, Cred-wad), so information contained herein may be out of date at any given time (and, admittedly, it probably was at the time of printing). We may also make improvements and/or changes in the products and/or programs described in this information at any time and without notice *(like when you're sleeping, motherfucker)*. Important risk factors could cause actual Cred results and other future Cred-related events to differ materially from those estimated by the publication, including failure to achieve desired sperm rate increases and/or profitable Cred growth due to significant competition, reputational issues or other factors in key geographic markets where cool ass motherfuckers are concentrated; unanticipated increases in Cred costs (including increased Cred utilization, increased hair gel costs, increases resulting from unfavorable changes in contracting or re-contracting with good labels, changes in guys you hang around with, or that new girl who is kinda quiet but real cool, or membership in a Cred-adverse group like the NBA, PBA or NHL; as well as changes in high-end drug cost estimates due to the necessary extensive poor judgment that is used in picking out a dealer, the considerable variability inherent in such estimates, and the sensitivity of such estimates to changes in Cred payment patterns and changes in Cred cost trends); and the ability to reduce administrative expenses while maintaining targeted levels of service and operating performance. Other important risk factors include, but are not limited to: the ability to improve relations with readers while taking actions to reduce pizza and beer costs; the ability to successfully implement multiple strategic and operational initiatives simultaneously, or write 80 articles in one month; reduced levels of investment from parents and friends income due to low interest rates; adverse government regulations on publishing, changes in size, weight, sexual dysfunction, Cred experience in key markets; our ability to integrate, simplify, and enhance our existing information technology systems and platforms to keep pace with changing Cred regulatory needs; the outcome of various litigation and regulatory matters, including litigation and ongoing reviews of business practices by various regulatory authorities; and increases in Cred costs or Group Cred affiliation claims resulting from any acts of terrorism, epidemics or other extreme events. Under no circumstances will the second party be liable in any way for damages ensuing, including but not limited to liability for errors, omissions, or for any loss or damage of any kind incurred as a result of the misuse of any Communication espoused, transmitted, revealed, confessed, acknowledged, uttered, proclaimed, divulged, imparted, imbued or otherwise written via the publication. Save that shit for your next fake slip-and-fall lawsuit lest you incur the wrath of the Baby-Killer, which ain't pretty. In fact, the first party admits that the second party should just come over and have one big party, to be held at a site of mutual agreement, taking into account that Gubby's place is bigger while Mary has the keg, or at a neutral site, perhaps J&M Tap or other equidistant dive bar with "reasonable" (equal to or less than two dollars for the least expensive beer available, adjusted for inflation in New York or Los Angeles) pricing, and further, if combined party should remain on private property (either of the above-mentioned private property sites), any beer or other alcohol bought should be split among those partaking without regard to previous party affiliation and pot and/or any other illicit legal prescription drug or illegal drug distribution to be determined at the sole discretion of the owner of such substances. When reading this publication, please be certain that you are in a comfortable (preferably fetal) position; are not currently intoxicated, tweaking, tripping, sleepwalking or over-medicated; or are prone to behavior which may compromise your personal safety. Do not write your name, phone number, postal or e-mail address, passwords, or any other personally-identifying information on the inside or outside covers of this publication, as the microchips we've implanted in your scalp are already tracking you just fine. If reading the publication inspires palpable feelings of shame or self-derision, calmly close the book, piss in your own mouth, throw yourself down a flight of stairs, and resume reading. Readers under the age of 18 must have parental consent before reading the publication. Did you ask your parents for permission? If you did, you now have zero Cred. Don't be so gullible, and stop being such a pussy. The publication is not recommended as source material for research papers, book reports, parenthetical references or bathroom reading. No warranties or commitments shall be considered binding upon the writers, editors, typesetters, printers, publishers, their imaginary friends, and/or booty calls. All statements in this book have been evaluated by a crack research team appointed by the second party and are in no way intended to bear resemblance to any individuals living or dead, real or imagined, or those pilfered from a subordinate's notebook and used without permission or credit. If you believe any statements do bear resemblance to you, you should probably visit www.dictionary.com and search for the term "narcissism." Should there be any dispute as to the accuracy of any facts or statements in this publication, or should any claim harm caused by inclusion in the publication, the second party remains indemnified from litigation through the magic of impenetrable legalese and a smokescreen of barely-intelligible threats lobbied by the second party's chainsaw-toting neighbor Jesse. (Note: Jesse will be compensated for any service by means of grain alcohol in an amount not less than his body weight, at the expense of the first party.) Should apparently damaged parties seek recourse in the form of an out-of-court settlement for said damages, the second party will provide those parties with favors including but not limited to paper hats, cake (white with chocolate icing only), personalized paper napkins designed by the second party, and a choice of three songs to be determined at random via the shuffle feature on the second party's iPhone. Upon receipt of this publication the first party is expected to adhere to all international copyright laws in reproducing portions of said book for the amusement of friends (hereafter referred to as Random People You Work With Or Are Trying To Bed) or online acquaintances (hereafter referred to Former Classmates and Ex-Girlfriends You're Stalking On Facebook). If sufficient cause is found to enforce intellectual property laws pursuant to dissemination of this book's copyrighted material, Random People You Work With Or Are Trying To Bed and Ex-Girlfriends You're Stalking On Facebook may be subject to fines (levied at the discretion of relevant municipal judges) as well as a potpourri of savage group beatings (levied at the discretion of the second party's friends not afraid to go to jail for killing a shameless thief with their bare fucking hands). Former Classmates are exempted under Sections IV and V of the Star Wars films. Still reading this shit? Wow, you *really* need a hobby. All Cred is not available in all areas and in many instances may be offered only through friends, older siblings, or other plan sponsors. Results not valid in Missouri, Utah, Kentucky, or Harford County, Maryland. Test results will be returned within a time frame inversely proportional to the number of bands-per-square-mile in the Initiate's home zip code. Initiates who have over two (2) years work experience in record stores, live music venues, independent cinemas, or college radio stations will receive a -10% handicap upon their final score (prior to any extra credit). Nothing in this publication should be construed as a solicitation or offer to purchase Cred. It must be earned. Got all that? Good, now please rise for our national anthem...

MEET THE STAFF

FROM LEFT TO RIGHT.

"LUSCIOUS" LUCY PENDANG
(Reception Intern)

Sweet as wine cooler pie, Lucy spends most of her time freelancing for photographers and internet photo sites. Her time at reception is mostly spent checking for bedbugs and complaining about Facebook on Facebook 11 hours a day. For a plus-sized woman with four fully formed nipples she makes an outstanding front piece for the organization, and if we could we would all get behind her various endeavors.

HENRY HERRICK
(Chief Operating Officer)

Mr. Herrick was an original member of the Chunklet staff when the magazine still had staples in it. He still recalls the time when he understood what was going on, and where he put last week's payroll. But things have changed. Yes, the music has changed...but not Henry! He still has on the same britches he wore to the scallop plate benefit for dummies last month. When asked what he loved most about the publishing industry, Henry humbly replied, "I like apples. Granny Smiths, Braeburns, even those upstart Jona-Golds. Hep." We'll miss you soon enough.

JASON MASK
(Interoffice Stress Regenerator)

The second Jason's coworkers are happy and feel secure with their jobs, he goes by each of their desks and helps them to remember that they can be fired, decapitated, or prison-shanked at any given moment. Dick.

TOBY TURDSTROM
(Accountant / Daydreamer)

Remember that scene in Dirty Dancing where everyone freaks out and starts grinding their naughty bits on each other like rabid teenagers? So does Toby. Also: accounting.

JACK "THE RIPPER" RIPLOUSKI
(Resident Shamus)

Jack always knows what is going on with everyone. If someone is ill, Jack is the first one to chime in that they might be actually visiting an aunt in Ft. Lauderdale, or when an interoffice romance is budding Jack is the first one to lay odds on the success. Although Jack doesn't say much he doesn't have to; as keeper of the internet passwords and controller of the security tapes and log books, he truly is our Big Brother silently watching over us and judging. It's probably all the work-jerk-juice he spills into the trash can under his desk all day that keeps him in such high spirits.

LI'L CRONCHY
(Fridge Nazi)

Cronchy is what doctors would describe as a "Super-Duper Fatty Fatpants." She monitors what goes in and out of the office refrigerator by way of her own gastrointestinal system. We once busted her shittingin the office restroom while barefoot and eating someone else's cheeseburger, and we won't let her live it down for shit. She also won't hesitate to reach her butt-scratching claws into your beverage and select a piece of ice to suckle on, so use a lid. Just an F.Y.I.

FAITH PROMISCUITY
(Senior Internal Auditor)

With a combined MBA/J.D. from Hamburger U. Technical Inst., Ms. Promiscuity came to us incredibly overqualified. Thankfully, she's done an excellent job dispelling our expectations. Her work with staff monitoring revolutionized several procedures for greater efficiency and increasing what she memorably termed "reconstitutionalized tea work decompliance." Also, revenue is up 12% in our past quarter (or so she claims). Hey, we hired her so we wouldn't have to figure out the math ourselves!

MARIE ST. BLISTER
(Internet Security)

Marie is responsible for making sure no one in the Chunklet office is surfing the wrong kind of porn (y'know, the kind that gives your computer viruses). Her iron pudgy fist on the Internet filters, as well her constant questioning of everyone else's patriotism, earns her the nickname "Star Spangled Blister." Also, her haircut is reminiscent of Jeff Beck's circa Blow By Blow, so her nickname may actually be "Jeff Beck." No one really talks to her enough to care.

DINKUS FLEBBINS
(Janitor)

The office commode's been running with duct tape and vacuum cleaner hose for three months, but by all means, Dinkus, drop by anytime to bitch that we're just writing about a bunch of drug-smokin' fancy boys and don't do no interviews with "The Nuge."

LARRYOLA COTTONFEATHER
(Receptionist)

Larryola Cottonfeather is a true Southern belle. She still talks like Penelope Pitstop even though no one's talked like that since the abolition of slavery, and she often brings some kind of English Fart Pudding and/or Onion Soufflé for lunch that's so offensively fetid that we all swear it's made up of decomposed feet. And onions.

ANONYMOUS
(Failed Blackmailer)

Thank you for not sending us anything truly dangerous in the mail. Although you are most likely an intern we fired or a vendor we neglected to pay, your threatening letters cut from local papers and magazines keep us in stitches all day long. Readers will note that the only reason we continue to publish is because you let us. We can tell by the jagged and harried way you cut out those words and assemble them into threatening sentences you are truly committed. We just wish you would put a little more DNA in there for us. *(Wink!)* We love you, buddy! Keep those letters coming and inspiring the whole darn staff!

PONCHO "PUNCHYA" VILANCHE
(Graphic Design Consultant)

With a background in prison economics and a foreground in blurry, oversaturated pastels, Poncho is every layout editor's best nightmare. Vector or raster? How about neither and gimme your fuckin' corn bread!

P. RICK SCHLONGSON
(Publishing Operations)

Rick is a total pro at his job, and nobody rocks the three-piece denim suit better, but he has not listened to any new music since 1976. He'll often ask interns if they've heard the groovy new Three Dog Night 45.

MAGDALENA DONG CHIANG-CHUKWUKAWUK
(Staple Shiner)

Fulfills Chunklet's industry obligation that all magazines must employ a beautiful, trilingual Afro-Asian with a bizarre fashion sense who refuses to speak to anyone in the office.

BLARNAMUS J. THROCKWHIPPLE IV
(Advisor)

The 68-year old heir to the Throckwhipple Mustard fortune, Blarny advises us to lay off the salsa, and to make loud noises in the presence of his 91-year old father.

SPARKLES SLAPSTEAK
(Part-Time Columnist / Former Groupie)

Originally hired to share great stories and anecdotes from her groupie days in the '60s, '70s and a few terribly misguided months in 2002. These days she wanders in drunk and turns in crumpled pieces of paper containing rants about her landlady, teaching her cat to use the toilet and how she was 'this close' to being in The GTO's.

THE INDIE CRED TEST

TYRONICUS MCMANIS
(Inside Sales)
An exchange student, Tyronicus hails from dreary Sconesborough-Pockmarkington in the U.K. where he got his toe-hold into the scene by forging an H1-B visa and landing a job at Last Gasp Records in Mexicali, CA. From there, he was able to parlay his distinctively crisp accent into lucrative voice-over work, which lasted until the economy went into ye old shitter recently. To those who'd judge him (and us) for taking a job away from a "real American," we'd like to remind you that he's a part of our ChunkAbroad training program, where talented bottom-feeders from all across the globe have a chance to learn "networking" skills in an international setting, free loading off of host families all across America, Africa and the techno-listening hellhole known as Europe. Take that, Nicholas Kristof!

BOOGSIE "GALT" DIMAGGIO
(Mail Room Intern)
Boogsie DiMaggio (no relation) is a twenty-something-year-old college student, currently going through the typical Ayn Rand obsession. He has a framed photo of Alan Greenspan at his desk, and carries a dog-eared copy of *Atlas Shrugged* everywhere he goes with nude pictures of Rush Limbaugh as bookmarks. He is happy to discuss objectivism with you, but only if you refrain from criticizing the gaping holes in the theory. He hopes one day to help eliminate big government, but until he can afford to, he's hoping for unemployment because, well, you gotta do what you gotta do.

DR. NED "NEEDLES" DEEDLES
(On-Call Doctor)
He handles everything from the common cold to over-the-counter steroid use. We cannot thank him enough for curing that episode of the slow clap that kept going around after our Bar League softball game was rained out three weeks in a row. He always knows what to say during amputations and is a whiz at Sudoku! Needles! Although his smiling face is the first and last one we see during the local anesthetic portion of our annual check-ups, he appears to all of us in the recollected nightmares we share in the lunchroom.

MARE JELLISON
(Real Estate Advisor)
Leasing half of Chunklet's corporate headquarters keeps Jellison on her sloppily manicured toes for half the year. The other half consists of soggy cereal lunches and 8-bit Nintendo cartridge-blowing challenges. Hey, it's a living.

FARI KERRELL
(Hipster Asian Chick)
We never checked out Fari's resume. We never checked out her references. But whatever, she's just awesome to have around. You always hope you'll be the person she'll make some played out and obviously insincere sexual innuendo to.

JIM "FLEX" WILSON
(Sports Ringer / Jars and Bottles)
While far from a musclehead, Jim works out daily and, as such, is like a '70s Lou Ferrigno compared to the rest of the pasty and flabby Chunklet staff. Jim is called in when staff members can't open bottles and jars, and is also the primary ringer when the Chunklet staff is asked to play any sport that requires athletic conditioning.

TARA NUÑEZ-MARTIN
(Project Manager)
After recovering last year from constant migraine headaches, sinus and allergy irritation, sudden onset clubfoot and "Faulty Torso," Tara has triumphed over her Johnson County, Kansas parents' wildest dreams. Without her, we never could have rebounded from missing a deadline by six months, since she had the doctor's notes to back it up.

ROGER "MIREPOIX" CRAPPERTON
(Microfische Archives)
Roger is obsessed with cooking shows on television, although he rarely eats anything other than Lebanon bologna sandwiches slathered with French's mustard. He regularly makes comments about food shows that are normally reserved for sporting events ("Did you see the way Iron Chef Flay came back last night?") and claims to be perfecting his own perfected recipe for mirepoix, which, of course, has been perfected for hundreds of years.

RANDALL "GREEN TEA" TOMPKINS
(Environmental Consultant)
In an attempt to be "green," Chunklet hired Randall. Several of his important suggestions (a copy machine powered by PBR, a machine that harnesses sarcasm into electricity, the ability to turn unrequested shitty band promo CDs into brand spankin' new Whirlyball scoops, a car that runs solely on Craig Finn's sweat) have yet to come to fruition, but he did start an office recycling program that, sadly, Paco, Pedro and Ramon don't use.

GWEN-BEN "OCEANIC FLIGHT 815" PUFFINBERGER
(Graveyard Shift Fact-Checker)
Ostensibly, Gwen-Ben (yes, he has a hyphenated first name) checks facts for the Chunklet team, but since the TV debut of Lost in September '04, Gwen-Ben hasn't done much but update his ridiculously detailed Lost blog, "Dharma Chameleon." While his theories about what the show means have changed from week to week, he is adamant in his belief that, at some point, the dude from To Catch A Predator will make an appearance and battle the Smoke Monster.

SCRATCH TUMBLEWEED
(Mail Room Overlord)
Scratch hasn't said a single word in this goddamned office in over five years, and would appreciate it if everyone would continue to fuck off.

COL. STERLING R. FOLEY
(Retired)
This ex-CIA operative first encountered the hipster underground in 1965, as he worked deep undercover in various hippie sects in order create the ideal rubber bullet. He then spent the next several decades producing and designing number station broadcasts, inadvertently making him an ambient/noise pioneer. He retired from active duty following the fall of the Soviet Union. He's also the original Toynbee Tiler, and recently produced the last three Morrissey albums, uncredited.

JEZ CELERADO
(Photo Retoucher)
Miss Celerado is currently on extended medical leave after we asked her to find the world's most unpleasant photo of G.G. Allin. Godspeed your recovery, Jez.

TRAVISTINA LEBLECH
("C" Org. Team Coordinator)
Having recently signed a trillion-year contract with Hen Ron Chunkard, Travistina is plenty busy around our offices. She's in charge of hooking subscribers and writers up to the FM (financial monitoring) meters, plus cleaning, oiling the Whirlyball carts to give H. Ron the competitive edge befitting his position. Also, silencing dissenters and union organizers is one of her favorite work-related hobbies. Travistina was also recently betrothed to Esmonondo LeBlech in a massive hipster wedding of 300 couples held at the 40 Watt Club and presided over by our feckless leader himself. (Esmonondo is currently posted to Calais on hip-missionary work, attempting to convince the French not to get up and dance while jazz performers are trying to play).

HIRAM JEOSEPHAT
(Subscriptions)
In his back corner closet of an office, Gordon is surrounded by piles and piles of old issues of *Crawdaddy, Hit Parader* and *Cat Fancy*. A one time mover and shaker in the underground Cleveland Performance Art scene, Gordon has written two books whose names are so offensive they can't even be printed in this bio. Gordon has never missed a day of work in his life and lives with his two cats Shitty-Pie and Blorgb.

CHET FRAMPTON
(Back Rub Specialist)
A veteran of dozens of Leo Buscaglia seminars, Chet is a key member of the team. Using his vast array of drug connections, Chet fuels us through many a late night semi-psychotic writing session as well as giving the office a general feel good vibe not seen around here since the Browns won the Super Bowl. Chet has only been sued for sexual harassment four times.

TITO "DANGLE BALLS" BRENNAN
(Custodial Services)
At 5'4", Chunklet's longtime janitor is a tight little bundle of joy, tears, drool, inexplicable odors, and sing-songy screams, and may or may not live in our service closet.

FRATRICK GILBAIR
(Freelance Illustrator)
Fratrick came to us after creating a new descender for the letter "R." I shit you negative, it's going to blow your goddamned mind. We could only fit in into the book like once, but man... when you see it. It's like, "Blammo! Who the fuck even cares about X-heights anymore?" For real. This motherfucker's gonna dump typography on its ass.

KAREN KRIEDERMANN
(Director of Superficial Optimism)
Karen always has, like, the craziest ring tones. This past week it was the opening guitar riff from "Bad To The Bone" by George Thorogood. That's actually a step up from that month she was obsessed with *Pulp Fiction*. She gets a *lot* of calls. And one can only suffer through "Chill that bitch out!" so many times. I mean, that doesn't even make sense as a ring tone.

VLADIMIR "THE HUMAN THUMB" BLOTSKI
(Accounts Receivable)
To quote Vlad, "Just pay your bill, okay? Okay."

CRAMPOON SPLIFF
(Regional Editor, Mid-Atlantic)
Nobody has actually seen this guy around since he blew through his last three deadlines. But for some reason, his Netflix account has been redirected to the Chunklet offices. Cramps is out there somewhere not watching season three of Gilmore Girls.

GRAIG HORSLEY
(Graphic Production)
Greg can only express his opinion about things by making reference to fonts. He once sheepishly muttered that the latest Wilco album was "totally Arial Narrow."

RICARDO JEFFERS
(Odd Time Signatures / Spiritual Support)
Ricardo's master's degree in musicology at the University of West South Carolina included hours of John Cage-style aural experiments, which stripped him of his ability to be in any way accessible or friendly. His musical vision guides Chunklet through its roughest, most sycophant-infested waters.

HELEN ST. MOUNT
(Graphic Design / Free Jazz fan)
Helen is from New York, so naturally she goes on and on about how she can't get a good piece of pizza anywhere near the office. Helen hasn't figured out why her turn to play music on the stereo is when everyone is at lunch.

RONNIE RAY RILEY
(Vending Machine Guy)
Ronnie Ray, who moonlights as the acting assistant gun polisher for the local Militia, can frequently be heard screaming things like "Who put goddamned pesetas in this thing? DON'CHALL GOT 'MURICAN MONEY? Jesus Christ!"

DINA ARBUTUS
(Mayor)
We didn't know we needed a Mayor, and we sure as hell don't recall electing one. We also don't remember Dina at all either. Seriously. Not one of us can ever recall seeing her. But according to Foursquare she's the Mayor of the Chunklet Offices because she checks in here at least once a day. Even on days when the offices are closed.

GIL FORLACHES
(Senior Senior Account Manager)
Gil manages accounts the Old Fashioned way: by drinking at least three Old Fashioneds before every client meeting. Frequently takes "lunch" breaks where he disappears for three hours, only to return with six new clients and breath that could degrease a tractor engine. Don't like it? Go fuck yourself, Junior! He's passed kidney stones bigger than your commission checks.

DR. "DIS" SPENCE NOSTRUM, PH.D.
(Clinical Psychologist)
Dr. Nostrum has been a critical ally when the need for doctor-approved medications arise. Slightly more than just a human-pill dispensary, Dr. Nostrum's compulsory talk-therapy sessions and staff retreats have debatably lifted the psyches of our workers, while also providing senior management with information on muckrakers revealed during the "unburdening" coal-walking sessions.

JOLENE PINDERWELL
(Forensic Accounting)
Though her first love is the numbers game, Jolene is relentlessly addicted to crime-scene television dramas. She's been trying for years without luck to develop a catch-phrase for whenever she resolves bookkeeping inconsistencies. Her best so far: Windmilling her arms around in Townsendian tribute, yelling, "WE WON'T GET FOOLED AGAIN!"

CHIP SCHLITZFORD
(Trade Show Associate)
Chip's assistance and backline support have been assets to all manner of Chunklet-approved events. Indeed, whether unloading cases of "Captain Henry's Special Tarter-Q Sauce" to unsuspecting grocers, or selling t-shirts at the merch table in the bathroom, his experience "making change" as an Obama '08 intern has really come in handy when those Ben Franks and Magic Jacksons start to fly in. (Full disclosure: we did have some minor unpleasantness with Chip due to some missing hoodies and counterfeit fifties, but after a unwritten telepathic warning, H.R. now considers the matter closed).

"MADDY"
(Warehouse / Fork Lift Operator)
Look, Maddy has a great attitude and work ethic, as well as possessing the appropriate class of license for this type of work. And we've never really figured out whether it's supposed to be "Matty" and somehow the name got confused over the years, or whether "Maddy" is short for Madelyn or something like that. We really couldn't tell you more, and we're sure as hell not going to ask, either.

CLOBBERT SLAMERSON
(Animal Husbandry)
We have video surveillance footage where Clobbert belched on every phone in the office. If he likes you, he only does it to the earpiece.

MINDY (OR MAYBE IT'S "WENDY") "SOMETHING"
(Assistant Receptionist)
She's dumb as a bag of hair. She has a god-awful dye job. She types 9 wpm. NINE! We're not sure what she does all day, except that she logs a lot of phone time. But she wears tank tops and mini-skirts to work, in the middle of December, and some of our executives find goose bumps "vulnerable... and sexy."

LEMONGELO FARNSWORTH
(Permissions)
Lemongelo has been a Wikipedia volunteer editor for over a decade, and is responsible for the fact that the site's entry on Sevendust is longer than its entry on World War II.

MARSHALL GOGGINS
(Regulator)
If you've got a problem with us, go to "Sheriff Marsh." If you stain his all-white suit, imitate his accent, or say anything about his mustache, that's your ass.

YVES CELINE
(Envoy to Quebec Emeritus)
During the fallout from our "Things We Hate About Canada" thread, we brought in Yves as a diplomat. He wasn't much help, and we did not part amicably. Yves, if you're reading this, you're welcome to drop in, rant incoherently in French and pass out in our office fish tank whenever.

THE INDIE CRED TEST

DEDICATED TO THE
LOVING MEMORY OF
JERRY FUCHS

1974–2009

PHOTO: BRIAN MCCALL

THE
INDIE
CRED TEST

OTHERWISE KNOWN AS...

EVERYTHING YOU NEED TO KNOW ABOUT
KNOWING EVERYTHING YOU NEED TO KNOW

ANOTHER PRODUCT
FROM THE BRAIN OF

CHUNKLET INDUSTRIES

QUALITY LITERARY
ACHIEVEMENTS

A PERIGEE BOOK

THE INDIE CRED TEST

PRINTED WITH 100% AMERICAN PRIDE BY A PROUD PEOPLE RIGHT HERE ON AMERICAN SOIL.

FROM THE STAFF AT CHUNKLET INDUSTRIES, ATLANTA, GEO. U.S.A.

PRODUCED AND APPROVED BY NOTED AUTHORITIES.

PLEASE READ THESE WORDS CAREFULLY: WE'RE ALL IN THIS TOGETHER. EXCEPT YOU. YOU'RE A DICK.

SECOND EDITION. INTENDED FOR ALL SKILL LEVELS.

ANOTHER QUALITY PRODUCT. HOME OF COUNTLESS SUPERIOR LITERARY ACHIEVEMENTS.

EVERYTHING YOU NEED TO KNOW ABOUT KNOWING EVERYTHING YOU NEED TO KNOW

From Mustaches to Mirrored Shades:
Why Irony Just Makes You Look Like a Dick

Sports for the Physically Weak

Surviving Your Lo-Fi Phase with Dignity

Tax Law for the Crust-Punk

101 Things to Do Instead of "Gettin' the Band Back Together"

Choosing the Right Font for Your Death Metal Band

Living with a Hybrid Owner

Everything You Wanted to Know About Hip-Hop
(But Were Afraid to Axe)

Stop Being a Jerk and Start Being an Asshole

Feigning Disdain for Everything

The Un-sanctimonious Vegan and Other Myths

Improv for Funerals

Thinking Twice About Your Podcast

So You've Resigned Yourself to Learning The Tambourine

Saying Goodbye to Money:
The Beginner's Guide to Documentary Filmmaking

Stoplights and Cigarettes: What You Need to Know

Our Bodies, Our Vintage Turntables, Ourselves

Erasing Your Rockabilly Phase

The Path of Mainstream Resistance

Sarcasm for the Deaf

Judging Me, Judging You: Dispatches from a Record Store Clerk

This Thing Smells Funny: Figuring Out What's on Your Clothes

PBR vs. NPR: How to Be Cheap and Intellectual

Blind, Black and Old: An Authenticity Primer

TABLE OF CONTENTS

A WORD FROM OUR LEADER 10
A MESSAGE TO THE HIPSTER IN AMERICA 13
THE EVOLUTION OF THE HIPSTER 15
THE BRIEF HISTORY OF COOL 16
TEST INSTRUCTIONS 18
GENERAL PROFILE 20

SECTION I
THE X, Y AND Z OF WHATEVER: FEEDING, CLOTHING AND LIVING WITH THE AFFECTED

CHAPTER 1: GENERAL LIFESTYLE 24
Acceptable Reasons To Get Married 27
Hipster or Homo? 28
Acceptable Reasons To Have Children 29
Are You Raising a Hipster Baby? 33
Evaluating Your Partner 34
Cred Indulgences 35
Recreational Substance Evaluation 36
Home Life 39

CHAPTER 2: WARDROBE 40
Getting a Tattoo (flowchart) 47
Wardrobe Checklist 48

CHAPTER 3: HEALTH & FITNESS 50
Acceptable Reasons To Quit Drinking 55

CHAPTER 4: FOOD & DRINK 56

SECTION II
JUSTIFIED & ANCIENT: GETTING PAID. GETTING LAID. GETTING OLD.

CHAPTER 5: CAREER & OCCUPATION 64
Acceptable Reasons To Get a Divorce 70
Online Music Journalist Application Form 71

CHAPTER 6: OLDER CRED 80
Acceptable Reasons To Commit Suicide 86

CHAPTER 7: NOTORIETY 88

CHAPTER 8: NETWORK & SCHMOOZE 92

SPECIAL ADVERTISING SUPPLEMENT 96

CHAPTER 9: EXTRACURRICULAR ACTIVITIES 100
Cred Proximity 104

SECTION III
FORGET HIGH SCHOOL. REMEMBER THE SCENE. IT'S ALL ABOUT THE MUSIC.

CHAPTER 10: MUSIC AFFINITY 108
Cred Test For Girls 119
Genre Test 120
Death Metal Quiz 121
Ultra Impossible Band Trivia 126

CHAPTER 11: SHOWS, GIGS & CONCERTS 122

CHAPTER 12: MUSIC ACTIVITY 130
Should You Be In a Band? (flowchart) 137
The Live Cred Score And Your Entertainment Dollar 139
So, You Guys Wanna Jam? 142
Multiple Choice 143

CHAPTER 13: DJ CULTURE 144
Hip-Hop Checklist 149

CHAPTER 14: RECORD COLLECTION 150
Acceptable Reasons To Sell Your Record Collection 156

SECTION IV
UNLOADING MORE IRONY UPON THE SHELVES: ARTS & ENTERTAINMENT

CHAPTER 15: CINEMA 164
Movie Checklist 170

CHAPTER 16: LITERATURE 172
Author Checklist 178

SECTION V
WRAPPING IT UP: HOW TO KNOW A LOT WHILE LEARNING ABSOLUTELY NOTHING

CALCULATING YOUR SCORE 184
TERMS OF AGREEMENT 186
WARRANTY AND DISCLAIMER 187
MEET THE STAFF 188

the Chunklet Industries Testing Staff

CONCEPT/EDITOR
Henry H. Owings

SENIOR CONTRIBUTORS
Chad Baker
Guion Bentley
Shane Gillis

ILLUSTRATOR
Jesse LeDoux

MAJOR CONTRIBUTORS
Emerson Dameron
Daniel Del Ben
Derek Fricano
Randy Harward
Neil Jendon
Eric Rovie
John Wenzel

ART DIRECTORS
Aaron James Draplin
Henry H. Owings

ADDITIONAL DESIGN
Nick Hollomon
Scott Sosebee

EDITORS/PROOFREADERS
Molly Ellis
Arthur Johnson
Benn Ray
Jonathan G. Williams

LEGAL COUNSEL
Lisa Fortune Moore

CONTRIBUTORS

Mike Appelstein	Thomas Davies	Ben Johnson	Stoat Mixen	Pete Schreiner
Matt Armstrong	Jeremy DeVine	Matty Karas	Ross Morgan	John Shields
Ben Arnold	Marah Eakin	Kris Kasperowski	Aaron Mullan	Ethan Stanislawski
J. Christopher Arrison	Jeffrey Ellinger	Kip Kelgard	Dan Nadolny	Mark Stelmach
Michael J. Barber II	Michael Faloon	Kim Kelly	Amanda Nichols	Ken Taylor
Maryann Bayer	Ian Fitzpatrick	Dryw Keltz	Ashley Nix	Jack Teague
Jeffrey Bergstrom	Michael T. Fournier	John Kenyon	Dan Norris	Brian Teasley
Stuart Berman	Gregory Franklin	Alex Koenig	Adam Oliansky	Matthew Tomich
Chris Bilheimer	Aron Gagliardo	Mark Konwinski	Brendan O'Sullivan	Monica Topping
Steve Birmingham	Leor Galil	Molly Lambert	Chris Pacifico	Aaron Turney
Ben Blackwell	Patrick Gough	Alex LaRoche	Tony Party	Mark Von Frankenstine
Nick Blakey	Jason Graham	Mike LaVella	Andrew Pearson	Dr. Jonathan Waks
Chris Brooks	P. William Grimm	Aaron Lefkove	Leonard Pierce	Rob Warmowski
Tom Brookes	Meseret Haddis	Jaron Loggins	Andrew Pope	Jeff Waye
Paul Bruno	Tim Hinely	Mike Madrigale	Benn Ray	Christopher R. Weingarten
Christian Campagna	Marc Horton	Don Malkemes	Patrick Reed	Curt Wells
Billy Carter	Erin Huntley	Bob Massey	Adam Reach	John White
Frank Cassidy	Wm. Huntley	Heath McFarland	Seb Roberts	Terrence White
Vincent Chung	Seth Jabour	Jeff McLeod	Levi Rubeck	Pete Wilkins
Ian Cone	Johnny Jimenez	Sean McTiernan	BJ Rubin	Jonathan G. Williams
Jasmine Cook	Myke Johns	Steven Mirkin	Vern Schleyer	James Wilson

...and the many nameless people that posted anonymously to chunklet.com

A WORD FROM OUR LEADER

Oh, hello. Come on in. Can I interest you in a glass of water? Perhaps a refreshing Fresca? Please, have a seat.

I'd personally like to welcome you to the newest product to roll off the assembly line at Chunklet Industries: *The Indie Cred Test*. Originally thought up by me during a hunting weekend with some old college buddies, the entirety of the test was written and rewritten and re-rewritten by our exhaustively huge staff. Our goal? To give you, the reader, a crystal clear glimpse into the inner realm of cool. Sure, you can spend your entire life accumulating stuff: memories, photographs, downloads, tour laminates, notches on your bed post…. But why take all that time out of your hectic schedule? Let the fully licensed and bonded staff at Chunklet Industries *(that would be us)* afford the masses *(that would be you)* the ability to get a leg up on the competition from the comfort of your own home.

There's no doubt in my mind you're going to find yourself amazed, titillated and (perhaps even) bewildered by *The Indie Cred Test*. Embrace your knowledge, and please, don't be ashamed by your shortcomings. Because, let's face it, you can't become a graceful swan (read: "cool") without being a black duckling (read: "loser") first. Start off with any of the 16 chapters, invite failure and learn from your mistakes. Give the lessons time to sink in. You can't be expected to become fully vested with your cred in a few days. For some people, it takes weeks. Some people, it takes months. Then there are those who will never fully achieve their cred. And well, we feel sad for them, but really, screw those losers. Screw them all! Screw them right in the face.

Now, there's one very important thing my father taught me. One thing that is so important that he'd tell it to me every night when he was tucking me between the sheets and reading me bedtime stories. One thing that was so pivotal to Chunklet Industries that it's on our welcome mat as you walk into our 142,000 square foot factory. One thing that is so critical that it's drilled into our employees' heads during our trust building retreats. One thing that our customer service reps greet customers with when they pick up the phone. Are you dying to know what that one thing is?

Indie cred is serious business.

And, after my years in the family business, I would take that one step farther: Indie cred is *really really* serious business.

Way back, back before I was born, when my father started this company, how would anybody know that Chunklet Industries would be the multinational conglomerate it is today? My father didn't have an easy time of building the family empire. I clearly remember countless nights when he would burn the midnight oil trying to keep business afloat. But let's be frank, the '70s and '80s were a kickass time to build a company and with our family's signature tenacity and grit, Chunklet Industries flourished. And then, about seven years ago, shortly after squeaking through community college, my father brought me in as CEO. However, when I took over the company for my ailing father, things were far from perfect. No, no, no. Actually, I was required to do things. Things like think of stuff…the kind of stuff that would keep us in business. If I knew that work was going to be this hard, I would've actually stuck around and graduated. But, live and learn. Am I right?

And hey, I think the business has done pretty okay with me running it. I mean, heck, look at the size of this boardroom! It's freakin' huge! And look at this chair I'm sitting in. I bet you it cost more than a nice used car. Or what I'd imagine normal people spend on a used car. But yeah, I bet I could throw a sweet kegger in here! And *then* let's watch the cops shut it down! No way.

Recent years have been quite a challenge to Chunklet Industries. The cred market has bottomed out several times. The big ones were first with the death of print, and then with the birth of those stupid bloggers. Man, you talk about a one-two punch! And it's not even like a blogger adds to the cred market. But I digress. As with everything we have done, we've endured. And with that accomplishment comes this celebration: *The Indie Cred Test*.

Keep this book near you. Let it guide you through the crowded mall parking lot known as life. Let it keep you safe. Let it keep you informed. And yes, let it maintain your credibility at all times.

Now, if you wouldn't mind, I have to get back to work as I'm incredibly successful and wealthy. My female assistant will see you out. And no, we don't validate parking.

H₂O

— HENRY H. OWINGS
(dictated)

"For every credibility gap, there is a gullibility fill."
— *Richard Clopton*

The struggle for acceptance while conveying the idea that you have no desire whatsoever to be accepted can be quite the tricky venture. It calls for a plenitude of both self and peer imposed rules, and the false impression that anyone besides you really gives a shit. While you're commended (slightly) for digging deeper than say, whatever mind-numbing scat television and radio are shoving down your throat, by the same token, your über hipness is both laughable and infuriating. With your gourmet shoes, designer measuring cups, and overabundance of ac"siss"ories, you are merely a horribly-put-together Voltron of a douchebag. Remember that. Seriously. On the unforgiving, side-splitting pages that follow, you can look forward to being undermined and humbled. Your very existence is a myth. Have a nice day.

— **CHAD BAKER**

A MESSAGE TO THE
HIPSTER IN AMERICA

WHAT DO YOU KNOW, what do you do, and what is your place in this world? Don't kid yourself, you have no idea, even though you have access to many times more information than any generation before you. (When I started college, all we had was Netscape. Forget nudie pictures; I couldn't even see emoticons.) You are the first and the last of your kind. The first, because parents just don't understand. The last, because you don't seem to really like sex all that much, and if you have kids, you won't have any control over them. You have the best to offer; better than any human beings who have ever lived. So let's do this.

You descended from heroes. People like Walt Whitman, Henry David Thoreau, Herman Melville, Groucho Marx, Jim Jones, OJ Simpson and that one guy who did that thing. People who pushed themselves to the outer limits of human experience, tested their thresholds for pain, and sucked it up when people broke into their cars and stole their stereos. But you realized you needed to somehow propagate your seed. And there wasn't much of a bar scene on Walden Pond. So you moved toward the cities.

The proto-hipsters were Depression-era diehards who set up shop in decrepit Hoovervilles around Manhattan, taking the only route they could find away from the already, even then, preposterously insane rents. As industry and shipping drew mixed multitudes to the cities, there was increasing crosstalk between mingling cultures and ethnicities. The nightclubs were the new social frontier. Interesting people got drunk and spilled their guts to each other. Some took notes, which created some cool books and a canon of stock gestures, phrases and affectations that weren't that hard to simply parrot and memorize, you dig, brah?

So of course the tourists showed up. You had your real outsiders: hobos, junkies, carnies, persecuted minorities, hydrophobics, burnouts, toothless hookers and other for-real outcasts. Then you had the ones who actively chose that status, who hung out with those people and gave up their connections back home. (This category includes, of all people, clarinetist Bing Crosby, whom Archie Shepp described as "the first hip white person born in the United States." And I'm going to let that stand, because I can't really argue with Archie Shepp.) And you had the tourists, the children of relative privilege who could sample this shit and still go back to the suburbs for Thanksgiving. And that's cool. If that's you, your ranks include William S. Burroughs, Joe Strummer, and a lot of other people who made plenty of interesting things happen. If you could pay for my sandwich, that would be great.

Capitalism is a cold bitch. Some people are too eccentric to work in the same office for 50 years. But we've all got to make a living, and there's only so many dumpsters worth diving in. So the smarter eccentrics found ways of selling

their eccentricities. Which meant the better eccentricities were bigger sellers, which meant it was a good idea to spend some time crafting (or outright faking) your eccentricities, which turned out to be a decent job. If a bit of a grind, when the hangover kicked in, you remembered your antics from last night, and no one was particularly sorry that your rib was fractured or that you have herpes on your cornea.

Anyway, hipsters of all kinds thrived in cities. Thus, their descendents choose to inhabit happening hellholes like Echo Park, Logan Square, Fishtown or Williamsburg. Actually, fuck Williamsburg. I'm sure everyone has moved on by now.

You are by and large educated, clever, frugal (if your idea of frugal is spending $75 on a Swans import LP), supportive of our nearby fellow humans, and authorities on exotic beer brands. You make fun of each other a lot because you know you can handle it, although sometimes, in truth it hurts your li'l emo-queen feelings, though you're way too hip to admit it. You're each unique, and also the same, which you don't talk about because you already had that stupid debate when you got stoned in freshman dorm, from which you still bear a scar or a slight limp. You'll dance to anything, which we fully support, because you dance funny and we like to laugh at you.

You are, for the most part, white. But you are shameless appropriators of African, African-American, and other zesty cultures, so when the white man finally bows out of the evolutionary scheme, you'll still be here. The word "hip" originated in Africa, derived from a Wolof word meaning "to see." That, or it was an inside thing for junkies. Either way, the UV rays will probably brown you out as much as you need. Melanoma is totally the next big thing for white America, trust me.

You've heard about "The White Negro" by Norman Mailer. It's a good read. Obnoxious, yes, but the guy got laid a lot. Steve Albini and Thomas Frank also wrote some painfully brilliant stuff about you, but they didn't get laid nearly as much. Then there's that dude who does Beetle Bailey…but that's a different story.

Food. Let's talk about this. Many of you choose to treat your bodies like garbage disposals, living off $2 hot dogs and PBRs. Let's cut that shit. Listen to the teetotalers and vegetarians. They're not sick all the time. They come in three categories: the easily grossed out; the ones who don't want to fuck with animals; and the ones who listen to

Morrissey like your step mom listens to Oprah. They all pretty much suck, and they're self-righteous assholes, but they're onto something, or at least they're not dying of heart attacks in their 40s. Meditating isn't a bad idea either. It keeps you from beating up random strangers. If you're having a hard time, risk being a hippie for a minute. It beats the shit out of dying. And just stop smoking. You're edgy. We get it. It's an incredibly stupid habit, and you stink worse than most hippies. Seriously. My eyes are watering from it.

We need to figure out how to not have to drive cars anymore. Many of you ride bikes, which is great. However, I don't know if you know this, but riding a "fixie" in an urban area while blackout-drunk is incredibly dangerous, and it's amazing that you haven't had a concussion yet. The Jewfro doesn't count as a helmet. No wonder the townies like to shoot BB guns at you.

A lot of people just despise you. You're living in the last days. You're the butt-end of postmodernism, the ultimate shipwreck of American culture, the embodiment of self-absorbed nihilism with a dumb 'haircut. Some of you are just bored conformists. Some of you have a point. Don't sweat it too hard. This is an incredibly difficult time to be alive. Just keep moving. You're up, and making art and serving my coffee. You are enough.

Let's say you quit binge drinking, start eating right, find someone you can stand not to cheat on, and hone some kind of a skill. What happens then? There's really no endgame. You could have been a yuppie, but you opted for this, and now you're going to have to spend some time sitting on the porch, telling tour stories and listening to car alarms on Sunday afternoons. It's cool. You've got the rest of us, and the entire Dead C catalogue.

We here at Chunklet Industries like hipsters. You are our source material, but you're also the only ones who will put up with us.

While we're here, let's figure out who's who in the hipster kingdom. Like Mims, we need to know who's hot and who's not, and back it up with numbers, because quantification is the only paradigm we've got. And that's where Chunklet comes in. While you've been out there with your ass hanging out, we've been in the lab. We've been distilling this whole hipster business down to a painfully accurate science. We will put your sexy outsider stance to the test. Who wants to step up?

—EMERSON DAMERON

THE EVOLUTION OF THE HIPSTER

YOU'RE NOT GETTING ANY COOLER...

It's clear to anyone playing with two full lobes that human life has a course with a beginning, a middle, and an end. Well, friend, so does your indie cred. So, using a vague mash-up of Freud/Erickson terms we don't really understand, we will hereby identify the Stages of Hipster Evolution.

01 ORAL STAGE
(aka 'The New Guy' and/or 'The Wannabe Hipster')

This is scene infancy. Like mother's breast, hipster music becomes the center of all experience, beginning when the awesome power of sonic art awakens the creative potential within an individual, showing them just how much tail can be netted with a few out of tune Iron Maiden riffs. The Wannabe Hipster is often voracious in his new fandom. The record and too-tight t-shirt collection begins to develop, but with little discrimination. At this stage the New Guy often falls prey to faux-indie bands on Astroturf labels secretly owned by "the man." These corporate doppelgangers act as decoys, seeking to stray the New Guy from the enlightened White Belted Path, thus diverting their allowances into the dreaded Corporate Coffers of Conformity.

02 ANAL STAGE
(aka 'Fan Boy')

Like a booger wiped on a handrail, the Fan Boy's musical taste is solidifying rapidly during the Anal phase. The subject experiences singular pleasure in hoarding records, 'zines, stickers, flyers, hats, coozies, one hitters, frisbees, embroidered socks and anything else with a band logo in it. In this stage, the Fan Boy often dismisses those still in the Oral stage as "poseurs," "conformist wankers," and assorted derogatory colloquialisms hyphenated with the word "douche." Semi-radical style makeovers of the "look at me, I got two toned hair and a 10 oz. bar thru my tongue" variety are a sort of final larval transformation to the next phase of development.

03 PHALLIC/PUBERTY STAGE
(aka 'The Frontman' or 'Rockstar')

At this point, the developing scenesters begin to realize that, much like Jakob Dylan, they too feel "stuff" about "things." This often results in a desire to express themselves creatively, sometimes self consciously and/or painfully for one's intended audience. A hipster's first band typically forms at this stage and adverse experiences such as heckling or mass disinterest during this stage of development may have a profound effect on the subject's artistic direction, financial stability, pants tightness and the overtness/ridiculousness of tattoo symbolism.

04 LATENCY STAGE
(aka 'Enigmatic Asshole')

During this stage, the subject falls into a state of creative dormancy, instead focusing, frequently too late, on developing *actual musical skills*. In punk rock circles, this is sometimes referred to as "crossing over" or "dumping the punk." At times the 'Enigmatic Asshole' begins to feel jaded, and disconnected from the scene and 'the kids' dismissing them as "robo-poseurs who are too busy playing Guitar Hero to financially reward my precious, misunderstood genius." These feelings can often be traced to a slowly dawning understanding that one's music sucks through a very rusty swizzle stick.

05 ADULTHOOD
(aka 'The Decline')

At this stage, one is faced not only with their physical and financial mortality, but with their cred mortality. The silver-lined clouds of madness descend on the adult in Decline, who will enter into senseless mundanity like "meaningful relationships" and "jobs where you don't wear name tags" followed by surprise bouts of childbirth and house buying. At this point, most Rock n' Roll Fathers become 'Black Flag Dads' *(see below)* and Music Snob Moms, well, let's be honest, we never hear from these broads again post-childbirth.

SO HERE'S THE BAD NEWS, YOUNG HIPSTER...

Unless you get hit by Glen Danzig's big bat-winged tour bus, the Black Flag Dad future awaits *you* as well. Look around next time you're at a show and you'll likely see ol' Gramps and Roses, his once super-boss 'do now a three-hair combover, kicking back at the bar with an ice cold O'Doul's, trying to impress Motörhead Mom *(aka Lemmy Lady)* and sweet li'l old Gorguts Granny with his late bloom virility. And venues all along this big, flat world of ours are full of similar scenes and haggard old scenesters. It's like my dear old Aunt the Gates used to say before she sacrificed her tongue to Lucifer: "Nobody beats the clock, buttnut."

SO, SEE YOU IN ABOUT 10 TO 15 YEARS WHEN THEY CALL YOU UNCLE CRUNK-CORE AKA "OL' UNKLE CRUNKLE."

WHO IS "BLACK FLAG DAD"?

He's the middle-aged guy standing, arms crossed, by the bar or near the door guy at rock shows. He's drinking responsibly, not macking chicks and he doesn't recognize a mosh pit unless it's moving in a circular direction. Upon closer inspection, his personal style can usually be seen to consist of an old but still cred-worthy t-shirt, regular fit jeans and a haircut, unnoteworthy in both color and architecture, sitting atop his unpierced face.

As his lack of hipititude will probably make clear, the Black Flag Dad is not here for the show. He is simply paying the price for turning his son into a band-nerd at an early age, thereby putting himself into the undignified position of playing "the cool father" as his twittering tween rages stylishly in the pit to the likes of Avenged Sevenfold or (most likely) worse, while lamenting, silently or out loud, about "how much cooler it was when people didn't mosh with Roman candles," and "when underground scenes weren't just a big fashion show."

A BRIEF HISTORY OF COOL

WALK INTO ANY COOL COFFEE SHOP, or a bar with the *Garden State* soundtrack on constant rotation, and the tension is impenetrable. With every creak of the door, everyone peeks, seemingly to judge with derisive wrath. One can't escape the self-conscious rambling: Am I wearing white after Labor Day? Are there crumbs in my beard? Have I forgotten pants again? It's hard not to feel insecure, or at least defensive enough to walk in with both middle fingers extended.

It's always the young'uns, with entitlement as smug as their pants are snug, downloading whatever new band informed by a three-year old musical knowledge and acting superior about it, and exercising hyper-consumerism indirectly learned from Japanese teens.

Or, it's always the crotchety old fart, railing about "back in the day" like it was an ex he never got over. A dinosaur of a bachelor, his "that one time I saw Magazine at this warehouse party" line is long spent.

Or, it's always the anti-establishment punk with his liberty spikes, menacingly mouthing "yuppie," but when it comes down to it, you know how to sing more Discharge songs than he knows Against Me! riffs.

Or, it's always the scholarly film buff, collared shirt buttoned to the top, reading shallow philosophy, but never actually willing to discuss it. The kind of pal who uses the word "criterion" only as a proper noun.

But it's not ever you. No, never you. Cool people are, like, *soooooo* annoying. You're cool, but you don't care about cool. Cool's overrated. Cool sucks. Cool is *so* over. You liked Cool's early stuff better. Whatever. You're not even trying to be cool.

That would affect your carefree nonchalance—the same disaffected attitude you take towards your hair. The one that states, "I'm me. A unique individual, free from pigeonholing." And when it's pointed out that you're sporting the same Fred Perry track jacket as five other folks in the vicinity, you reply, "Get bent, it was on sale!" In desperate moments, such conversations always end with the classic exclamation: "Don't you even know who I am?!"

Welcome to our subculture, with a social climate so potent with oneupsmanship, it's why you picked up this book. It's what happens when one throws a bunch of awkwardly anti-social nerds into a room where they quickly skip to condescending conversations about the most obscure thing, ever.

People got into indie cred because it was a subculture for alienated outsiders, disaffected youth music cultures carry so many names: the hepcat, teddy boys, beats, hippies, rockers, mods, punks, skins, SHARPS, straight edge, crusties, alternative; Where have all the rude boys gone?

Then there's the hipster. Wasn't it kind of a catch-all phrase for all the kids that were into underground shit? Of course, with the advent of the Internet, everyone is into underground shit. If you think hipsters are strictly the overly-ironic kids on track bikes and skinny jeans, that means you haven't paid attention to underground culture prior to 2003.

Hipsters have had a long evolution, with its etymology dating back to '40s jazz aficionados. Like when "alternative" finally became a section card in record stores (remember those?), its original meaning is forever lost. So much, that *The New York Times* put an editorial call to lower its usage. Now, as society's whipping boy, it's a catch-all phrase for everything that sucks. At least amongst those suffering strictly from First World Problems.

Coupled with Dickies, Converse All-Stars, and retro thick-rimmed glasses, each commodity is an inane part of our subculture's uniform. Today's uniform is tomorrow's ironic punchline. Each genre has its own sense of style, made up of small artifacts loaded with stigma. And that stigma means something to our social capital. Not just with records and material goods, but in knowledge and ambition. Really, it's no different than 'roided-out club brahs gloating in $100 bedazzled Affliction t-shirts and learning the names and work-out regimens of their favorite MMA fighters.

When subverting The Man becomes a popular idea, it's an exercise in hegemony. It's where influence becomes consent and trends are born. It's like everyone in the exclusive navel

THE FIVE STAGES OF BECOMING COOL

This scientific-philosophical-sociological condition

CIRCLE COMPLETE!
The subject should now remove themselves from the gene pool with a rusty rake.

STAGE ONE
The subject starts out doing an activity in an ironic, hipster way (listening to Lady Gaga, wearing trucker hats, drinking PBR) in an attempt to confound the obviously unironic sensibilities of the under-pierced proles. Should someone who actually likes the thing in question be encountered, scoffs, eye-rolling and vicious blogging are the standard response.

STAGE TWO
Time passes, and the subject begins to enthusiastically enjoy the thing in question. PBR starts to appear in the home fridge not out of economic necessity, but because it tastes good to the subject. PBR is ordered even in situations where there is no shock value to doing so (like at a local bar or Captain D's).

STAGE THREE
At some level, the thing in question begins to become more popular and accepted. Lady Gaga starts getting love from all the blogs, and johnny-come-lately-hipsters climb onboard. PBR starts selling ads in *Vanity Fair*. High-end clothing stores begin to stock the trucker hat.

STAGE FOUR
The subject, now officially fond of the thing in question, sees the cultural upswing and reacts by dismissing it from his life. He burns his trucker hats, switches back to micro brews, and sells his Lady Gaga for old Public Image Limited records. Still, the desire lingers...

STAGE FIVE
With the thing in question now a full-fledged cultural phenomenon, the subject can begin pretending to enjoy it ironically in full view of the proles while secretly enjoying it for real.

gazing suddenly turned around and said, "Hey man, y'gotta get in on this!" Only then does capitalism take notice. While "subculture" is subversive from the straight world, "culture" is what keeps it conformist. True subversives are the eccentrics.

Each subculture is a refraction of its predecessors, and with information so accessible, there's a lot to filter. What used to be a collection of niche subcultures one had to seek is now available with a few keyboard strokes. It's instant knowledge. When everybody knows everything about anything then cool is about a reference followed by a wink, then acknowledged with a nod.

If punk rock style was a distillation of all the major post-war subcultures, then today's hipster could be of the post-Internet age. Do you remember the underground before the Internet? If not, it doesn't matter how much you've read on Wikipedia—you have already failed this book. Please shut it, place it neatly back on the shelf, and resume ironically watching juggalo videos on your iPhone while marching headlong into interstate traffic. However, if you remember having to write checks to some address in the back pages of *MRR*, and glues-ticking the stamps so that kid in that garage can reuse them, then you haven't wholly cheated your way towards cred.

A fellow writer once told me that anyone who derides hipsters at a party automatically cops to being the straightest person in the room. Stigma lives in stereotypes and that's a slippery slope towards a prejudice—another symptom of "Us-versus-Them" chauvinism. Everyone hates entitled pretentious people. Hell, even pretentious people hate pretentious people. But in any aggressive climate run by social capital, pretension rules all.

So, old fogey, it's time to indulge that superiority complex and really check your worth. Take the test and consider your credibility. As exemplified by the coffee shop chatter surrounding us, these are all very important issues. Even if you're not trying to be the coolest person in the room, all eyes are on you.

—VINCENT CHUNG

TEST INSTRUCTIONS

THESE NOTES ARE FOR THE TEST TAKERS. NOT 'TESTEES.' THAT'D JUST BE A CHEAP JOKE.

GETTING STARTED!

This test is designed to assess your credliness using traditional paper-based testing materials. The test is self-adjusting and self-correcting. It also knows where you live, what kind of car you drive and is licensed to carry concealed firearms.

Once you have started the test, it is not recommended that you finish. This test is not organized, analytical or concise.

Rather it is an expensive exercise in random, freeform assertion of baseless conjecture and hyperbole, carefully strip-mined of any actual demonstrable knowledge.

This test will not be easy, but it will make a fucking man out of you (but only if you're a woman).

ANSWERING PROTOCOL

There are no right answers.

Answer all questions to the best of your (or your neighbor who you are cheating from's) ability.

Do not check your work or launch projectiles at your instructor.

Bonus points will be awarded if the bribe is adequate.

No bathroom breaks. Students are required to supply their own catheters and bedpans.

IF YOU ANSWER QUESTIONS **IN**CORRECTLY

- Your score goes down
- You become less attractive
- You make less money

IF YOU ANSWER QUESTIONS **CORRECTLY**

- Your sex appeal increases dramatically
- Your poop begins to smell slightly better
- Your score still goes down *(nobody likes a know-it-all)*

 OBTAIN A NO. 2 PENCIL, ACUMINATE IT UP REAL GOOD WITH YOUR BOOT KNIFE AND MAYBE CHEW ON IT A BIT. NEXT, LIGHT THE ERASER ON FIRE AND SMELL IT. INHALE DEEPLY. NEXT, DRINK THREE (3) EXPENSIVE BEERS, SMOKE A BOWL OF CAT HAIR AND THROW A DEAD WOMBAT THROUGH A WINDOW. CONGRATULATIONS, YOU ARE NOW READY TO EMBARK ON THE MOST IMPORTANT PSEUDO-ANALYSIS OF YOUR ENTIRE EXISTENCE.   STAB YOUR SELF

ACCEPTABLE LOCATIONS FOR ADMINISTERING THIS TEST INCLUDE:

A. Near highway construction

B. Ringside at Monday Night Raw (preferably holding a sign that reads: "Whip his ASS!")

C. Up a music critic's ass on taco night

DO NOT FIND A QUIET ROOM IN WHICH TO TAKE THIS TEST

FOR STUDENTS WITH DISABILITIES, THE FOLLOWING ALTERNATE TESTING FORMATS WILL BE PROVIDED:

A. Those with learning disabilities will be mocked in inverse-proportion to their ability to speak a coherent sentence. Learning disabilities are generally complemented by retard-strength, so we're prepared to call you "sir" if need be.

B. For students who are blind and cannot read printed tests in standard-size print, a death metal audio format of the test is available. Chris Barnes is the narrator. Good luck with that.

C. Students who are hard of hearing or deaf may have difficulty understanding verbal instructions. This is proof that you have rocked so hard that you don't need to take this test.

D. Kryptonians can request a kryptonite-free testing facility, but must do so in writing three (3) weeks after the test was administered.

E. No fatties. Dear God, **PLEASE** no fatties.

PLEASE, IF YOU GET STUMPED, JUST REMEMBER THAT YOU'RE NOT ALONE. YOU'RE JUST STUPID! GOOD LUCK, SCHMUCK!

QUESTIONS? CALL 1-900-CHUNK-LT OR VISIT US ONLINE AT CHUNKLET.COM

This test is administered by Chunklet Industries, a licensed vendor of the United States Department of Creducation, credquartered in the cred-light district of Shoe Horn, Mississippi, where it is the very credrock of the community. All cred-blooded examinees are subject to an abundance of credicule, resulting in the occasional migraine credache. Subjects who pass the test will receive a certificate credeemable for a lengthy stay at the nearest cred and breakfast, while those that fail will be treated as credneeks and credophiles, and be promptly becreded in a public display of credlam, by Crederick Credwards, the current reigning Credliest Warrior champion, with live musical performances by Right Said Cred and The Cred Milkmen.

THE INDIE CRED TEST

PRELIMINARY ESSAY QUESTION:

What makes you think you're good enough to read this book/take this test?

(FEEL FREE TO USE MORE PAPER IF NECESSARY)

GENERAL PROFILE

Name:_____

Current city of residence:_____

From what suburban hellhole did you move?

_____

_____

INCOME

Declared [,   ]   Undeclared [,   ]

Let's get this out of the way first. What's the address of your shitty blog?

_____

And what is the name of your shitty band?

_____

_____

ASTROLOGICAL SIGN

☐ Aquarius   ☐ Pisces   ☐ Aries   ☐ Taurus   ☐ Gemini
☐ Cancer   ☐ Leo   ☐ Virgo   ☐ Libra   ☐ Scorpio
☐ Sagittarius   ☐ Stradivarius   ☐ Capricorn

CB Radio Handle: _____

Favorite US President: _____

Date of last sexual encounter: _____

RACIALITY

☐ White   ☐ Albino (extra-extra white)   ☐ Asian/Ornamental
☐ Creole   ☐ African American   ☐ African African   ☐ Latino
☐ Eskimo/Inuit   ☐ Arabic   ☐ Frenchy   ☐ Jew   ☐ Juggalo
☐ Jewgalo   ☐ Tiger Woods (black and Asian)   ☐ Just plain fat
☐ Rae Dawn Chong (black and Latino)   ☐ Halle Barry (black and white)
☐ Lucy Liu (white and Asian)   ☐ Anime (blonde Asian with *huge* blue eyes)
☐ Elf   ☐ Magical midget   ☐ It's complicated   ☐ Other_____

MARITAL STATUS

☐ Married   ☐ Gay Married   ☐ Single   ☐ Widow   ☐ Wait, *what?*
☐ Separated, but living together because of finances
☐ It depends who's asking (*Are you a cop?*)   ☐ I am my husband's property

EDUCATION

☐ Junior High drop-out   ☐ Home schooled (by junior high drop out)
☐ High school drop-out (because teachers were "mean")
☐ High school diploma   ☐ College drop-out (because of sheer laziness)
☐ Pretended to go to college but didn't really, just took parents' money
☐ Associates or Trade degree   ☐ Liberal Arts something or other
☐ In 6th year plus of 4 year college degree   ☐ College graduate
☐ Hamburger U. graduate   ☐ Graduate School or something
☐ School of LIFE, man

If you have attended college and beyond, what was/were the determining factor(s) that influenced your decision to pursue post-secondary ed?
(check all that apply)
☐ Needed specific training that only a university education could provide
☐ Close proximity of school to a geographical area that provided
    significant cultural opportunities unavailable in hometown
☐ Close proximity to surfing/the beach

☐ Desire to escape parents or generally stifling family dynamic
☐ Inability to resist lemming-like behavior of age cohort
☐ Increased quality/availability of recreational drugs and 'tang
☐ Uncertainty about what to do with life was able to be postponed for
    at least four years
☐ Expectations of parents made the decision pretty much a given
☐ You always wanted to start a band
☐ All of the above   ☐ None of the above

YOU CURRENTLY RESIDING AT/IN

☐ Your parents' house   ☐ A tent behind parents' house
☐ A college dorm   ☐ An apartment (>2 roommates)
☐ An apartment (<2 roommates)   ☐ A squat
☐ A house (>6 house mates)   ☐ A house (<6 house mates)
☐ Under a highway overpass   ☐ Your band's practice space   ☐ A yurt
☐ The back room at the record store   ☐ A friend's couch
☐ On the road, following some horrible band
☐ A smelly hippy commune   ☐ Somewhere in the boonies
☐ The shed   ☐ An old, immobile school bus   ☐ Loft/"Alternative" Space

A DAY OF WORK FOR YOU CONSISTS OF

☐ Working with children   ☐ Working with the poor
☐ Standing on the poor   ☐ "Art"   ☐ Playing on a cash register
☐ Pricing newly arrived records   ☐ Telemarketing
☐ Calling parents and asking for a check
☐ Waiting for check to arrive from parents
☐ Walking to mailbox to retrieve check from parents
☐ Health food store   ☐ Placing pepperoni on things
☐ Placing alcohol in people   ☐ Computers   ☐ Pulling coffee
☐ Trying to hide your pirate radio station from the FCC
☐ Distributing your DIY zine throughout the community
☐ Massage therapist/reiki master   ☐ Dancing naked on tables
☐ Being a corporate stooge   ☐ Wearing a stupid costume/uniform
☐ Crying uncontrollably   ☐ Going on imaginary killing sprees
☐ Taking tickets at the Children's Museum   ☐ Driving a machine
☐ Washing things   ☐ Ignoring patrons' wishes
☐ Scraping up interstate roadkill
☐ Doorman for a hipster bar or rock club where you hope to one day tend bar
☐ Adjunct faculty at some shitty college that will never give you tenure
☐ Sound man   ☐ Smell man   ☐ Managing children in a classroom setting
☐ Managing children in a classroom setting while trying to figure out
    how to go around web block to get to Facebook and Twitter
☐ Turning the sign from stop to slow during repave
☐ Supervising the guy turning the sign from stop to slow during repave
☐ Youngest person handing out samples at a Sam's Club or Costco
☐ Hauling stuff for a moving company or hoarder-trash removal company
☐ One of those people that collects pallets on a shopping cart
☐ "Actor"/"Comedian"/"Improv"/"Lifelong temp"
☐ Yelling, "Welcome to Moe's" about 378 times
☐ Finding the right pair of old shades
☐ Pretending to work on job-related things while reading (and
    believing) Pitchfork and/or buying thrifty/shitty clothes on eBay
☐ Other: _____

IN THE LAST TWO PRESIDENTIAL ELECTIONS, YOU VOTED

- ☐ Democrat/Liberal   ☐ Republican/Conservative
- ☐ Third Party (Green, Libertarian, etc.)
- ☐ Humorous/ironic write in, such as Richard Ramirez or Mario Van Peebles
- ☐ Not at all; was busy sleeping off the previous night's pre-election drinks
- ☐ I voted to make Ted Nugent Lord of Earth

PLEASE CHOOSE THE CATEGORY THAT BEST DESCRIBES YOUR HIGH SCHOOL-ERA PERSONA

- ☐ Jock   ☐ Preppie   ☐ Neo-hippie   ☐ Daddy's princessy cheerleader
- ☐ Bullied Velvet Underground fan
- ☐ Methalhead (i.e., both a hard drugs and *Sabbath Vol. 4* user)
- ☐ Science fair bait   ☐ Gang banger   ☐ Teacher banger   ☐ Drug dealer
- ☐ Late convert to R.E.M.   ☐ A/V helper   ☐ "That pregnant chick"
- ☐ Magic the Gathering/Dungeons And Dragons player   ☐ Library cruiser
- ☐ Oldest non-graduating senior in history   ☐ Grease-Monkey/Motorhead
- ☐ Teen scene queen   ☐ Gutter punk-in-training   ☐ Margin-writer
- ☐ Pimploma, The Human Pimple Of Indeterminate Gender
- ☐ Hate-filled poetess in black, black, black   ☐ Dude who said "whooooo!" a lot
- ☐ Grim survivor of coach-induced psychoses

WHICH OF THE FOLLOWING WERE YOU WELL-VERSED IN BEFORE YOU DISCOVERED THE WORTH OF YOUR CRED?

- ☐ Comic books   ☐ D&D   ☐ Theft   ☐ "Punk"   ☐ Metal   ☐ Drama
- ☐ Your pillow   ☐ Hip-Hop/R&B   ☐ The Smiths   ☐ Glam Rock   ☐ Poetry
- ☐ Interpretive Dance   ☐ Tying a tie/looking presentable   ☐ Drugs
- ☐ Booze   ☐ Pretentious booze   ☐ Local sports bar trivia   ☐ Fantasy
- ☐ Football   ☐ Weekend paintball warrior   ☐ Backyard wrestling
- ☐ Trying to communicate with the opposite sex   ☐ Action movies
- ☐ Video games   ☐ Nunchucks   ☐ Titty books   ☐ Pokemon
- ☐ Food   ☐ Vomiting   ☐ Stalking

WHICH SELF-AGGRANDIZING BEHAVIOR DO YOU DISPLAY?

- ☐ Paint   ☐ Take photos   ☐ Make sculptures   ☐ Dance
- ☐ Write (god help you)   ☐ Streak   ☐ Other _____

PREFERRED STYLE OF BARBECUE

- ☐ North Carolina (vinegar)   ☐ South Carolina (mustard)
- ☐ Memphis (sloppy)   ☐ Kansas City (turpentine)   ☐ Central Texas ("zesty")
- ☐ East Texas (secessionist)   ☐ Saigon (white phosphorous)
- ☐ Other _____

TECHNOLOGY ITEMS WITH YOU AT ALL TIME
(CHECK ALL THAT APPLY)

- ☐ None   ☐ A pencil   ☐ A stamp and postcard   ☐ Basic cellphone
- ☐ Smartphone with internet   ☐ Laptop   ☐ Smartphone   ☐ Blackberry
- ☐ iPad   ☐ DAT player   ☐ VCR   ☐ Pager   ☐ Pedometer   ☐ Abacus
- ☐ Wrist watch   ☐ Other _____

MODE OF TRANSPORTATION

- ☐ Car   ☐ Bus   ☐ Bike   ☐ Bipedal locomotion   ☐ Homeless piggy back
- ☐ Coattails   ☐ Magic carpet   ☐ Tauntaun   ☐ Other _____

WHICH CHOICE BEST DESCRIBES YOUR FINANCES

- ☐ Parents' generosity   ☐ Street hustled   ☐ Student loan-based
- ☐ Limited by the number of promo CDs the local record store will buy

WHAT BEST DESCRIBES YOUR CHOICE OF EYEWEAR

- ☐ Contact lenses   ☐ Beer goggles   ☐ Prescription
- ☐ Cosmetic   ☐ Thrift store   ☐ Hank Williams Jr.

DIET

- ☐ Omnivore   ☐ Carnivore   ☐ Pescatarian (veggies and fish)
- ☐ Vegetarian   ☐ Vegan   ☐ Ramen and candy bars
- ☐ Heroin 'n' hot dogs   ☐ Other *(write here)* _____

HOW MANY PETS DO YOU HAVE?

- ☐ None (allergies)   ☐ None (court order)   ☐ 1 to 3 (a few)
- ☐ 3 to 5 (a gaggle)   ☐ 5 to 7 (a herd)   ☐ 7 to 10 (a stampede)
- ☐ I have no human friends (a shitload)

PETS YOU OWN (CHECK ALL THAT APPLY)

- ☐ Dog   ☐ Cat   ☐ Bird   ☐ Fish   ☐ Reptile   ☐ Amphibian
- ☐ Robot   ☐ Alf   ☐ Sam Donaldson look-alike
- ☐ Other _____

WHERE DO YOU GO WHEN YOU NEED A HAIRCUT?

- ☐ Salon   ☐ Stylist   ☐ Hairdresser   ☐ Garden store
- ☐ The bathroom   ☐ The chemo-lab

FILL IN THE BLANK

Self described level of psychological stability on a scale of one (stable) to 100 (batshit nuts): _____

Sexuality: _____

Location: _____

Politics: _____

Square inches of skin covered by tattoos: _____

Number of sexual partners (in the last 12 months): _____

Number of sexual partners (career total): _____

List all non-music related hobbies: _____

Favorite color: _____

Favorite religion: _____

Favorite asinine Charles Barkley quote: _____

Approximate ERA: _____

Favorite sexual position: _____

Current and/or former bands: _____

Language(s) spoken at the level of conversational fluency: _____

Myers-Brigg: _____

Enneagram: _____

Diagnosed psychological problem: _____

Diagnosed gastro-intestinal problem: _____

Ideal occupation: _____

Actual occupation: _____

Preferred musical instrument: _____

Preferred instrument of torture: _____

Ringtone: _____

Arrest record: _____

Favorite ethnic group: _____

Favorite crotch aroma: _____

What personal inadequacy are you compensating for by engaging in all this superfluous hipster bullshit? _____

Is there someone hipper than you we should be talking to instead? *(please list top five)*

_____

THE INDIE CRED TEST

SECTION I

THE X,Y&Z OF WHATEVER: FEEDING, CLOTHING AND LIVING WITH THE AFFECTED

CHAPTER 1

MODUS VIVENDI & OPERANDI

CRED DOESN'T ALWAYS CONSTRAIN ITSELF to the clubs and record stores. No way. Remember the heinously aloof, grandma-sweater-clad longhair buying paper plates behind you at the gas station last week? His or hers infuriating mishmash of bad taste and bad attitude was actually prime evidence of the cred-hunter lifestyle. To the dedicated, bullshitting the size of your record collection from a sticky bar stool no longer passes muster. No, every instant is an opportunity to glean cred — be it showing off your antiquated coffee press, commuting by unicycle or blogging the details of your obscurely-named cat's raw food diet. However eccentric, the 'indie advanced' among us excel by taking that brand of nonsense to the streets. Like a peacock who always forgets to retract its plumage...just in case someone cool is (indeed) watching.

YES/NO

THE INDIE CRED TEST   THE INDIE CRED TEST

COMPLETE THE FOLLOWING QUESTIONS WITH A YES/NO ANSWER OR YOU GET NO CAKE AND/OR PUDDING.

YES NO

01. Do you decide when you get up in the morning, or afternoon?

02. Are you an active member of a political party that doesn't begin with "D"? *(Note: If you're not American, we don't care.)*

03. Do you get upset when people fail to see how weird you are?

04. Have you ever committed yourself whole-heartedly to veganism and animal rights only to renounce them by lunch time?

05. Did you used to be environmentally friendly, but now use the world as your personal dumpster?

06. Do you curse to downplay your extensive vocabulary?

07. Are you constantly mistaken for a member of a band you hate?

08. Have you ever asked a person of color what time it is just to show how comfortable with him or her you are?

09. Have you ever intentionally looked away from an attractive person just to show how secure you are with yourself?

10. Do you have a semi-legendary criminal record?

11. Do you generally leave a trail of used and abused broads in your wake?

12. Do you keep score of how many times you've been thrown out of various clubs?

13. Are you "that guy"?

14. Do you own a gun?

15. Do you dig into the booger sugar?

16. Do you have any other addictions *(e.g.: pills, food, meth, hospital visits, etc.)*?

17. Have you squatted in London for a year to find your roots?

18. Did those experiences lead to the loss of any teeth?

19. Are you familiar with cheap eats like rats, squirrels and cockroaches?

YES NO

20. When you get into collecting something, does it become mainstream six to twelve months later?

21. Do you then renounce having ever had any interest in it at all?

22. Did you choose what city to live in based on something that happened there 30 years before you were born?

23. Is the driving force in both your professional and personal life inertia?

24. Are you obsessed with being "different"?

25. Conversely, are you obsessed with being "just a regular person"?

26. Are you obsessive over your love of childhood cultural influences like Scooby Doo or *Road House*?

27. Does your license plate reflect your lifestyle with stupid shit like 2HIP4U, LAKEGUY, VINTIJ, 4VINYL or STR8DIY?

28. Does your name come with a modifier that identifies you to others but can also be applied to the music you listen to/champion, like "Psychedelic" Steve or "Black Metal" Bob?

DWELLING

29. Can you see the floor in your house?

30. Do you brag about not owning a TV, microwave, or dishwasher?

31. Do you have any pets named after musicians, beat poets, or serial killers?

32. Have you ever corrected someone by saying, "No, my *parents* live with *me*"?

33. Do you tell people you're the only white person in your apartment building?

34. Is it important to you that people know you've got real hardwood, not laminate?

35. Were the drums to any good records tracked in your house because your real hardwood sounds so good?

36. Did you burn down the house next door because it blocked your view of Starbucks?

37. Does your hot neighbor play sitar late at night, causing you to stay there even though you haven't had running water for three months?

ACCEPTABLE REASONS TO
GET MARRIED

The potential merging of record collections will create a super-collection, impervious to attacks from even the most discerning of taste-makers.

Peer pressure + howling loneliness = I do.

She's cool with the anime porn and titty-shaped baking pans.

You're both the same size = doubling your phalanx of thick scarves, semi-ironic baseball caps, and purple corduroys.

Because your mom just died.

It's the best showcase for that new set of breasts you just bought.

Shotgun.

You need more Crock-ware and Kitchen-Aid attachments.

As part of your religion you have to take something that used to be sacred and turn it into something profane.

For the collection of paperback novels, teddy bears, letters, mix tapes, softball trophies, license plates, year books, Friday Night Videos and Night Tracks VHS tapes, old curling irons, and photo albums that will live in your garage until you die.

Kickass stereo.

To stay in the country.

He is the rare man who bravely accepts and supports your bisexuality.

Because no one else knows exactly how you like your turkey club prepared.

How else are you going to get divorced?

For spite.

To slowly watch someone you love get really old and ornery.

What's the point of a home decorated with semi-antique kitsch when there's no one else to appreciate/comment on it?

His and hers Criterion Collection editions of Metropolis and The Holy Mountain means never having to buff scratched DVDs.

Dinner doesn't just make itself.

That beer gut isn't going away, but that mildly attractive, semi-intelligent person willing to settle for you might.

So I can get on her health insurance and get this oozing-leg thing looked at.

She's got a bunch of androgynous horn rimmed frames you can use.

His employee discount at Guitar Center.

Her employee discount at Urban Outfitters.

He responded to your Craigslist personal with something other than a picture of his schlong (because he couldn't get far enough away to fit the entire thing in the frame).

Your future in-laws have a van they're not using.

It's so much easier to make ends meet with two trust funds.

Ironic babies are totally *teh shit* in Brooklyn right now.

The survival of the white, hetero race depends on it.

He'll haul your ginormous '70s arena-rock bass amp upstairs for you, no questions asked. Pro tip: Walk a few steps ahead and wear a short skirt if you want that magic to last.

He's claims to be satisfied with a garden variety roll in the hay and doesn't inflict some humiliating act named after a city and described in Urban Dictionary.

She's a Juggalo, you're a Juggalo. That makeup is going to be everywhere, but who *really* cares?

Your spouse-to-be has a reputation on the scene, and you'll be able to glom onto it.

Regular access to sex.

Creating the illusion of regular access to sex.

The possibility of lots of iTunes gift certificates as wedding presents.

Instant excuse to blow off your friends' lame concerts, art openings and poetry readings.

She believes you when you say you'll quit (add habit, whatever) if she lets you buy (add *very* expensive item(s)). If she does it more than three times over five years, you *have* to marry her.

She is obsessive-compulsive about cleaning and other things that in no way affect you drinking, smoking and watching TV all day.

You need a new dishwasher, washing machine, dryer, vacuum, cook.

She was a lesbian in high school, so with time, who knows what you can accomplish when her friends come over.

Spouse-to-be works at a trendy bar where he/she can smuggle as much PBR as they can fit into a purse/back pack every night after closing.

It finally dawned on you that "friends with benefits" doesn't extend to frequent visits to the gastroenterologist.

You need a guaranteed place to stay after rehab.

She's your soulmate, dude. (And hey, she also gave you a gnarly case of crabs.)

You use the same hair products, so that's like $6 a month saved.

He's cute and little, just like you.

She owns a liquor store.

He runs a brewery.

The idea of having money makes you physically ill.

Because we don't get along too well, so naturally it'd be a good idea to take it to the next level: Pure hate.

She is loaded and willing to finance your dream of running a concert venue.

ARE YOU "COOL" ENOUGH TO BE MISTAKEN FOR A "HOMO"?
"GAY" ENOUGH TO BE MISTAKEN FOR A "HIPSTER"?

HIPSTER OR HOMO?

IN MANY CASES, THERE IS A FINE LINE between "hipster" and "homosexual." Maybe you don't even know if you're straight or gay. Does that big beard of yours make you look like a Brooklynite, a "bear" or just a particularly fashionable homeless guy? It may also be that you're just another metrosexual trying to look gay so the ladies will find you irresistible, in which case, do us a favor and go read your copy of *Details* and puke into your Jack Spade messenger bag while listening to whatever painfully lame racket you choose on your stupid iPod dock.

Fortunately there exists a very simple, yet unfathomably complicated test to determine where you stand: in line lamely for Fleet Foxes tickets or sheepishly in a giant pool of man goo while Depeche Mode blares, or by yourself in a bar wondering why guys *and* gals think you're a total tool. We are not here to judge you—only to gauge (*gayge*, get it?) you.

So this is what's called a short answer test. It's what professional psychologicals call a "subjective" thingy. So don't read too much into the queries. (Get it, *queeries*? Ha!) One question means nothing. One sub-question means even less. One implied question not directly asked means *everything*, but only sometimes. It's a tricky, icky formula we use to figure you out and you wouldn't understand. Anyway, straight, gay or simply handsome, you're okay and people love you. So let's crack on...

01. How big is your record collection? How big is your roommate's record collection? Who would win in a fight, your roommate's or your record collection?

02. Do you prefer movies or films? What's the difference? And why do you think there's a difference?

03. Can you name every Hüsker Dü album in order? Who do you prefer: Bob Mould, Grant Hart or Greg Norton? Are you aware that the only straight member of the band is a professional chef with a handlebar mustache? Why are you aware of that?

04. Do you like sports? No? Thank God.

05. Can you hear your parents arguing upstairs right now? For real or in your head?

06. Do you have any flannel shirts? Flannel sheets? Grey Flannel cologne? *The Man in the Grey Flannel Suit* on DVD?

07. Ever had Panther Burns?

08. Nobody admits they like Guns n Roses. Why exactly don't you like them?

09. Do you ever think about Stephen Malkmus when you aren't listening to Pavement?

10. Who is Rob Halford— and why?

11. Do you have a beard? If yes, does she have a name?

12. Are skinny jeans any different than tight jeans? How so?

13. Why do your shoes/boots look like that?

14. Do you like Magnetic Fields?

15. Do you own Dennis Wilson's *Pacific Blue* on vinyl? What do you think of the tri-fold cover? Do you think it's a seminal album? What do you think of the word "seminal"? Should it be spelled differently?

16. Why do your girl friends and/or girlfriends' friends like you so much?

17. What magazines do you read regularly? (*"Gotcha" question!*) What magazines do you *look* at regularly?

18. What were the Descendents always going on about? What are you always going on about?

19. Why are you so goddamn thin/fat/normal?

20. Can you recommend a good framer or gay lion tamer?

21. Have you ever won a fight?

22. Can one easily read your nipple-braille through your At The Drive-In shirt without squinting? What does it say?

23. Do you feel that Klaus Nomi would have been a better recipient for all those merchandising deals KISS got?

24. Have you ever described a boring band as being "monocepage"?

25. Are you of the opinion that Boris' *Pink* could have been a little pinker?

26. Were you upset to find out Drag City wasn't a real city at all?

27. Do you have the 12" of Fugazi's *Margin Walker*? Did you first have it on cassette, but then think, "I need a bigger picture of this"? Do you gaze into Ian MacKaye's eyes on the cover and hope he really took a few ropes across the face for art's sake?

28. Do you shave your feet so they'll be prettier in your flip flops?

29. Is PBR the only beer you can drink?

30. Were you excited to know that Benicio Del Toro was playing Che Guevara in *Che* because he's hot when he's not fat?

31. So really, what's your favorite Faith No More song? Is Roddy Bottum your favorite member because his lyrics make you tingle? Do you ever picture Mike Patton practicing all those ingenious mouth noises while Roddy Bottum pounds his bottom?

32. Do you shave daily? Are you clean-shaven by choice or by design? How's that working out?

33. Does your girlfriend sleep around? With members of bands you like? Was it your idea?

34. Do you wear eyeliner? As a joke? At home, alone, in front of the mirror?

35. Are you *really* a lesbian? Or are you just trying to impress Mark Robinson and/or Robert Christgau?

36. Are you a girl? Are you into Ariel Schrag? Does her No Doubt fixation bug you? Did you just Google her?

37. When in a bookstore that carries it, do you always have to point out *Butt Magazine* and how heeelarious it is that it exists?

38. Are you still excited by DJ nights?

ACCEPTABLE REASONS TO
HAVE CHILDREN

Christ-like awesomeness.

You don't really use the X-Box anymore, but it cost like $300, so....

Need a solid excuse for not going to shows anymore.

You're getting too old to go to shows anyway.

You're *not* Catholic.

The guy who checks IDs at your bar just up and quit.

To dress them in band onesies that match your old metal shirts you gave up on fitting into 12 years ago. Nostalgia, man.

To give the world more absurd first names like Sandlot or Eno.

For the toys!

Little hands are great at retrieving screens that pop out of your pipe and roll under the couch.

Someone has to be sacrificed to the Kraken.

As a distraction from your every day job as a kindergarten teacher.

Because everyone else's kids like your beard.

For England!

You work in a Similac factory and you hate to feel like an Amish dude in Radio Shack.

Race-mixing. Take *that*, Dad!

The cactus lived. The cat lived. The kid should be fine.

If they fall out of a window, maybe you'll pen the next "Tears In Heaven."

Airport security doesn't want to reach into a soiled diaper any more than you do.

The line between breast-feeding and indecent exposure is murky at best.

Have you seen the price of condoms lately?

Got to have something to keep her busy while you fuck around.

Milk spots are the new ironic mustache.

You get tired of telling people what's up with Teasley.

It's the only way to prove how kvlt you are in the blackened natural childbirth doom metal scene.

There's no better place to raise a kid than a one-room apartment in Williamsburg.

You can raise the baby vegan and have one more thing to be smug and insufferable about.

Your own vegan diet already looks and tastes like baby food.

No one else will name their child Sleater-Kinney Please-Reunite Goldstein.

You feel like those Jesus Lizard shows prepared you for life with a screaming naked creature that can't control its bowels or bladder.

To use "baby weight" as an excuse for your fatness.

Friends and relatives will have to chip in for your new amp if it's on a baby registry.

The doc won't let you have any more abortions.

In case, one day, you think you might run out of food.

So you can finally move out of that sketchy neighborhood and not look like a racist due to the better school district argument.

Because you secretly hate your friends and want something better to do.

Ineffable joy of watching child discover, then hate, then come around again to the Beatles.

Conversational topic for hated Buddhist friends of spouse.

Another fresh mind to dump Bill Hicks into.

Your coke-induced insomnia means you're up all night anyway, and sometimes it gets lonely.

You need at least one child in order to play the "Go Get Dad a Beer From the Fridge" game.

You really need someone to talk to who will look over your shoulder instead of really paying attention to you.

You've got so much wisdom about useless bullshit that it'd be a shame for it to just die with you.

There's no substitute for a child's love, or their free labor.

You've grown tired of buying records, going to shows, taking vacations and living a free and fulfilling life.

Her family is old-money loaded and a nanny/au pair is all but guaranteed for dung duty and perhaps actual parenting.

It's the easiest way to fix a broken marriage. *Trust me.*

A lot of times kids get in free, so they can just bring you some shit back.

You like being puked on.

So you can make sure his first word is "Slayer!!"

Cuz a baby is worth like, 500 bucks on the Australian black market or something.

You export child laborers.

Drinking in public is so much easier with a crying baby.

Your parents will give you some money, which you will promptly spend on a new Rickenbacker bass and some ProTools plug-ins.

All you really feel comfortable driving is a mini-van.

You are totally going to circuit-bend those baby monitors when they are all grown up, or before.

You want to experiment with running your baby monitors through your pedal board.

You need an excuse to stop driving drunk.

You're married, but looking to get less satisfaction from the whole thing.

You're looking for an iron-clad reason to miss crucial gigs for the next 1,100 weekends.

You secretly want to see all the things you love destroyed by a narcissistic shit machine.

Because it's the only way to get in to a "Rock-n-Romp."

You have always wondered what the center of the universe is like, and now you can be legally responsible for it.

Try as you might, your argument that pets of any kind are "just like kids" dies at the foot of a ticking biological clock.

Both you and your mate possess the co-dominant hipster gene, thereby enabling you to produce über-hipsters.

So you'll have a toddler to mash makeup into and poison with your own failed dreams before they're old enough to realize that you dressed them like a homeless person.

Who else were you going to leave your record collection to when you die?

To build your own Partridge Family. Or maybe Jonas Brothers. Or at the very least, maybe you'll get a Justin Bieber out of the deal.

Two words. "Chick magnet."

All of your favorite bands have made appearances on *Yo! Gabba Gabba*, and you have way too much pride to ask any of your bros to watch it with you.

Because you wanted to name someone Freddy Cougar Mellencamp.

So glances from elderly strangers in public will go from a "tattooed ex-con" scowl to a pleasant "oh, look at that hip new dad!"

You (albino) + mate (huge port-wine stain) = Prettiest hipster ever.

Youngster in the house = forever plugged in to what's cool.

Irony, spite and/or love.

She's gorgeous (even in the morning), has a smoking body, and a killer sense of humor. Plus when you met, she was wearing a Cows t-shirt, for chrissakes. So if she wants to spawn, knock her the fuck up when you know in your heart of hearts you could never possibly do better.

YES NO

38. Do you have a skinny robe to lounge around in at home when you're not wearing other clothes that are too small for you?

39. Do you feel forced to turn up your stereo just to drown out the FOX News seeping through your walls because of your hard-of-hearing, ancient next door neighbors who stubbornly refuse to die?

40. While looking at houses to buy, is your first concern where the studio will go?

41. Do you have odd hours of the day, say 2:00 to 4:00 PM, where you can play drums in the house because the neighbors are all gone at that time? Is that life? Is that style?

42. Do you recreationally landscape?

MUSIC

43. Do you feel people value your musical opinion?

44. Do you scoff at those who value your musical opinion?

45. Are you a tech snob with no knowledge of how to play any musical instrument?

46. Has anyone you hung out with in college been signed?

47. Are they on a shitty indie label so small that it's run out of a hatchback vehicle?

48. Have you ever had an extended visit from a crusty punk band's stench long after they've left?

49. Do you often refer to things as being pre- or post-Nirvana?

50. When you found "Sky Vindaloo: Psych/Garage Rock From Kerala, India, Vol. 16" in a thrift store bin for $2, did you put it down because you don't already own volumes 1 through 15?

51. You didn't buy your turntable from Urban Outfitters, did you?

52. Do you turn your nose up at things that aren't "tube driven"?

53. Are you working on a documentary about the Roland TR-808 drum machine?

(IN)SIGNIFICANT OTHER

54. Did you choose your mate based on their ability to pay your bills and/or carry your amp?

55. Do you secretly suspect you're better at everything than your significant other?

56. Do you feel threatened because your significant other once made out with someone whose record you own? And do you secretly hate them a little bit because their slutty ways have ruined that record for you?

YES NO

57. Does your significant other poster for your shows?

58. Does your significant other let you fuck your other significant others?

59. Is your significant other a little too hot for you, but too dumb to know it? *If so, good job!*

TRANSPORTATION

60. When you take mass transit, are you making a point?

61. Are you obsessed with cars but don't know how to drive?

62. Do you have more band stickers on your car than your 14-year old neighbor has on his skateboard?

63. Do you drive a hybrid? Don't you wish everyone could?

64. Do you pine away for a car made before you were born?

65. Are you embarrassed of how nice your car is? Are you aware of what a stupid thing this is to be embarrassed about? Are you also embarrassed about getting laid "too often"?

66. Is a bike your primary form of transportation?

67. Did you buy it new or did you build your own "fixie" from spare lawn mower and leaf blower parts?

68. Do you spend more time tweaking your bike than you do riding it?

69. Do you wear any of that ludicrous looking Spandex bikey gear?

70. Do you wear those ridiculous, mini beanie-looking biker's caps out to the pub, even if you didn't actually ride a bike to the pub?

71. Do you own a one-of-a-kind Wesley Willis signature mountain bike?

72. Do you have the exact same car, down to the pin stripes, as someone you work with, only yours is just a little faster?

73. Did you buy one of the 17 Challengers used in season three of "The Dukes of Hazzard" from some guy in Arizona? *(Me too.)*

COMPUTERS/INTERHOLE

74. Do you downplay how much you know about computers, hygiene, and most things?

75. Does that modesty impress you?

76. Have you ever blogged about the influence of pre-war Bentonia blues on German minimalist techno?

	YES	NO

77. Is there any correlation between your MP3 purchases and Internetting while high? ☐ ☐

78. Do you use emoticons in the place of real emotions? ☐ ☐

79. Do you always build a personal profile on whatever the hot, new social networking site is? ☐ ☐

80. If so, do you think people really give a fuck about your status updates? ☐ ☐

81. Did you totally make Manny's EZ Margaritas for Cinco de Mayo like you posted before, during, and after? ☐ ☐

82. Do you spell "your" "yr"? ☐ ☐

83. Do you ever type "LOL" when you don't actually LOL? ☐ ☐

84. Do you think an emoticon at the end of a sentence negates any vile nasty thing you might say in the sentence itself? Really? You're a bicycle seat smeller. ;-) ☐ ☐

85. Do you brag to non-record collectors about your greatest score on eBay? ☐ ☐

86. Do you know more people on 4chan, ilx, or somethingawful.com than you do in real life? ☐ ☐

87. Do you use your Mac that barely runs because it looks more sleek and is far cooler than the perfectly fine, twice as fast, twice as tricked out PC collecting dust in the corner? ☐ ☐

88. Do you believe YouPorn took YouTube and made it better? ☐ ☐

89. Are you jacking off right now? ☐ ☐

SPORTS/ACTIVITY

90. Have you ever won a trophy? *(Baseball, chess, moshing, laundry, etc.)* ☐ ☐

91. Did you flunk Phys Ed in high school? ☐ ☐

92. Do you enjoy any professional sports besides baseball? ☐ ☐

93. Is it acceptable to mock football culture but not football itself? ☐ ☐

94. Do you still pretend to like soccer even though you haven't played it since high school? ☐ ☐

95. Do you think hockey is actually something more than soccer Ice Capades? ☐ ☐

THE INDIE CRED TEST

MULTIPLE CHOICE

THE INDIE CRED TEST

EVALUATE. AJUDICATE. DESIGNATE.

01. The first thing I see when I wake up is:
A. A band poster.
B. That tranny I mistakenly nailed last night.
C. The inside of the toilet.
D. My cellmate.

02. I first knew Rob Halford was gay:
A. When it was officially announced.
B. When I saw the video that takes place in a bath house.
C. About two minutes before he knew, when I invited him back to my room for "drinks and whatever."
D. Wait? What? Uh, Halford is gay?

03. "Straight Edge" is:
A. A song by seminal hardcore band Minor Threat.
B. The razor I shave with.
C. A lifestyle that disavows harmful intoxicants.
D. A bunch of fruitcakes who wouldn't know fun if it blew them in the bathroom at the 40 Watt Club.
E. Wound up people with control issues.
F. Embarrassing.

04. Which of the following descriptions or labels do you find *most* irritating when a "normal person" references metal or punk music?
A. Devil music
B. Headbanging music
C. That crazy shit
D. Kill Your Momma music

05. I get my pot from:
A. Street dealers in dime bags.
B. Some guy who stays at home all day.
C. Delivery service.
D. My basement garden.
E. School kids.

06. I smoke my pot in:
A. Regular size Jay's.
B. My car before going to work to help cushion the misery.
C. A crushed tin can converted into a bowl.
D. A homemade bong.
E. A metal screw-together pipe.
F. A glass pipe that resembles my mom a bit too much.
G. Plexiglas bongs.
H. A $250 electric contraption with a 28-page instruction manual.

FILL IN THE BLANK

UNBLANKIFY THE EMPTY SPOTS.

01. How many members of the opposite sex do you know on a first name basis? *(Note: Family does not count.)*

02. What quirky local organizations claim you as a dues-paying member?

03. How long does it take you to get to work, and how do you get there?

04. Name five places you visit where you never see somebody you'd deem as "cool." *(Note: Your parents' house doesn't count.)*
LOCATION No.01:

LOCATION No.02:

LOCATION No.03:

LOCATION No.04:

LOCATION No.05:

05. What is your position on sports?

06. Describe any nervous ticks you may have:
(e.g.: profane outbursts, uncontrollable snorts, irrepressible fisticuffs, etc.).

07. Describe any random body malfunctions you may have:
(e.g.: inward vomiting, involuntary scream-singing, spontaneous projectile limbs, etc.)

08. How many dead homies' names or faces are tattooed on your body?

09. How often do you find yourself fighting invisible assailants?

10. How often do you bathe?

11. How often do you bathe in the blood of your enemies?

12. When you hear "pits, pole and hole," what comes to mind?

13. Explain why you have a Yeah Yeah Yeahs CD.
(We know it's not a promo copy.)

14. You're flipping through the punk bin at a used record store. The bin starts with some promising stuff, but soon you realize you're wrist-deep in a pile of Blink 182, Sum 41 and the Mighty Mighty Bosstones. How deep and soul-searing is your momentary shame?

15. When Steve Albini mentions the make and model of a microphone, how many seconds is it before you're searching eBay?

16. How many websites do you check in the morning before taking a shower?

17. When you're the only non-Mexican in a Mexican restaurant, how good does that make you feel?

18. What were you listening to when you lost your virginity?

19. You lost your virginity in a trailer, but you lie and tell people you lost it in a _____.

20. You first tried these drugs in this order:

☐ Marijuana　☐ Cocaine/pills (uppers + downers)
☐ PCP　☐ Heroin
☐ LSD　☐ Methamphetamine
☐ HGH　☐ Over-The-Counter Decongestants

21. Did Thom Yorke leave a weird stain on your couch that you won't clean up because…well…it's Thom Yorke?

22. What's the most interesting place you've ever had food poisoning?

23. How often do you use the phrase "analog warmth"?

24. When did your appreciation of Hall and Oates stop being ironic?

ARE YOU RAISING A
HIPSTER BABY?

JUST BECAUSE YOU SHOVED ALL OF your hipster hopes and dreams into some poor broad and then watched them shoot back out in the form of a screaming, soul-sucking bag of fluids like some kind of miraculous enema doesn't mean the little tyke was born with any cred. Fact is, if want your kid to amount to anything more than Schneider from *One Day at a Time* you'd better damn well be stuffing cred in all its holes from second one. Will your child grow up to wear non-prescription frappuccino glasses or camo-pattern Mossy Oak beer goggles? Will they sport Big Daddy Roth tattoos or pock marks from an extensive steroid habit? It's time to calculate the cred of those who sprung from your fertile loins.

YOUR CHILD...	MORNIN', WHITE TRASH!	A NORMAL, SENSIBLE (YET ULTIMATELY DULL) CHILD.	CONGRATULATIONS! YOU'VE GOT YOURSELF A HIPSTER BABY.
WAS CONCEIVED...	Against the wall of McDonald's (inner or outer wall).	In a bed (romantic candlelight optional).	Following a Panda Bear gig.
SUITABLE NAMES	Boy, Girl, Hey You.	Something sensible, easily pronounceable, or the name of one of your parents.	Rothko, Camus, Zooey, Natas, Oops.
WORE [BLANK] HOME FROM THE HOSPITAL	A pair of cutoff shorts and a Bocephus temporary tattoo.	A monogrammed sweater hand-knitted by Grandma.	A custom-made Animal Collective onesie printed on American Apparel.
MOST COMFORTED BY	The sound of Mama being banged, beaten, or both simultaneously.	A pacifier and Mother's soothing touch.	An organic cotton vegan pillow.
DO YOU FEED IT ORGANIC, ETHICALLY SOURCED, VEGAN FOOD?	Feed them?	When affordable. A balanced diet is essential.	Of course. Anything else would be tantamount to child abuse.
SPENT THEIR FIRST NINE MONTHS...	Teething on a dirty syringe.	Filling diapers.	Wondering when Kevin Shields is going to come off the next My Bloody Valentine record.
WHILE CHANGING A DIAPER, S/HE IS MOST LIKELY TO...	Fart out a Toby Keith tune.	Be pissed off because you interrupted *Yo Gabba Gabba*.	Stare at the sparkles randomly sprinkled across the popcorn ceiling, making connections to a Stephen Hawking theory.
EASTER	Hunt eggs and eat all 32 immediately.	Hunt eggs and only cares about the ones with money.	Skip the hunt and talk about more post-modern things, like flip-flops and Elvis Costello.
"DAYCARE"	"Archie" comics, cold fish sticks and a tire swing by the rusted scrap iron pile in the back yard.	A somewhat-attentive stay-at-home parent who periodically checks on the kid in between "Dog the Bounty Hunter" marathons and Zoloft refills.	A bouncy-seat next to your documentary video editing station in your loft.
ASKED SANTA FOR...	A box of "Spicy Hot" Twinkies, a shotgun and a cubic zirconia mouth-grill.	A set of "Rock 'Em Sock 'Em" Robots: Taliban vs. USMC edition.	Nothing. My child does not believe in Santa, Jesus or corporatized Christmas consumerism. At least, that's what we tell him every time he asks for some "Rock 'Em Sock 'Em" Robots.
FAVORITE SPORT	He likes to play "Dodge Daddy's Beer Bottles." He's really good, I can hardly even hit him any more.	Football. And even if he hates it, he's playing, by God. And he better win! I didn't raise no damn queer bait! C'mon, boy! Set...hutt!!!	My child disdains competitive sports. He prefers crystal channeling, trancing and sensory deprivation flotation tanks. He was the first kindergartner ever to achieve "divine emptiness."
BEDROOM WALLS ARE DECORATED WITH	Firearms.	Posters of latest teen pin-ups (Robert Pattinson, Megan Fox, Bill O'Reilly, etc.).	Black and white photos of infamous heroin addicts.

EVALUATING YOUR PARTNER

What line of work is your partner in?
A. Graphic designer
B. Booking agent at a rock club
C. Data entry
D. Knitting/selling scarves on Etsy

What's your partner's highest level of education?
A. Graduate degree, NYU film school
B. M.B.A., the University of Michigan
C. Associates Degree in Scrappin', The School of Hard-Knocks
D. B.A. in English, The Bartending Institute of North Hollywood

Your partner's avenue of expression is:
A. making decent art.
B. a competent blog.
C. steady gossip.
D. repeatedly breaking into your neighbor's house to shit on their computer.

Your partner's big dream is:
A. to get published.
B. to run a solvent small business.
C. being an Amway success story.
D. being too confused to die.

Your pet name for your partner:
A. Morrissey
B. Lovey-Biscuits
C. Bitchface
D. Aunt Thunderballs

You met your partner:
A. at an unannounced Fucked Up show at last year's South By Southwest.
B. at a Chuck Close retrospective/wine tasting at the Art Institute of Chicago.
C. in the drunk tank after a Chickenfoot concert.
D. doing lines off the toilet tank at Slick Rick's apartment.

For your first date, your partner took you:
A. on a walk through the park, followed by lunch at a carbon-neutral raw vegan restaurant.
B. to the Chili's on the "nice" side of town for Fajita-Rita Monday.
C. to a martini bar where everything went black after the first drink.
D. to the loading docks at the abandoned steel refinery to share a bottle of SoCo and some Parliaments.

Before you met your partner, their last hook-up was with someone they met on:
A. a Belle & Sebastian fan site message board.
B. the "Missed Connections" section of the Chicago Reader.
C. Craigslist "Casual Encounters."
D. death row.

You'd be least surprised to hear that your partner previously hooked up with:
A. David Yow.
B. Julian Casablancas.
C. Gibby Haynes.
D. Pig Champion.

Your partner's hairstyle is most like:
A. Taka from Boris.
B. Joanna Newsom.
C. Kimya Dawson.
D. Richard Dawson.

Your partner exclusively wear:
A. vintage Levis.
B. vintage corduroys.
C. vintage Skidz.
D. vintage fishing waders.

Your partner thinks your tattoo is:
A. evidence of some aspect or flavor of individuality on your part.
B. a childish but forgivable indulgence.
C. preventing your upward mobility into management.
D. an affront to their Amish sensibilities, and turn off those lights.

Your partner carries:
A. your DJ gear so you can protect your hands
B. your business card, to help get you some referrals
C. your rent and student loan payments.
D. your roommate's seed.

Your partner says you look "good," which really means:
A. you look like the kind of person (s)he would fuck in the bathroom at a bar.
B. you look relatively healthy and stylish.
C. you look only mildly retarded.
D. you look like you need to shave something that's not visible to onlookers.

Your partner's favorite song to initiate sex is:
A. "Ace Of Spades."
B. "Ignition" (Remix).
C. "The Humpty Dance."
D. the theme from The Match Game.

Your partner's favorite euphemism for intercourse is:
A. "exchanging pleasantries."
B. "stocking the pantry."
C. "exploring our shame."
D. "the 'ol Tijuana crime scene."

During sex, your partner thinks of:
A. how awesome you are.
B. cast members of Gossip Girl.
C. Ralph Nader.
D. Swiffering.

After sex, your partner likes to:
A. smoke a joint and play Houses of the Holy.
B. balance pillow-talk with practicality and turn the TV on at a low volume.
C. motion for a high-five.
D. leap out of bed and curse you in a foreign language.

Your partner's record collection is primarily:
A. indie rock, '70s soul, and Blue Note jazz.
B. crusty punk with some early '90s industrial.
C. unlabeled MP3s they've copped from various friends' iPods.
D. every volume of Now That's What I Call Music.

When entering a record shop, does your partner:
A. starts at the opposite end of the stacks to help you cover ground faster.
B. blankly follows you around the store.
C. buys up all of the records on your want list before you can get them, then offers to sell them to you at double the price.
D. tries to score with the hot clerk by making "RPM" and "twelve-incher" innuendos.

When introduced to your parents, your partner is:
A. genuinely nice to them while appreciating their endearing cluelessness.
B. patiently willing to listen to their stories about your legendary childhood.
C. struggling to maintain a smile while the rage slowly builds.
D. constantly going to the bathroom to snort cocaine with the family dog.

The best thing about moving in with your partner is:
A. impromptu steamy showers together.
B. lip-synching in the mirror together to the morning radio.
C. comparing your lists of medications and pills.
D. flossing each other's teeth as a bonding exercise.

Happy Holidays! Your partner gave you:
A. paid airfare and tickets to All Tomorrow's Parties.
B. the coffee-table *Odermatt* compendium you had on your Amazon Wish List.
C. socks.
D. a gallon of expired milk and a box of syringes.

When your partner says "wedding," they mean:
A. a small Unitarian ceremony conducted by one of your friends, with a garden reception afterward.
B. several hundred people, several thousand dollars, and several months of planning.
C. a festival of fire-and-brimstone guilt, bookended by several days of "suck-for-a-buck" tee shirts and Hooters catering.
D. "Honey, there's a ring on the night stand. Put it on and then can we go back to bed"?

The first real argument with your partner was over:
A. String Theory.
B. "Why can't you help me pick up around the goddamn house already?"
C. whether Herr Metal would be the perfect name for your Scorpions tribute band.
D. whether "professional wrestling" is either "professional" or "wrestling."

When you go out to eat, your partner wants to:
A. hit up the taco truck and share a bottle of wine by the river.
B. visit the locally-sourced mom-and-pop restaurant around the corner.
C. see if those jalapeño poppers at Old Chicago taste as good as they look on TV.
D. control their urge to cut you just long enough to get some food in their belly.

When it comes to movies, your partner is:
A. as passionate about obscure foreign films as (s)he is about *Big Trouble In Little China.*
B. the equivalent of Roger Ebert: articulate and fair but ultimately populist.
C. the proud owner of the Joel Schumacher canon on Blu-ray.
D. adamant that movies will never reclaim the majesty of *The Best Little Whorehouse in Texas.*

On vacation, your partner likes to:
A. test the locals' sense of propriety.
B. plan ahead but remain open to fun, low-stress spontaneity.
C. criticize everyone who served you food or drinks that day.
D. drunkenly reminisce about how much better it was to vacation with their ex.

You are at a party trying to demonstrate how important, comfortable, and well-known a face you are in the local scene. Your partner:
A. stands next to you, laughing at your blend of clever humor and understated intellect.
B. stands next to you, looking for an opening at the bar.
C. continuously thumbs through texts on their Blackberry.
D. interjects randomly about Corn Nuts and "menses."

Why is your partner calling you at 4a.m.?
A. "There's this amazing warehouse party going on, get your ass down here!"
B. Wasted after DJ friend's set and needs you to pick them up.
C. Calling from a sales conference on west coast and forgot about time difference.
D. Propositioned an undercover cop, needs you to come bail them out (again).

CRED INDULGENCES

All of us have skeletons in our closets. For some, however, the transgressions of the past shadow their every move, consigning them to a life wholly devoid of cred. Is there any way to wash away the shame?

Why, yes there is. In the spirit of papal indulgences—donations once made to ensure a sinner's path into the kingdom of Heaven—the following cred indulgences can neutralize the past, boost your cred, and silence even your harshest critics.

IF YOU...	THEN...
Played in an all-white ska band from Florida	Working the door at Common Grounds or the Earl (whichever is farthest from where you currently reside) for two years while being paid in high fives
Owned a Steinberger	Perform Cinderella covers with a Mosrite utilizing four strings (non-standard tuning)
Followed Smashing Pumpkins on tour (post-*Gish*)	Six months wearing a Spice Girls camisole while working merch for Immortal, during which you're completely out of XL shirts and spiked pro-wrestling belts
Ever championed the bands Live, Fuel, or Bush	Provoke a fight with Brent Hinds. Start by shouting, "Well, if it isn't Eddie Van Hobo!" then toss him a crowbar and charge headfirst
Owned *Reality Bites* on VHS	Watch the nine-hour Holocaust documentary *Shoah* while blogging about it in real time
Succeeded in getting your band signed to a major label	The job you currently hold, serving at a restaurant, will suffice
Fucked Matt Dillon	Seduce Elijah Wood
Dissed Chunklet on Twitter	Things probably couldn't get much worse
Have a stated preference for Rush's eighties output	Discover the opposite sex
Attended (sans irony) a Dane Cook concert	Sorry. Sounds like you're absolutely screwed.
Eulogized a friend with a Nickelback song at his/her funeral	They'll be awaiting you in Hell, so get your apology ready.

RECREATIONAL SUBSTANCE EVALUATION
(BOTH LICIT AND ILLICIT)

HAS ANY DECENT STORY BEEN TOLD THAT DIDN'T INVOLVE DRUGS? Of course not! Why? 'Cuz chances are that person's vices are the only interesting thing about them. And, really, other than getting struck down by a runaway golf cart, what could be more exciting and/or death defying than a tummy filled with recreational narcotics? Nothing! So gander at this here chart to see what you've been enjoying and/or missing.*

SUBSTANCE	SLANG	BEGINNER	NOVICE	JOURNEYMAN	EXPERT
BEER	Piss Water, Brewski, Liquid Confidence, Fire Starter, Froth Dogger, Ice Tiger, Blockhead, Iced Bronson, Hip Hip Hooray	Heightened Sense of Awesomeness	Groupie Groped	More Brain-Dead Babies on the Way	Lengthy Incarceration Due to the Picking of a Fight With the Anamatronic Mouse at Chucky Cheese During Your Child's Birthday Party Because He Refused to Take Your Song Request
HARD LIQUOR	Shithead, Scottish Hate Crime, Paddy Juice, Date Rape Serum, Irish Gatorade	3 a.m. Jams in the Trailer Park	Shitzkrieg	Multiple, Simultaneous, Overlapping Court Dates	Sudden, Violent Procreation
MOONSHINE	Inevitable Disagreement, Highwaters, Liver Eraser	Became Proficient at the Banjo and Jew's Harp	Fought the Entire Earth	Seducing Your Own Couch	Dying from Ingestion Before Getting Murdered by Some Dude Named Donnie Ray
MARIJUANA	Da Grinch, Broccoli, Chillums, Ganja, Killa	Mastered the Rainstick	Had Sex with a White Chick with Dreads	Consumed a Graham Cracker and Spaghetti Sandwich	Wore Tie-Dyed Business Suit
LSD	Strobe, Bark at the Moon, Rain Dance, Keys to the Kingdom, Electric Kool-Aid	Learned, Then Forgot How to Play a Sitar	Opened a Junk Shop	Hallucinations That Lead to Eating Your Own Eyeball	Flashbacks Caused You to Eat Your Other Eyeball
MUSHROOMS	Glory Spores, Smurf Houses, Dogma-nure	Repeated the Phrase "Bob Moog is God!" While Holding Down the Lowest Key on Your Mini Moog for Three Hours	Puke-Giggled	White-Knuckled The Couch for Five Hours With the Phone Unplugged	Nipple Migration
PEYOTE	Cactus, Spewphoria, Dragon Hunter, Please Don't Eat My Mother	Participated in Crop Circle Sized Drum Circle	Engaged in a 48-hour Solo (on any instrument)	Involuntary High Fiving	Projectile Vomited from either nose or ear
ECSTASY	Any expensive car of your choice (e.g. Benz, Mitsubishi), $25 Orgasm, Brain Auger	Unreasonably/ Unseasonably Humongous Pants	Thought That Douchebag You Hate is "Alright"	Rubbed an Inappropriate Impression Into a Park Bench	Got Da Jock Ache
COCAINE	Peruvian Marching Powder, Hittin' the Slopes (in August), Nose Whiskey, Racehorse Charlie	Socialized with Dregs You Would Never Talk to Under Normal Circumstances	Told the Same God Damn Story Over and Over and Over and Over Again	Turned Two Nostrils Into One	Sneezed Out an Entire Coca Plant and a Small Peruvian Family
CRACK	Apple Jacks, Bobo Bullion, Devil's Dandruff, ODB	All Musical Equipment has Been Pawned for Six Bucks	Bouts of Giving the Best Damn Deals on Electronics in Town	Experienced a Strong Desire to Murder People for Their Loose Change and Recyclable Aluminum	Won a Two Month Unpaid Cell-Block Vacation

* NOTE THE AUTHORS OF THE INDIE CRED TEST ARE NOT ENCOURAGING DRUG USE. HOWEVER, LIFE IS FOR THE LIVING AND THE HUMAN MIND IS MEANT TO BE EXPANDED. DECIDE FOR YOURSELF. AND PLEASE, PLEASE, PLEASE DON'T SUE US BECAUSE WE'RE AUTHORITIES IN YET ANOTHER FIELD OF STUDY.

DRUG	SLANG	BEGINNER	NOVICE	JOURNEYMAN	EXPERT
METH	Dentist Boat Payment, Mullet Vitamins, Jail House Coffee, Baby Face, Potential Eraser	Got Some Shit DONE, No Matter the Cost	Endured Sternum Shattering Heart Palpitations	Arrrgh! Bugs!	Jelly Teeth
ANGEL DUST/ PCP	Amoeba, Crazy Eddie, Gorilla Biscuits, Pig Killer	Attended a Juggalo-Oriented Social Gathering	Achieved the Strength of Six Baboons	Demolished Four City Blocks in a Radioactive Fireball	Got Your Teeth Pushed in by Your Cell Mate, "Luther"
HEROIN	1000 Yard Stare, Judas Yeast, Rambo, Scag	Got over Fear of Needles	Nodded off While Playing a Guitar Solo	Didn't Shit for Two Whole Months	Got Mistaken for a Zombie and Shot Nineteen Times by Eight Different Rednecks
METHADONE	Dolophine™, Amidone™, Methadose™, Physeptone™, Heptadon™, Henna Heroin	Asked Your Doctor if Being a Methadone Addict is Right For You	Experienced Extremely Inopportune Bouts of Narcolepsy	Clown Feet	Accomplished No Sex or Enjoyment of Life Whatsoever for 12 to 20 Hours
OXYCONTIN	Hillbilly Heroin, Cotton Balls, Moccasins, Peter Rabbit	Eased That Cancer	Believed You Could Fly, Learned That You Were Incorrect.	Played in an '80s Cover Band Where All the Songs are About Wang Dang, to Make Up for the Fact that Your Dick is Doomed to the Noodle-y Nature of a Breadstick in a Pool	Never Shat Again
LORTAB/ VICODIN	Flea Market Smack, The Dean, Sweet Dreams, Co-Diddy, Robotrip	Experienced a Deliciously False Sense of Well-Being	Talked to People you Wouldn't Even Talk to While on Cocaine	Played "In the Groove" That No One Else Heard	Wrote a Concept Record, Minus the Concept
MORPHINE	The Quitter, Slooooow, Morf From Orf	Played a Single Guitar Note that You Were Positive No One Else Had Ever Played Before	Clearly Understood Conversations 30 Yards Away, but Ignored the One Being Directed at You	Rubber Bones	Died on a Toilet
ADDERALL/ VYVANSE	Honor Roll, Flowers for Algernon, The Amphetamine Babysitter	Won Employee of the Month	Learned Absolutely Positively Everything There is to Know About Mrs. Dalloway, the Many Uses of New Tide With Color Guard™ or Any Other Shit you Normally Wouldn't Care About	Translated all Tolstoy's War and Peace into Binary Code. Y'know, for "Fun"	Thought a Gaping Hole into Solid Matter
DOWNERS/ SLEEPING PILLS	Slo-Mo, Blue Suede Shoes, Blankie, Freddy Krueger, Livin' on a Prayer	Bitchin' Snore Solo, Dude	Publicly Exhibited Elevated Levels of Saliva Expulsion	Got 37 Consecutive Hours of Sleep	Snooze-Drove Your SUV Through the First Floor of a Mall While Blaring Journey's "Separate Ways" and had Zero Recollection of it the Next Morning
BARBITURATES	Apple-Piss, Bbu8, Hunter Thompson's Bone Marrow	Formed a Kickass Bob Seger Cover Band With Your Bowling Buddies	Foot Raced a Dead Guy, Lost	Sleep Pooped	Yawned 'til Your Head Folded Over Backwards
QUAALUDES	Shag, Rainbow Van, Doc Holiday, Altamont	Feathered Hair	Feathered Hair, Sweet Molestache	Feathered Hair, Sweet Molestache, Badass ponytail	Convicted of Third-Degree Nap-Rape
INHALANTS	The Huff, Hippie Crack, Whipple Nipple, Bloomin' Onion	Metallic Blue Lips	Perfected "The Stare"	4 + 4 = Mayonnaise	Brain Cell Holocaust
OPIUM	Black Jesus, Curly Bill, Opey, Alex Treblack	Spent 18 hours in a Bathtub	Itchiness Leading to Self-Induced Pitchfork Lacerations	Painful and Laborious Shitting of Play-Doh Cans	Witnessed Slow Motion Hurricanes Moving Backwards (Or Did You?)
CARBS	Swole, Bearclaw, Hot Pocket, Pachyderm, Chris Farley	Raw, Peeling Fat-Folds	Jowls	XXXXL	Step, Undulate, Inhale. Step, Undulate, Exhale

THE INDIE CRED TEST

"There I was: Death Cab was on a major, we were enjoying moderate success, and people knew me by name. But I was like, 'Fuck this, I demand more!' Thanks to my affiliation with the Bank of Indie Cred, I was able to acquire a top-of-the-line pixie actress, and then I was like, 'This is more like it!' Since our split, I now get what membership offers: Interview talking points, cyber-stalkers and orchestras. Yes, life is good! Thanks, BIC!"

Ben Gibbard
Gold Card member since 2007

HELPING NICE GUYS NOT FINISH LAST SINCE 1979.

On the surface, you're earnest, humble, harmless. You write songs about how many times your heart's been broken, and you've inspired more hopeless, defeated fans than the LA Clippers. But what sets you apart from your horn-rimmed competition? Your Bank of Indie Cred membership, which you've parlayed into the fastest cars, the biggest venues and the doe-eyed-iest women. With our help, even blasting from a super-credible indie to the same soulless major that Kid Rock and Matchbox 20 call home barely left a powder-burn on your cred rating. If you're ready to get a real return on that fake "sensitive" schtick you've fronted for years, call us today.

Visit **chunklet.com** today to see what **you** can acquire.

BANK OF INDIE CRED

BIC

CELEBRATING GENERATIONS OF INVESTING IN YOUR CREDIBILITY FOR OUR FUTURE

DON'T PLAY A NOTE WITHOUT IT. ™

HOME LIFE

LET'S FACE IT, WHEN ONE IS OUT AND ABOUT, it can be easy to pretend to be whoever we want to be, but nobody goes out every night. It's home life that can really define one as a person. Here's a quick guide to how your life is going at the place you are spending most of it. Are you pretentious? Are things not going so well? Or are you that baby bear hipster where everything is juuuuuuuuuust right?

	OVER COMPENSATING	JUST RIGHT!	UNDER SHOOTING
AUDIO	"The receiver isn't top of the line, but I figured for six grand, it was too good a deal to pass up. Plus, with the Indonesian gold plated speaker cables, you can't really tell the difference unless you are listening for it."	"I paid a ton for the turntable, but I got the rest on Amazon. I think I might have paid more for my computer speakers."	"I found it in the alley next to a raped, half eaten human corpse. You can use that screwdriver to jiggle open the cassette player."
DECOR	"I wouldn't mind trying La Maison Parfaite for a new gazebo trellis, but not after that little pissant valet messed with my sunroof."	"A guy was packing up shop at the Dogwood Festival and sold me some pretty cool prints at half-price."	"This Gone in 60 Seconds promotional poster really pulls the kitchen together."
FOOD	"Whole Foods had fresh duck breast flown in from Long Island. I'm going to make a red wine reduction and pair it with some haricot vert."	"I got some nice looking stuff at Dan's Fruit Market on the way home. Up for a stir fry?"	"Can you please pay the gas bill so we can at least boil water?"
INTERIOR DESIGN	"Yeah, we actually patterned the bedroom, living room and den after Neil Young's house in the Canyon."	"Our bar has the same kind of stools they use at the Rainbow Room in L.A."	"See this? It's the exact same brand of shitter that Elvis died on."
MOVIES	"I've been getting into a lot of Korean directors lately. Domestic films are getting way too overbudgeted and predictable."	"TNT's showing The Bourne Supremacy again tonight — grab a sixer and stop by!"	"Yeah, I grabbed a porno and a bag of Cheetos on the way home from work and had another evening of sitting prostrate in Cheeto dust."
PETS	"These are my Chinese water pythons, Robyn Hitchcock and Kid Koala."	"These are my Norwegian forest cats, Gaahl and Fenriz."	"These are my pit bulls, Michael Vick and GG Allin."
SHAVING	"It is from the Art of Shaving, a kind of soft mercurial blend of Kiel's mint hair raising formula and natural jojoba. The brush is Sri Lankan ostrich plumes and when you use it on your genitals it feels so wrong it's just gotta be right."	"I use an organic toner and papaya kiwi blend, and my Sensor Excel has a hybrid solar-Biodiesel motor!"	"How many times do you use your Bic before you start bleeding everywhere? Like twenty, right? They say disposable, but I think otherwise."
SLEEPING ARRANGEMENTS	"Yuck, 1500 thread count? I suppose we can use these in the mother-in-law suite."	"There's nothing quite like falling asleep to Music For Airports on a body pillow."	"Sorry 'bout the skid marks. Our last guest slept naked."
SLEEP	"I fall asleep to a tape of people clapping."	"I get in my 6-8 hours."	"Sleep is the cousin of death, and the next-door neighbor of meth-addicted unemployment."
WORK AT HOME	"I just want to finish the end-of-year financials before I take off for that week in Bali."	"They want like three more looks to decide from by tomorrow for the new logo treatment. My friend is coming over with beer and some My Morning Jacket bootlegs and we're going to bust 'em out."	"I bet there's a lot of copper pipe in that abandoned building across the alley."
YARD WORK	"Chuy, I hate to be a drip, but it's fifty pounds of lime pellets per 1000 square feet of lawn."	"I got some free compost from the county site. Let's get our organic plot started!"	"If Jesus wanted us to make use of city sanitation services, he wouldn't have invented the burn barrel."

CHAPTER 2

GET IT ON.
WEAR A THONG.
GET IT ON.

CLOTHES MAKE THE MAN, and in rare cases, they make the man-boobs less apparent. What began for humanity as a mere fig leaf has exploded into vast, overstuffed closets of sartorial lunacy. Having a wardrobe malfunction? Wear it until it becomes iconic. Are those moon boots trending up or down? Does it pop? Does it clash? Are you *trying* to resemble a vagrant? Function over form, right? *Wrong!* Discover how "put together" you truly are...

YES/NO

EITHER COMPLETE THE FOLLOWING QUESTIONS WITH A YES/NO ANSWER OR SUFFER THE CONSEQUENCES.

01. Do you want people to be able to discern your sexuality from your clothing?

02. Do Japanese kids ever offer to buy the clothes off your back?

03. Do you have any velour or terrycloth in your wardrobe?

03A. Do you know what velour or terrycloth is?

04. Do you buy clothing one size smaller just to "accentuate" and/or asphyxiate?

05. Did you get into hip-hop solely because you could buy fashionable clothes in size XXL, XXXL, and circus tent/tarpaulin sizes?

06. Do you think there should be a skateboarding test required to wear skateboard company clothing?

07. Do you secretly fear that when you die, your burial suit will be unstylish?

08. Do you look cooler in a suit than a Chihuahua does in a sweater?

09. Have you ever turned your work uniform into a fashion statement?

10. Do you tie a flannel shirt around your waist?

10A. If so, do you tie your socks around your ankles too?

11. Have you ever worn clothing cut for the opposite gender because "it fits better"?

12. Do you feel inadequate at music festivals when not wearing something neon?

13. Do zippers need to be functional?

14. Does your swimsuit have a turtleneck?

15. Leather jackets: black only, or some hue from the brown spectrum?

16. Has anyone ever told you that you dress like a rock star? How about a rock critic?

16A. If so, did that seem like a backhanded compliment to you?
('Cuz it probably was. Just sayin'.)

SHIRTS

17. Has your spouse/mate ever addressed (or "objected to") your t-shirt choice for family gatherings?

18. In retrospect, was it a good idea to wear that Eyehategod t-shirt to church?

19. Did you wear a Sub Pop "Loser" shirt in the '90s with obvious irony because you're clearly a total "winner"?

20. Do you wear t-shirts that you tell people are or are not ironic, depending on who you're talking to, such as a D.A.R.E. shirt?

21. Did you ever get into a band just because you liked their t-shirt?

22. Did a band ever get into you because they liked your shirt?

23. Should wearing the Misfits shirts with the big skull be limited to people who own at least one album by the Misfits with Danzig as the singer?

24. Do you wear tighter shirts so you don't look as fat? You do know that doesn't work, right?

25. Do you own any shirts with laces, ruffles or vampire collars?

26. Have borderline pedophile ads convinced you that crap called "brushed cotton" is worth ten bucks more than you would ordinarily pay for a t-shirt?

27. Do you own a bowling shirt and/or bowling shoes, despite having never bowled?

28. Have you ever worn a worn-out shirt for a joke band like Dread Zeppelin?

28A. Did you not wear it ironically?

28B. Did that explanation stop those Mexican dudes from beating your ass?

29. Do you consider having muscles to be a prerequisite for wearing muscle shirts?

30. Do you wear v-necks to show off your chest hair highlights or your "American bald eagle raping a snake" tattoo?

<u>31.</u> Is there any kind of t-shirt that can't be worn ironically?   YES ☐   NO ☐

<u>32.</u> Do you own a Daniel Johnston "Hi! How Are You?" t-shirt because Kurt Cobain wore one first?   ☐ ☐

<u>33.</u> Did you wear a shotgun blast to your face because Kurt Cobain wore one first?   ☐ ☐

JEANS/PANTS/ETC

<u>34.</u> Will you admit that you miss raver pants?   ☐ ☐

<u>34A.</u> How about now?   ☐ ☐

<u>35.</u> Do you believe there is such thing as a gender-neutral pant?   ☐ ☐

<u>36.</u> Can you make corduroy look rock'n'roll somehow? Are you quite sure?   ☐ ☐

<u>37.</u> Are you so fucking rock'n'roll you can pull off white jeans?   ☐ ☐

<u>37A.</u> Even if so, is it really a good idea?   ☐ ☐

<u>38.</u> Do you really think those black stovepipe jeans look good on those fleshy legs of yours?   ☐ ☐

<u>39.</u> Do you agree with the adage, "If you Dock, you can't rock"?   ☐ ☐

<u>40.</u> Have you ever worn khaki, even if it was only for a job interview? *(If so, put down the book and walk away.)*   ☐ ☐

VINTAGE CLOTHING

<u>41.</u> Do you know your exact pit-to-pit and collar-to-hem measurements specifically for buying vintage t-shirts on eBay?   ☐ ☐

<u>42.</u> Have you managed to convince yourself that you're not a douche for shopping at "vintage" clothing stores?   ☐ ☐

<u>43.</u> Do you own athletic apparel for teams that have not existed during your entire lifetime?   ☐ ☐

<u>44.</u> Do you own t-shirts featuring product mascots that have not existed during your entire lifetime?   ☐ ☐

<u>45.</u> Have you ever paid $25 at a boutique clothing store for an article of clothing that looks like you bought it for $3 at a thrift store?   ☐ ☐

<u>46.</u> Do you draw the line at underwear?   ☐ ☐

<u>47.</u> Do you shop for exclusively new clothes because old vintage clothing can't even possibly fit your sizable carriage?   ☐ ☐

<u>48.</u> Would you drive 40-50 miles from your home for a "virgin" thrift store not picked over by hipsters?   ☐ ☐

<u>49.</u> When short on cash, do you hide clothing in the racks for an future time when you're not short on cash so you can come back and buy it?   YES ☐   NO ☐

<u>50.</u> Have you been wearing a handful of your parents' "cooler" clothes since high school or college?   ☐ ☐

<u>51.</u> Do you really think that *Slip It In* t-shirt covers your muffin top?   ☐ ☐

<u>52.</u> Do you vintage-ize everything?   ☐ ☐

FOOTWEAR

<u>53.</u> Do you have a shoe room?   ☐ ☐

<u>54.</u> Do you wear cowboy or motorcycle boots?   ☐ ☐

<u>55.</u> Did you wear checkered slip-on Vans?   ☐ ☐

<u>56.</u> Did you continue to do so after you turned 30?   ☐ ☐

<u>57.</u> Did you ever put on roller blades for any reason, even if it was 1991?   ☐ ☐

<u>57A.</u> Did you tell everyone they were "inline hockey skates" to appear less lame?   ☐ ☐

<u>57B.</u> Did it work?   ☐ ☐

<u>58.</u> Do you *think* you're so fucking rock n' roll you can pull off white cowboy boots, à la Lemmy?   ☐ ☐

<u>58A.</u> If so, are you aware of how astonishingly wrong you are?   ☐ ☐

<u>59.</u> Do you wear pointy shoes in an effort to look more like a stylish European?   ☐ ☐

<u>60.</u> Do you wear combat boots?   ☐ ☐

<u>60A.</u> If you do, is your household income below the poverty line?   ☐ ☐

<u>61.</u> Did you wear Converse All-Stars when they were cheap and made in the States?   ☐ ☐

<u>62.</u> If so, do you continue to wear them now that they're expensive and made by starving, legless orphan sex slaves in a Burmese sweatshop?   ☐ ☐

<u>63.</u> If so, do you feel good about supporting their "way of life"?   ☐ ☐

<u>64.</u> Argyle: Completely stylish?   ☐ ☐

<u>65.</u> There are two types of socks...dress (black) and everything else (white). *This is not a question.*

<u>66.</u> Do you wear Timberland boots but don't work in construction? If so, is it because you are a trendy yuppie, an outdoorsy hippie, or a hardcore gangsta?   ☐ ☐

<u>67.</u> Are you punk enough to wear Crocs?   ☐ ☐

THE INDIE CRED TEST

	YES	NO
68. Have you ever worn Crocs to a show?	☐	☐
68A. Did you have the balls to get into the pit and do the "crock mosh"?	☐	☐
69. Do you think you understand homophobia, sexism, or racism more now that you own multiple pairs of Crocs?	☐	☐
70. Do you still think clogs will make a comeback?	☐	☐
71. Do you have a display case of rare shoes much in the same way your basement-dwelling, mouthbreather best friend has a display case of Star Wars action figures?	☐	☐

HAIR

	YES	NO
72. Does long hair facilitate rockin'?	☐	☐
73. Do you use gel and spray hair products to compose your head pubes into a helmet-like structure?	☐	☐
74. Did you stop dyeing your hair when they started selling Manic Panic at the mall?	☐	☐
75. Do you rock a comb over, sans any signs of baldness?	☐	☐
76. Have your parents ever validated your haircut because they saw something similar to it on TV?	☐	☐
77. Have you ever used an album cover as reference for your hair stylist?	☐	☐
78. Have you ever called in sick because of a bad hair day?	☐	☐
79. Men, have you ever put curlers in your facial or head hair?	☐	☐
80. Have you ever sculpted your sideburns into the shape of something that kicks ass, like grenades or flames?	☐	☐
81. Have you ever rocked dread pubes?	☐	☐
82. Have you ever gotten your shoulder or back waxed so you look sweet with a wife-beater on?	☐	☐
83. Have you ever been advised by a female to "shave your fingers"?	☐	☐
84. Do you consider facial hair a form of self-expression?	☐	☐
85. Do you have a Zach Galifianakis-eseque beard and/or physique?	☐	☐
86. Do you flat iron your eyelashes?	☐	☐
87. Do you refer to that thing above your lip as "the sweet 'stache"?	☐	☐
88. Do you high-five complete strangers with beards?	☐	☐
89. Do you knuckle-bump chicks who hit on you for your beard?	☐	☐

	YES	NO
90. Do you non-ironically compete in mustache or beard competitions?	☐	☐
91. Do you encourage or reassure those with new facial hair?	☐	☐

TATTOOS/PIERCINGS

	YES	NO
92. Do you have a tattoo of a band that you no longer like?	☐	☐
93. Have you not gotten a tattoo because of the pain factor?	☐	☐
94. Are you regretting that Prince Albert piercing yet?	☐	☐
95. Do you ever get "gauge envy"?	☐	☐
96. Have you ever entertained the thought, no matter how fleeting, that not every cartoon character makes for a bad tattoo?	☐	☐
97. Do you have a former lover's name tattooed on you somewhere?	☐	☐

ACCESSORIES

	YES	NO
98. Do you carry exposed drum keys to look cool?	☐	☐
99. Do you wear eye makeup but give it a virile name like "manscara" or "guyliner" to convey ownership and hide the fact that you can't stay out of your girlfriend's belongings?	☐	☐
100. Do you wear a wallet chain? *Wait, still?!*	☐	☐
100A. Is there actually a wallet attached to the chain?	☐	☐
100B. Do you tell people your chain is a "theft deterrent"?	☐	☐
101. Spiky ("pyramid") belts: Do you wear them?	☐	☐
102. Do you wear your sunglasses at night and/or indoors? *(If so, are you aware that you are not, in fact, Corey Hart?)*	☐	☐
103. Do you wear skinny ties?	☐	☐
104. Do you carry earplugs in your pocket?	☐	☐
104A. On your keychain?	☐	☐
105. Has your sweet choker necklace ever rendered you unconscious when you turned your head too fast?	☐	☐
106. When you wear a ball cap, do you prefer to wear it flat-billed and catawampus to show how antagonistic you are?	☐	☐
107. Do you wear fingerless gloves?	☐	☐
107A. Why? _____		
107B. Do you own a pair of leather socks, too?	☐	☐

THE INDIE CRED TEST

	YES	NO

108. Did you ever silkscreen patches for your jacket and/or hoodie in high school? ☐ ☐

108A. Was it:
Slayer? ☐ ☐
The Exploited? ☐ ☐
The Subhumans? ☐ ☐
Guns & Roses? ☐ ☐
Don Henley? ☐ ☐
Dee-Lite? ☐ ☐

109. Do you wear hats bought at big box suburban strip mall stores because they kinda sorta look Fedora-y? ☐ ☐

110. Are you such a fat sweaty fuck that you need the additional sopping-up power that only a wristband can give? ☐ ☐

111. Do you think Mark Knopfler pulled off that headband? ☐ ☐

LADIES

	YES	NO

112. Do you visit Etsy at least once a day? ☐ ☐

113. Did you knit your own scarf? ☐ ☐

114. Have you ever worn little girls barrettes or baby doll dresses? ☐ ☐

115. Do you and your boyfriend share jeans? ☐ ☐

116. Have you ever tried using curlers to sculpt the "area"? ☐ ☐

117. Do you prefer fancy winklepickers to crusty fencehoppers? ☐ ☐

118. Ladies, be honest: the first time you wore a thong, did you put it on backwards, feeling a lot more comfortable with a small swatch of fabric over your pubes and the larger swatch of fabric over your ass? ☐ ☐

118A. Men: same question.

THE INDIE CRED TEST

MULTIPLE CHOICE

THE INDIE CRED TEST

CHOOSE THE MOST APPROPRIATE ANSWER, OR LIE AND CHOOSE THE ANSWER THAT IS MOST LIKELY TO GET YOU LAID, PAID OR MADE.

01. Is your shirt:
A. Tucked
B. Untucked
C. Front-tucked
D. Off

02. You got your last new T-shirt:
A. At a show.
B. At Value Village.
C. In a vintage tour memorabilia auction on eBay.
D. From the floor you woke up on last weekend.
E. From a buddy who was tired of seeing your man-nipples.

03. Which of the following best describes your haircut:
A. A jet black fauxhawk with ironic mullet and flat ironed devil lock.
B. Clipper guard number 3.
C. I'd sooner cut my wrist than cut my hair.
D. I'm just trying to go bald before I go gray.

04. My favorite accessory is:
A. A one eyed parrot named "Skittles."
B. A cigarette burn on my eyelid.
C. A fishing lure on my Hoobastank baseball cap.
D. A "Drug Free: Way To Be" bandana tied over my track marks.
E. Pins of bands I don't like so I can roll my eyes at and feel superior to anyone who compliments me on them.
F. A dirt stain from last year's Bonnaroo.
G. A Dale Earnhardt bolo tie.

05. The only thing better than a popped collar is:
A. Two popped collars!
B. A popped neck.
C. An ascot.

06. Have you ever....
A. Worn a visor at night?
B. How about indoors at night?
C. How about backwards, indoors and at night?
D. How about upside down, backwards, indoors and at night?
E. How do you expect God to forgive us for our sins with you dressed like that?

07. Your glasses look like something you'd buy off a Soviet carpet salesman because:
A. They're old-school ironic chic, like in Portland, Oregon in '00.
B. You don't have insurance and they're all you can afford.
C. You sold carpet in Leningrad back in the day.
D. They glow in the dark.
E. They're falling apart.

08. When choosing a t-shirt for a show, you wear a shirt from:
A. The headliner (current tour).
B. The headliner (previous tour).
C. The support act.
D. Headliner side-project.
E. Headliner label-mates or known friends.
F. Support act label mates.
G. Support from headliner's previous appearance.
H. A label itself.
I. Headliner's rival band.
J. Tool.
K. What was on top of the clean pile.
L. Same as the last three days.

09. After having bathed in a pair of jeans to get that perfect fit, how stupid did you feel afterwards?
A. Not at all, I rule no matter what.
B. I felt somewhat stupid.
C. Stupider than Sarah Palin addressing the Mensa All-Stars.
D. Unbearably stupid. I *literally* killed myself in shame and am writing this with a ghost pencil from beyond the grave.
E. Not stupid at all. I look at my corpsey, dyed-blue legs as a badge of pride.

THE INDIE
CRED TEST

FILL IN THE BLANK

THE INDIE
CRED TEST

COMPLETE THE FOLLOWING QUESTIONS BY FILLING IN THE BLANKS. BUT SMOKE OPIUM FIRST.

01. Describe how Converse Chuck Taylors and One Stars are different?

02. If so, please describe, in one word or less, how such useless information enriches your life in some way.

03. Please draw your hair style.

04. Ladies, how big of a role does animal print play in your wardrobe?

05. How many all-over-print (read: douche-print) shirts do you own?

06. How much longer is your beard than your hair?

07. How many more square inches of ink you have than skin?

08. Are sweater vests ironically cool or just dorky? Is there a difference?

09. Does the fact that you continue to shop for clothes at Hot Topic without any shame mean you have more or less cred than someone who either A) refuses to shop there or B) shops there secretly, perhaps disguised as Fred Durst?

10. How much were those glasses? Be honest.

THE INDIE
CRED TEST

IDENTIFICATION

THE INDIE
CRED TEST

WHICH RETRO LOOK DO YOU FOLLOW?

- ☐ 4th century Mongol Warrior
- ☐ Ronnie James Dio
- ☐ Medieval European Leper
- ☐ 1860s Carpetbagger
- ☐ 1870s Prospector
- ☐ 1890s British Chimney Sweep
- ☐ '20s Gangster
- ☐ '30s Golfer
- ☐ '40s Barbershop quartet

- ☐ '40s Sharecropper
- ☐ '50s Doo-wopper
- ☐ '50s Housewife
- ☐ '50s Gas Station Attendant
- ☐ '50s Milkman
- ☐ '60s Greaser
- ☐ '70s Doofus
- ☐ '70s ABA Basketball Star
- ☐ '70s Groupie

- ☐ '70s Disco(ke head)
- ☐ '80s Preppie
- ☐ '80s Flashdancer
- ☐ '90s Dirtbag
- ☐ '90s Babe in Toyland
- ☐ '90s Raver
- ☐ 2000s Bike messenger
- ☐ 2050 Robot Insect
- ☐ Ninja

- ☐ Hobo
- ☐ Hitchhiker
- ☐ Tad Doyle
- ☐ "Smuggler's Blues" Video Extra
- ☐ Post-Rapture Angel
- ☐ Other:_____
  _____
  _____

WHICH OF THE FOLLOWING TATTOOS DO YOU HAVE? *(CHECK ALL THAT APPLY)*

- ☐ Black Flag 'bars'
- ☐ Rocket From The Crypt logo
- ☐ Generic 'straightedge' X's
- ☐ Screeching Weasel logo
- ☐ "How Much Art Can You Take?"
- ☐ Avail's "Dixie" stick man logo
- ☐ Pearl Jam's stick man logo
- ☐ Morrissey lyrics
- ☐ The Postcard Records cat
- ☐ The Sarah Records cherries
- ☐ Misfits skull
- ☐ Nautical star(s)
- ☐ Chicago flag

- ☐ The DC stars and bars
- ☐ Anything inside your upper lip
- ☐ Anything on your knuckles
- ☐ Jawbreaker 4 F's cross
- ☐ Hot Water Music logo
- ☐ Crass logo
- ☐ A swastika in a circle with a slash
- ☐ A sea cucumber with a heart over it
- ☐ Dead Kennedys logo
- ☐ Generic or Emo stars
- ☐ Germs logo
- ☐ Minor Threat "Out Of Step" sheep
- ☐ NYHC

- ☐ Tales From the Crypt logo
- ☐ Starland Vocal Band *(they suck)*
- ☐ Factory Records logo
- ☐ A line from an R.E.M. song
- ☐ A line from a High Back Chairs song
- ☐ DRI skankin' man
- ☐ Hello Kitty
- ☐ Dukakis/Bentsen '88
- ☐ Dead Moon logo
- ☐ Barbed wire around arm or leg
- ☐ K Records logo
- ☐ Bad Brains self-titled album cover
- ☐ Anything covering up track marks

- ☐ Jesus Lizard "mouse on bomb" image
- ☐ Celtic or tribal anything
- ☐ AC/DC logo
- ☐ This Is Not A Fugazi Tattoo
- ☐ Schlong's Schlitz beer logo
- ☐ Fuel "Head and Gas Nozzle"
- ☐ Spitboy "Crying Woman"
- ☐ The cover of any Mastodon album
- ☐ Snake on your face
- ☐ Axl Rose's face *(back piece)*
- ☐ "Beer" and "Poon" on your knuckles
- ☐ Sewer Trout "Devil Trout & Pitchfork"
- ☐ Skankin' Pickle skankin' man

- ☐ Self-inflicted vertical knife scars on your wrists
- ☐ "No Bad Days" (you stanky-ass hippie)
- ☐ Yosemite Sam riding Falcor with a picket sign that says "Clikitat Ikatowi Cannot Be Stopped, Only Contained"
- ☐ Soulside logo, but only because actor Dax Shepard used to have it on his shoulder
- ☐ Anything Rick Froberg illustrated
- ☐ Very Small Records "Denny's 'Race Mixing Is Cool' Logo"
- ☐ Calvin pissing on the Urge Overkill logo
- ☐ Iron Maiden's Eddie hurting another band's mascot
- ☐ Joy Division *Unknown Pleasures* cover

SO YOU WANT TO GET A TATTOO

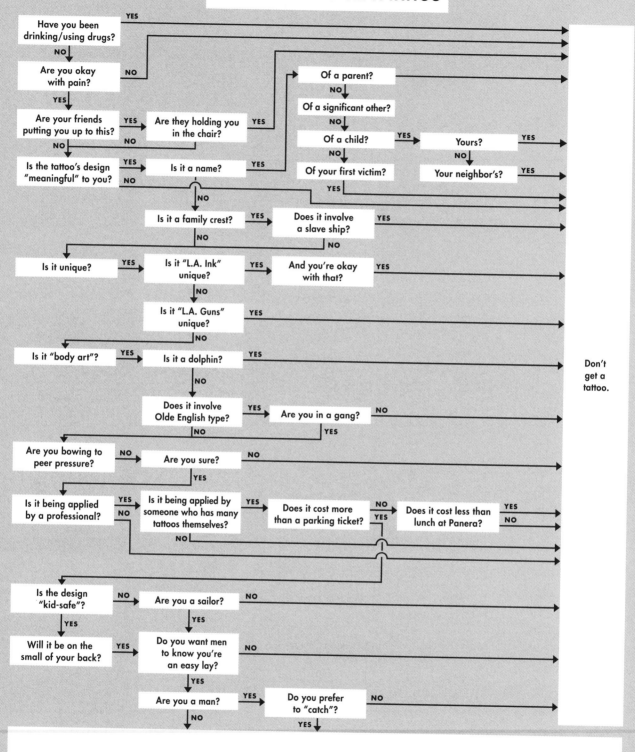

THE INDIE CRED TEST

WARDROBE CHECKLIST

CHECK ALL THAT APPLY.

SHOES

- [ ] Doc Martens *(14-hole or above)*
- [ ] Doc Martens *(before they were bought out by LA Gear)*
- [ ] Beatle Boots
- [ ] Combat boots
- [ ] Zubaz
- [ ] Moon boots
- [ ] Rubber kangaroo shoes
- [ ] Vision Street Wear shoes *(originals, not reissues)*
- [ ] Indoor soccer shoes
- [ ] Clunky shoes
- [ ] Chuck Taylors *(that were made in America)*
- [ ] Checkerboard Vans
- [ ] Chukka boots
- [ ] Saddle shoes
- [ ] British Knights shoes
- [ ] Light up knock-off Air Jordans
- [ ] Jelly sandals
- [ ] Jams
- [ ] Puma 'Clydes' *(list color combo)_____*
- [ ] Suede creepers
- [ ] Air Jordans *(pre-1995)*

SHIRT

- [ ] Coca-Cola rugby shirt
- [ ] Hawaiian shirt
- [ ] Minor League hockey jersey
- [ ] Marc Jacobs flannel shirt circa '92
- [ ] Bowling shirt that you only wear to Reverend Horton Heat shows
- [ ] Gas Station Attendant shirt with name patch of someone that absolutely can't have existed *(e.g. "Cradge")*
- [ ] Any Ralph Lauren Polo shirts
- [ ] V-neck shirt that other people just call a vest
- [ ] A plaid shirt for all the colors of the rainbow
- [ ] Cut-off mesh football jersey

T-SHIRT

- [ ] Hypercolor t-shirt
- [ ] "Where Were You When St. Helens Blew?" t-shirt
- [ ] "This Is Not A Fugazi Shirt" t-shirt
- [ ] "Wellstone!" or "Wellstone Action" t-shirt
- [ ] One "Lidsville" iron-on t-shirt, extra skinny
- [ ] "My Other Shirt is a Rolls Royce" t-shirt
- [ ] Original Black Flag "Slip it In" t-shirt
- [ ] Old Chunklet t-shirts that are now too small to fit over your ever-growing belly
- [ ] "I'm Stoned" t-shirt with a picture of someone having rocks thrown at them
- [ ] "Steak-Ummms" ringer
- [ ] Desert Storm shirt
- [ ] Panama Jack shirt
- [ ] Ocean Pacific shirt

- [ ] Black Smurfs shirt
- [ ] Sports team t-shirt from a high school you did not attend or a town you have never visited *(basketball or baseball preferred)*
- [ ] Big Johnson shirt
- [ ] One standard-issue "Velvet Underground And Nico" Warhol-Banana t-shirt *(should have received during freshman orientation)*
- [ ] Bloodstained Slayer shirt
- [ ] Nazi Punks Fuck Off shirt
- [ ] Ruffled tuxedo shirt
- [ ] Motorhead shirt
- [ ] SST "Corporate Rock Still Sucks" shirt
- [ ] Youth of Today shirt *(XXL or larger only)*
- [ ] White t-shirt
- [ ] D.A.R.E. t-shirt
- [ ] Priest t-shirt
- [ ] Death t-shirt
- [ ] Electric Wizard t-shirt
- [ ] Mayhem "True Norwegian Black Metal" t-shirt
- [ ] Championship t-shirt of now terribly shitty and/or nonexistent sports team *(likely from early/mid-'80s)*
- [ ] "Where's the Beef" t-shirt
- [ ] Vanilla Ice or New Kids On The Block Tour shirt
- [ ] 1987 Fun Run shirt that barely covers your PBR gut
- [ ] Tourist shirt from a city that barely has tourist attractions, much less a reason to be celebrated by a t-shirt *(Cincinnati, I'm looking at you!)*
- [ ] Any '70s cartoon t-shirt *(Underdog, Hong Kong Phooey, etc.)*
- [ ] Washed-up magician/prop comic shirt *(David Copperfield, Doug Henning, Gallagher and so on...)*
- [ ] The line of "Looney Tunes as thug/ghetto people" shirts *(the ones where it'd be Taz or whomever on the front with a backwards hat, cell phone, baggy jeans, etc.)*
- [ ] The t-shirt with the Black Flag roach spray logo *(not the bars or any band-related images)*
- [ ] Billy Corgan-style "ZERO" shirt
- [ ] Self-designed tee-fury shirt
- [ ] Thrifted hair metal band shirt *(extra points for loudness, nitro, or Lizzie Borden)*
- [ ] Vuarnet France t-shirt
- [ ] Phish t-shirt that doesn't have permanent pit stains
- [ ] Totally badass black metal t-shirt that you wore to work once, only to learn that no one looks at you long enough to read the bullshit on your chest
- [ ] "Who farted?" t-shirt
- [ ] "Button Your Fly" t-shirt
- [ ] "Button Your Own Fly, Dickhead" t-shirt
- [ ] White long sleeve shirts with black sleeves/collars
- [ ] "No Bozos" t-shirt, as worn by the brothers Van Halen on the '82 Diver Down tour
- [ ] T-Shirt from band you or your honey were in
- [ ] "Mustache rides 10¢" t-shirt
- [ ] Any sort of Grateful Dead themed parody of a product logo t-shirt

- [ ] Buy Olympia 'Reading Is Sexy' t-shirt
- [ ] Kid Robot hoodie/t-shirt *(preferably Kozik designed)*
- [ ] "If you ain't a duck hunter, you ain't shit" vintage t-shirt from *Uncle Buck*
- [ ] Original Soul Asylum "While You Were Out" t-shirt
- [ ] Original Replacements "Tim" t-shirt

JEWELRY

- [ ] Cassette-tape necklace
- [ ] Insane Clown Posse tie tack and cuff links
- [ ] Bear claw earring
- [ ] Chopstick necklace

SOCKS

- [ ] Tube socks of great length with many holes
- [ ] DayGlo socks

WRIST

- [ ] 2" wide leather banded watch
- [ ] Swatch
- [ ] Leather armbands
- [ ] Spiked bracelets
- [ ] Two Swatches with interlaced bands
- [ ] Dayglo snap-bracelet
- [ ] Fingerless gloves
- [ ] Calculator watch
- [ ] Swatch guards
- [ ] "X" Swatch
- [ ] Slap bracelets
- [ ] Wrist sweat band

PANTS

- [ ] Stone-washed jeans
- [ ] Guess jeans
- [ ] Parachute pants
- [ ] Girbaud cords
- [ ] Cargo pants
- [ ] Stone-washed Guess jeans
- [ ] Body Glove spandex
- [ ] High waters
- [ ] Sansabelt pants
- [ ] Skidz
- [ ] Dickies' shorts that were once Dickies' pants
- [ ] Stirrup pants
- [ ] Parachute pants
- [ ] Biking shorts
- [ ] MC Hammer pants
- [ ] A pair of too tight jeans that convinced you to try heroin
- [ ] Intentionally ripped jeans
- [ ] Culottes

BELT

- [ ] Bullet belt
- [ ] White belt
- [ ] Ethernet cord as a belt
- [ ] Vintage Swiss Army knife belt
- [ ] Spiked belt
- [ ] Olympia Beer belt buckle
- [ ] The Locust belt buckle
- [ ] Cartoonishly large belt buckle espousing a political ideal you find particularly hilarious/ironic

JACKET/SWEATER

- [ ] Nicaraguan hippie sweaters with the stench of patchouli
- [ ] Leather jacket *(plain)*
- [ ] Leather jacket *(with painted-on logos/patches)*
- [ ] Leather jacket *(with spikes/studs)*
- [ ] Suede "McCloud" jacket
- [ ] Jean jacket/vest covered in patches
- [ ] Michael Jackson Thriller/Beat It Jacket
- [ ] Dickies gas station jacket
- [ ] "Golden Girls" hoodie
- [ ] Black leather jacket, many-buckled
- [ ] Member's Only jacket
- [ ] Mondale/Ferraro Campaign Sweatshirt
- [ ] Biker jacket, even though you've never owned a motorcycle
- [ ] Dirty jean jacket *(this can be a vest if you are from the South)*
- [ ] Cardigan sweater *(list colors: you know you have at least three)*
- _____
- _____
- _____
- [ ] Real or faux animal print coat
- [ ] Hoodie promoting a now-extinct record store that went under due to gentrification/real estate "boom"

HAT

- [ ] PacMan snow cap
- [ ] Knitted beer can hat
- [ ] Multiple Lucha Libre wrestling masks
- [ ] Fisherman's hat
- [ ] Mesh hat
- [ ] Fitted baseball cap
- [ ] Snap-brim fedora
- [ ] Beer-can hat
- [ ] "X" cap
- [ ] Trucker hats
- [ ] Tennis visor
- [ ] Newsboy hat
- [ ] Fidel Castro hat
- [ ] Kangol hat
- [ ] Van Halen jobber hat
- [ ] Any animal print painter cap
- [ ] Negro League baseball cap that you simply don't have the balls to wear on the bus
- [ ] Fishnet hat

ACCESSORIES

- [ ] Operation Ivy back patch
- [ ] Leather fanny pack with dream catcher baubles
- [ ] Courier bag
- [ ] Headband with a hit of acid in it
- [ ] Piano keyboard scarf and/or tie
- [ ] Fishnet gloves
- [ ] Handmade scarf
- [ ] Skinny tie
- [ ] Cravat

- [ ] Chunky black-framed glasses *(with prescription lenses)*
- [ ] Chunky black-framed glasses *(with plain glass lenses)*
- [ ] "Brown in '92" pin
- [ ] Purse made from a cigar box
- [ ] Leg warmers *(what a feeling!)*
- [ ] Hoop skirt and parasol from your antebellum phase
- [ ] Welding goggles that match your electric violin
- [ ] Lunch box
- [ ] Sanrio accessories of any type

BRAND

- [ ] Bad Boy Club
- [ ] Carharrts
- [ ] Any Maui and Sons surf wear
- [ ] SB Dunks
- [ ] SB Bricks
- [ ] Croakies
- [ ] Vision Streetwear
- [ ] Wu Wear
- [ ] Built by Wendy anything
- [ ] Cross Colors
- [ ] British Knights

UNIFORM

- [ ] Cross Colors bib overalls *(circa '92)*
- [ ] Pizza Shuttle uniform
- [ ] Any 'leisure wear' à la Urge Overkill
- [ ] Costume/clothing elements for any member of Kiss
- [ ] Anarchy cheerleader outfit

UNDERWEAR

- [ ] Fishnet stockings
- [ ] TV on the Radio brand underwear
- [ ] Underoos

ANY ARTICLES OF CLOTHING WITH THE FOLLOWING ACCESSORIES

- [ ] Name patches *Bearing your own name, or a stranger's?*
- [ ] 1" pins *How many pins? How many articles of clothing are the pins on?*
- [ ] Canvas patches? *Are they sewn on with dental floss?*

ADULT

- [ ] Chastity belt
- [ ] "White Shadow" jock-strap
- [ ] Loincloth *(made of raw veal)*

OTHER

- [ ] Tie-dyed anything
- [ ] Anything with an iron-on
- [ ] Alf puppet
- [ ] Rolling papers and drum
- [ ] Rape whistle
- [ ] Lee Press-On nails
- [ ] Anything with a Crass logo on it
- [ ] Crutches
- [ ] Neck brace
- [ ] Any article of clothing advertising Pabst Blue Ribbon, Motel 6 or Kum 'n Go gasoline

---

THE INDIE CRED TEST

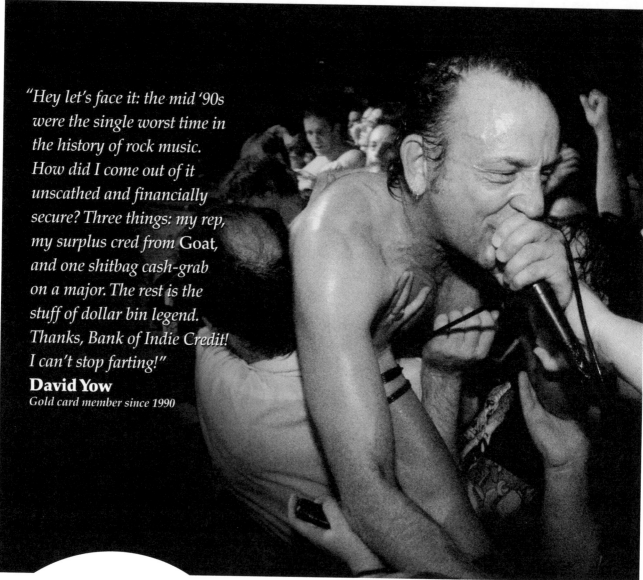

"Hey let's face it: the mid '90s were the single worst time in the history of rock music. How did I come out of it unscathed and financially secure? Three things: my rep, my surplus cred from Goat, and one shitbag cash-grab on a major. The rest is the stuff of dollar bin legend. Thanks, Bank of Indie Credit! I can't stop farting!"

David Yow
Gold card member since 1990

BANK OF INDIE CRED

BIC

CELEBRATING GENERATIONS OF INVESTING IN YOUR CREDIBILITY FOR OUR FUTURE

KEEPING YOU FAT. EVEN DURING LEAN TIMES.

It can happen in the blink of an eye: one moment you're riding high thanks to an album like *Liar*, and before you know it, even your friends are missing your gigs get on the guest list for that Smash Mouth/Third Eye Blind double-billing. But with membership, your cred level went untouched and your liquor cabinet was always well-stocked. How did you manage that? With the Bank of Indie Cred, it's never only one set of footprints in the sand — that was just where we were carrying you.

DON'T PLAY A NOTE WITHOUT IT. ™

Visit **chunklet.com** today to see what **you** can acquire.

CHAPTER 3

FIT (NIT)WIT

YOUR LIFESTYLE IMPACTS YOUR DEATHSTYLE. And weight loss always accompanies death. And since being skinny is cool, death is therefore also cool. To put it another way, being healthy is like being Rob Thomas, while being unhealthy is like being Rob Zombie. Either way, you're not all that great. So why try to live healthy? Wait. Don't answer that. But do answer these questions...

THE INDIE
CRED TEST

YES/NO

THE INDIE
CRED TEST

**COMPLETE THE FOLLOWING QUESTIONS WITH A
YES/NO ANSWER OR SUFFER THE CONSEQUENCES.**

01. Can you do 10 push-ups?

02. Can you do 10 punch-outs?

03. Can you do 1,000 anything?

04. Do you find that you only run if you're being chased?

05. Does the very idea of working out strike you as completely meritless?

06. Is your only form of exercise "rippin' up stages"?

07. Do you NOT work out, in a conspicuous fashion?

08. Do you find the term "squat thrusts" funny?

09. Do you secretly wish Nu Metal fashion would come back in vogue so you could jog to a show and not have to change clothes when you got there?

10. Did you have a beer gut by age 20?

11. Do you circulate the rumor that people who work out are perverts?

12. Do you circulate the rumor that people who work out are Catholics?

13. Do you scoff at magic voodoo words like "cholesterol" and "diabetes"?

14. Do you really go to yoga to exercise, or to pick up like-minded mates who listen to NPR, may own a couple of Sea and Cake CDs and put black turtlenecks on their cats?

WORKOUT MUSIC

15. Do you spend more time choosing the music for your workout than you do actually working out?

16. Have you ever quit a gym because of the music they played?

17. Were you excited (for exercise reasons) about the release of LCD Soundsystem's "45:33"?

18. Have you ever described a song as "the perfect running song"?

19. Have you ever described a song as "the perfect aerobic fighting song"?
Trick question, we ALL have.

WORKOUT EQUIPMENT

20. Is your amp the heaviest thing you've ever picked up?

21. Is your spouse/mate the heaviest thing you've ever picked up?

22. Do you own and use a pedometer?

23. Do you chuckle to yourself when you say the word "pedometer"?

24. Do you own any exercise equipment?

24A. Is it fighting for space with your band gear?

25. Have you ever sold any music equipment to buy exercise gear?

SUPPLEMENTS

26. Do you drink more than two energy drinks a day?

26A. If so, do you kick the bathroom wall's ass for gettin' lippy three or four times a day?

27. Do you ever slam protein shakes?

27A. Do they come from from a powdered mix, or do you just make a shake out of whatever you can find in Lou Ferrigno's garbage?

28. Have you ever taken a performance-enhancing drug?

29. Do you think "weed" qualifies as "performance enhancing"?

30. If so, what performance are you watching?

31. Have you ever eaten anybody on account of 'roid rage?

THE INDIE
CRED TEST

MULTIPLE CHOICE

THE INDIE
CRED TEST

CHOOSE THE MOST APPROPRIATE ANSWER, OR LIE AND CHOOSE THE ANSWER THAT WILL MAKE YOU SEEM COOLER THAN YOU REALLY ARE.

01. What is the first thing you do after a workout?
A. Check your pulse and calculate your calorie burn total.
B. Call the paramedics.
C. Smoke a cigarette.
D. Drop acid and hit a glory hole.

02. Which of the following best describes your workout apparel?
A. Old band t-shirt, crummy shorts, and low-top Converse one-stars.
B. Store-bought exercise gear that looks brand new because it gets used less often than Mars Volta writes a good song.
C. Jeans, hoodie, and water bottle filled with vodka.
D. I work out in the nude. The health club revoked my membership for some reason....
E. Ironic '80s sweatband/nut-huggers ensemble, which doubles as an on stage outfit and triples as a crime fighting costume.
F. The Stevenson: Sculpted back hair and teeny-tiny shorts.

03. Which fad have you most recently embraced and then bitterly discarded?
A. Atkins
B. P90X
C. The Master Cleanse
D. The Patch

04. Which vitamin is most important?
A. A
B. B
C. C
D. D, baby

05. How many hours of sleep do you require?
A. 8-10
B. 6-8
C. 3-5
D. The booze and meth decide

06. Where are you sore all the time?
A. Back
B. Head
C. Liver
D. Crotch

07. What condition holds you back?
A. Asthma
B. Sleep apnea
C. Fibromyalgia
D. Bipolar disorder

08. You quit smoking because...
A. You didn't want to die of cancer.
B. You were tired of coughing.
C. Your significant other disapproved.
D. Back off, squirt. I'm celebrating man's victory over fire.

09. What's the minimum that qualifies as a "workout"?
A. Two hours at the gym
B. One hour at the gym
C. Walking the dog
D. Getting out of bed before sunrise

10. What genre of music do you listen to on your headphones when you work out?
A. Hardcore punk
B. Hip hop
C. Speed metal
D. '70s and '80s classic rock
E. New wave and post punk
F. The theme from *Mork and Mindy*
G. Yanni

11. To monitor my fitness progress, I tend to tailor the length of my athletic endeavors to the average duration of:
A. Neurosis songs.
B. pre-*Agorapocalypse* Agoraphobic Nosebleed songs.
C. Beethoven symphonies.
D. TV commercial jingles.
E. The space between CD tracks.

12. Which of the following best describes your level of fitness?
A. Regular marathons and 10Ks.
B. Occasional hiking, usually when dating a granola-type outdoorsy person.
C. I don't usually worry about fitness, since my heroin addiction keeps me fit-and-trim.
D. Since I park in the free lots a mile or so from the clubs and venues, I get a fair amount of walking in.
E. I get most of my upper-body workouts lugging around vinyl crates to record shows and shops, and moving them from my various shitty apartments.
F. My major workout is walking from my car into the liquor store to buy alcohol and cigarettes.
G. I get cardio runnin' from the po-po. Taggin' bridges is a workout, yo.
H. Headbanging to *Reign In Blood*.

13. Thoughts on Yoga?
A. Daily Sun Salutations
B. Once a week with spouse/ girlfriend
C. Only when lookin' for chicks
D. Best watched in HD with sweatpants on

14. When you see other folks of indie ilk at the gym, do you:
A. Give a graceful, acknowledging nod that says, "Yeah, I've probably seen you at shows," but could be misinterpreted as, "Wanna go behind the dumpsters and party?"
B. Sneer condescendingly.
C. Pretend to be invisible in your all-over print hoodie.
D. Introduce yourself with a hi-five and staid compliment (*"Nice ink! That band rules! Sports!"*) and then exercise awkwardly with your really boring buddy, who is pretending to be invisible.

15. When doing any rigorous activity, what do you consume the most?
A. Water
B. Water with electrolytes
C. Beer
D. Energy drink with alcohol
E. Cocaine
F. Your own vomit

16. I own a fixed speed bike because:
A. I have been afraid of gears since I saw "A Nightmare on Gear Street" when I was seven.
B. The BMXers rejected me when I was 13, so it is nice to finally be accepted by the bike gang.
C. I saw Sufjan Stevens riding one in a Whole Foods commercial.
D. It goes better with fluorescent Ray Bans than a mountain bike.

17. When I buy a bike I look for:
A. A sturdy frame.
B. A colorful frame.
C. A colorful frame that matches my Chucks and Ray Bans.
D. A colorful frame that matches my Chucks, Ray Bans, messenger bag, and the wall in my apartment which it will occasionally not lean against.

18. I define exercise as:
   A. Walking to the American Apparel store.
   B. Pulling on a tight pair of jeans.
   C. Putting a new record on the turntable.
   D. Standing at a show for long periods of time with my arms folded.

19. Acceptable attire for any type of exercise is:
   A. Super-skinny jeans and a t-shirt.
   B. Super-skinny jeans (cut-off) and a t-shirt.
   C. Super-skinny jeans, no shirt, and a scarf.
   D. All of the above.

20. I play kickball because:
   A. Deep in my heart, I know I am a pussy.
   B. I am sick of the badminton crowd kicking my ass.
   C. I thought that basketball was the sport that had "touchdowns."
   D. Holding a bat tends to turn me on.
   E. I have no arms. Thanks, asshole.

21. Jocks suck because:
   A. They can't carry on a half hour debate about *Mass Romantic* being a better album than *The Electric Version*.
   B. They still beat me up when I try to get a drink at the water fountain, and I'm 42.
   C. They look better than me in skinny jeans.
   D. My girlfriend always makes me dress up like a baseball player so she can actually "get off" when we do it.

22. The last time I got exercise I was:
   A. Running to get in line to see Crystal Castles.
   B. Running to Starbucks to get a latte before they closed.
   C. Lifting a case of PBR cans into a shopping cart.
   D. Stapling a show flyer to a telephone pole.

23. If I was forced to play any team sport it would be _____, because:
   A. Field hockey/I already occasionally wear skirts.
   B. Soccer/my hands need to be free to flip through my iPod.
   C. Baseball/I could check the news on Pitchfork in the dugout or outfield.
   D. Basketball/it would give my phony love of rap increased credibility.

THE INDIE CRED TEST

FILL IN THE BLANK

THE INDIE CRED TEST

COMPLETE THE FOLLOWING QUESTIONS BY FILLING IN THE BLANKS. (DUH.)

01. How often do you go to the doctor? .. _____
   Dentist? .... _____
   Exorcist? .... _____
   Voodoo lady? .... _____

02. How often do you get your prostate checked?
   _____

03. How often do you get your prostate checked by a professional?
   _____

04. How often do you get your prostate checked by a professional wrestler?
   _____

05. How many times the recommended dosage of pseudoephedrine do you take when you have a cold?
   _____

05A. How much ass does that kick?
   _____

06. What's your max bench press?
   _____

07. What's your max bench press on Pantera? _____
   How about on Mariah Carey? _____

08. Number of "Ks" you brag to friends that you run: _____
   Percentage of that number that you actually run: _____

THE INDIE CRED TEST

CALCULATE

THE INDIE CRED TEST

CALCULATE (OR JUST MAKE SOME SHIT UP)

01. $$\frac{\text{(Length of time in the mosh pit before showing fatigue)} + \text{(average hours of sleep per night)} + \text{(\# of packs of cigarettes per day)}}{\text{(age)}} = \boxed{}$$

02. $$\frac{\text{(Grams of meth smuggled into the venue via "prison wallet")} + \text{(length of time it took to clean the bag)} + \text{(number of joules burned while tweaked and headbanging to the average-length Kirk Hammett solo)}}{\text{(number of vertebrae in need of realignment afterwards)}} = \boxed{}$$

THE INDIE CRED TEST

ACCEPTABLE REASONS TO
QUIT DRINKING

Drinking and driving isn't even a challenge anymore.

You realize you gave up on everything else you tried to do with your life.

Chris Berman is actually starting to make sense.

You wake up next to Courtney Love....two days in a row.

"It's all pink inside" goes from being a punch line to an excuse, to a motto, to a goal.

You're banned from the jazz club because sometimes saxophones look like urinals.

Keith Richards stages an intervention for you at his annual "All You Can Snort" coke party.

You find yourself having to negotiate a trade with a hobo in order to get your left eye back.

You routinely get mistaken for being a dead body.

You realize after recovering from a two-day drinking/Food Network bender that you've been throwing salt at people and yelling "bam!"

You routinely wake up on the other side of the state line with either a rash, a misspelled tattoo or a missing appendage.

Your mattress needs a few days for the piss to dry out.

Look in the mirror. You're not Bon Scott. You never will be. Move on with your life.

You've started to look like a cross between toilet Elvis, Jim Morrison, Mama Cass, and Flavor Flav.

The only mixer you have left is toilet water.

Boy Scouts use your breath to start fires.

Because teaching your son to be a prize-fighter at the age of four is frowned on by certain (asshole) government agencies.

Contrary to popular belief, it doesn't make you a better artist, just an asshole.

Your wardrobe consists entirely of sweatpants and free Miller Light t-shirts.

You pulled out your last good tooth opening that beer bottle, so how are you going to open another?

You paid $9.00 for a beer at a concert.

You've been cut off.

You vomited a condom.

You think that more liquor might be able to kill the tumor on your liver.

You find a turd, rolled neatly in someone else's monogrammed handkerchief, in your pocket.

There aren't any more wheels on your house to pawn.

You formed the opinion that if you snuggle with Melissa Gilbert, you will become magically sober. Just like that one time you drank gasoline to stop smoking.

You're finally ready to stop urinating for 45 minutes at a time.

You start enjoying G.G. Allin's music just a bit too much.

It's clear that Ian MacKaye would look cooler holding a diaper bag and twirling a baton than you do holding a longneck Bud.

Your fitness goal for the new year is to land somewhere in the Poison Idea range.

You're having second thoughts about hating most things.

Cops can't smell Vicodin on your breath.

You offer your bartender a blissed out night of shadow puppetry art for one last goddamned drink.

Liver bulge.

You die from alcohol poisoning.

FOOD & DRINK

CHAPTER 4

UP/DOWN THE HATCH

WHAT YOU PUT INTO YOUR BODY IS EQUALLY as important to your cred as what you drape over it and/or stick through it. We're not talking about Ben Wa balls here, we're talking about sustenance and nutrition. Are you a waifish vegan with Ethiopian tendencies or a rolling glob of mustard-stained-mayonnaise and body hair tightly wrapped in a Pantera shirt? Do you spend more time wandering the aisles of Barley Crumb's Whole Food and Supply, or waiting your sweaty mess of a self in line at Ye Olde Burger Joynt? Either way, that which is put into your body better damn well be cool. Let's find out if you're choking down enough cred.

YES/NO

COMPLETE THE FOLLOWING QUESTIONS WITH A YES/NO ANSWER OR SUFFER THE CONSEQUENCES.

YES NO

01. Do you argue with people who follow recipes?

02. Do you refuse to eat honey because you consider it to be "exploiting the bees"?

03. Do you run a community garden co-op on your property or in your neighborhood?

04. Do you consider yourself a specialist at cooking boxed dinners à la Hamburger Helper?

05. Do you have any professional experience as a line cook, sous-chef or school lunch lady?

06. Do you own a deep fryer big enough to cook a human body?

07. Are you mildly disgusted when a relative gives you meat they killed and butchered themselves?

08. Are you a professional musician who also blogs about food on the side, or a foodie who just happens to play bass?

09. Have you ever eaten roadkill just so "good meat won't go to waste"?

10. Do you consider yourself a "cereal specialist"?

11. Do you ever find yourself in heated discussions as to why BBQ is a noun and not a verb?

12. Have you ever participated at a secret/illegal culinary event where you pay a prix-fixe to dine on the homeless?

13. Have you ever taken a mid-meal shit to "make room"?

DINING OUT

YES NO

14. Are you a "regular" at any restaurant/bar?

15. Have you ever had a dish named after you at your favorite restaurant?

16. Are the words "gut buster" or "belt melter" found anywhere in that dish name?

17. Do you have a seat/table at your local eatery that's known, by the stains, to be yours?

18. Did you forgive McDonald's for being corporate shitbags once you tried those kickass Spicy Hyena Nuggets™?

19. And did you then forgive them for the gut-liquefying McDysentary™ that you got afterwards?

ALCOHOL

20. Is your picture on the wall of your favorite bar?

21. Does it say "do not serve this piece of shit" on that picture?

22. Do you really think people care to hear about your raunchy-assed home brew?

23. Have you ever paid more than a month's rent for a 12 oz. bottle of beer?

24. Do you drink unfiltered beer?

25. Do you ask to see a drink list before ordering?

26. Do you pay attention to the "legs" on a glass of wine?

27. How about the legs on the waitress who brought you the wine?

MULTIPLE CHOICE

CHOOSE THE MOST APPROPRIATE ANSWER AND SHUT YOUR PIE HOLE.

01. Who is the most famous hipster in your neighborhood CSA (community-supported agriculture) group?
A. John "I snort Patchouli" Robbins
B. That Japanese guy who eats 83 hotdogs in two minutes
C. Steve, who used to own a bike shop and likes to slip that into any conversation
D. Barney Frank's ex-lover's grandson.

02. How often do you eat fast food?
A. Only when on the road and starving
B. Monthly
C. Weekly
D. Daily
E. I'm sorry, can you repeat the question? I'm having a little trouble breathing.

03. When ordering fast food, my approach is:
   A. To scream "Meat is murder," hose down the whole restaurant with pig blood, thank them for their time, then leave.
   B. To get a couple of small items from the dollar menu.
   C. Just get the super-triple whatever and the phone number of a good cardiac surgeon.

04. What kind of beer snob are you?
   A. The kind that knows Schlitz has "just a kiss of the hops," thank you very much.
   B. I'm obnoxiously touting my fake Irish heritage by feigning extreme interest in Guinness snouts. Er, sprouts! I'm still learning.
   C. The Belgian trend is sooo overplayed, but I can't get enough of the Canadian copycats, eh.
   D. You're going to Darklord Day? Me too! Are you drinking your bottles or selling them on eBay?
   E. I listen to a lot of world music these days... hey, bartender, gimme something pretentious…I mean ethnic!

05. If you have eaten at Kuma's Corner, please select which of the following best describes your experience:
   A. I masticated a Mastodon.
   B. I pigged out on a Pig Destroyer.
   C. I swallowed a Goblin Cock.
   D. I'm far too hip to eat at a metal-music-themed restaurant, but let me know when Dinosaur Jr. opens a pasta house.

06. My favorite cocktail is:
   A. Gin and chronic
   B. Tequila and sweet tea
   C. Fancy Sauce™
   D. Vodka and Frankenberry
   E. Whatever you got. What's that, formaldehyde? Fine, gimme.

07. Has the recent economic downturn caused you to shift your enthusiasm from record collecting to becoming a connoisseur of any of the following?
   A. Hot dogs
   B. Rot dogs
   C. Scotch
   D. Human baby-cue

08. Please rate your level of meat consumption by choosing one of the following:
   A. All meat and only meat. No vegetables, starches or liquids that aren't blood. It hurts to poop. Is that normal?
   B. No beef or pork for dietary or crazy-ass religious reasons.
   C. Only fish but also dairy. Wait, is fish a vegetable?
   D. Vegetarian, aka vegan poseur. No meat of any kind but dairy products are OK, provided they contain no dairy.
   E. Vegan White Belt: no animal products of any kind.
   F. Vegan Yellow Belt: All organic, all the time.
   G. Vegan Green Belt: Only organic produce sourced from within one day's journey by horse.
   H. Vegan Brown Belt: All organic, locally sourced from Amish farmers who eschew combustion engines.
   I. Vegan Black Belt Master: I grow all my own food and eat it raw, while naked and crying.

09. You have an interview with Touring Band X over dinner.

Your choice of restaurant is:
   A. A vegan nacho cart.
   B. A corporate coffee shop.
   C. Squealers "Kill It Yourself" Slaughterhouse Cafe.
   D. Any place with a bar and no cover.
   E. Dumpster diving in the alley behind Homo's Pizza.

10. Your beer of choice is:
   A. PBR
   B. Bud Light (aka: the sucker's PBR).
   C. Meister Brau (the trust funder's PBR).
   D. Yuengling (the formerly-Chinese PBR).
   E. O'Doul's (the recovering alcoholic's PBR).
   F. Pretentious art student seaweed tasting crap.
   G. Anything I find left unattended at the bar.

11. Sorry, food wasn't on the rider. Guess you guys will be eating:
   A. Mexican (i.e.: Doritos)
   B. East Indian, so we can play "fart wars" in the van.
   C. Crumbs from the floorboard.
   D. Whatever we can shoplift at the gas station.
   E. Maybe we'll eat tomorrow.

12. Where do you keep your liquor?
   A. In my stomach!
   B. At a home bar I carved myself out of elephant ivory and hippo skulls.
   C. Under the sink.
   D. In a "quick draw" hip flask.
   E. Down the front of my shirt.

13. The name of my favorite restaurant ends in:
   A. Reve
   B. Puck's
   C. Garden
   D. Bell
   E. -11

14. My drinking habits are most comparable to those of:
   A. Carrie Nation
   B. Carrie Brownstein
   C. Drew Carey
   D. Don Draper
   E. Bon Scott
   F. Evan Williams

15. I am most likely to get drunk on:
   A. Champagne
   B. "Yack"
   C. "Martoonies"
   D. Jack Daniels straight from the bottle
   E. Paint thinner

16. Due to my eating habits, my physique is best described as:
   A. Boney
   B. Doughy
   C. Sweaty
   D. Juggalovian

17. The majority of my grocery money goes to:
   A. Whole Foods
   B. Ralph's
   C. Trader Joe's
   D. Safeway
   E. Subway
   F. 7-11
   G. My heroin dealer

18. When you suggest "the best slice in town," what you're really suggesting is:
 A. This place makes good pizza.
 B. This place makes "specialty" pizza, involving some shit that should never be on pizza, like pork rinds, whole avocados or macaroni.
 C. This place makes the biggest and cheapest slice of pizza.
 D. This place makes the best pizza that you don't have to wait an hour in line for.
 E. This place is a high quality whorehouse.

19. The hipster bar in town's most notable jukebox selection includes:
 A. Journey or Willie Nelson, sincerely.
 B. Slayer's blues cover album "Reign In Blues."
 C. Clarence Carter's "Strokin'."
 D. Mother Love Bone.
 E. Pavement.
 F. Gang of Four, ironically.

20. The default meal you make to impress others when they're over for dinner is:
 A. Thai curry.
 B. Fresh black bean hummus and pita.
 C. Insalata Caprese with field greens.
 D. Chili.
 E. Totino's party pizzas.
 F. Combos and Sierra Mist.

21. You switched from yellow corn chips to blue corn chips because:
 A. They're better for you.
 B. "Organic" appeared somewhere on the bag.
 C. You enjoy paying more for something that tastes like shit.
 D. You think blue looks more exotic.
 E. It's easier to assess the health of your bowel movements.

22. Without even thinking about it, you're typically in the mood for:
 A. Mexican and/or Asian food.
 B. Anything gluten-free.
 C. A syringe of spicy liquid cheese.
 D. Slow, belly-tightening starvation.

23. When you "pig out," you like to:
 A. Ignore your diet and dive into the fat and salt.
 B. Methodically shovel food into your face like a soulless, futuristic machine.
 C. Describing it requires the words "naked in a bathtub filled with…"
 D. Eat more than five gummy bears.
 E. See which part of a living pig you can most easily fit into your mouth.

24. Your best attribute in the kitchen is:
 A. Your fundamental grasp of cooking dynamics and measurements.
 B. Your nimble way with utensils and food processors.
 C. Your enviable upbeat attitude.
 D. You can always find the dishwasher.
 E. Your alcohol tolerance.

25. Your town's specialty is:
 A. Its own brewery.
 B. Three of its own breweries.
 C. Only to be found in the next town over.
 D. Food that makes outsiders sick.
 E. Variety, available in cannibal, vegan and kosher form.
 F. STDs.

26. Your female rocker dream date is:
 A. Grabbing a few drinks with Cristina from Pussy Galore and Boss Hog.
 B. Doing anything whatsoever with Debbie Harry circa 1978.
 C. Mama Cass and a gyro date circa 1968.
 D. A McDonalds dinner date with Courtney Love followed by some good ol' fashioned smack and a photo op nipple suck.

27. Your favorite kind of wine is:
 A. Red wine.
 B. White wine.
 C. Box wine.
 D. Toilet wine.
 E. Emo whine.

28. When you eat "spicy" food, you:
 A. Turn red/sweat.
 B. Shit/vomit uncontrollably.
 C. Have little/no reaction.
 D. Cry jalapeno tears that burn holes in the carpet.
 E. Talk to a camera crew about how miserable you are.

29. Organic food is:
 A. The only way to go.
 B. Nice when you've got a little extra money.
 C. Kinda gay.
 D. Not much of a concern when you mainly eat at gas stations on tour.
 E. A scam.
 F. Gross because it sounds like you're eating organs.

30. You're putting up a touring band for the night. You offer them:
 A. A date rape cocktail.
 B. Leftover Chinese Pizza.
 C. Organic, cruelty-free Vegan "air puffs."
 D. Lawn clippings.
 E. Leftover cat food.
 F. Purple stuff.

31. You start to brew your own beer instead of going to shows because you're old and every new band sucks. What do you name your first batch?
 A. Old Style.
 B. The Empty Bottle.
 C. Too Crowded Stout.
 D. Scared Ale.
 E. Nothing Good Has Been Released Since 1982 Lager.

32. To eat "ethically" you:
 A. Buy locally.
 B. Buy seasonally.
 C. Grow your own vegetables in the local community garden.
 D. Buy as much as possible at once from Sam's Club.
 E. Liberate foodstuffs from restaurant supply closets.

33. Coffee is:
 A. Unhealthy because caffeine is a drug.
 B. The number two legally-traded commodity on the planet.
 C. What courses through my veins.
 D. The flavor of my favorite Starbucks dessert beverage.
 E. Never worth $15 a cup no matter what animal shits out the beans.
 F. The reason my pee is chunky and my poo is 100% liquid.

34. You're a promoter in Europe and have to feed the headlining band.
What do you give them?
A. McDonalds so they don't get homesick.
B. Ramen so they don't get homesick.
C. Taco Bell and moonshine so they do get carsick.
D. Macaroni & Cheese-Its.
E. Drugs.

35. You're at the bar. You order:
A. Anchor Steam
B. Fancy British brew
C. Cocaine, some fruit juice and an underage hooker
D. Milwaukee's Best, ice and a puke bucket
E. Milk of Magnesia

36. When on tour, you:
A. Purchase/lift groceries at Whole Foods and cook at your host's house.
B. Go straight to hell with Taco Bell.
C. Ask Burger King if you can suck on their grease traps.
D. Hunt domestic cats and dogs.
E. Hit up the local slaughterhouses for spare head cheese.

37. What are your go-to value meal choices at the following chains (list by number):

McDONALD'S

01	02	03	04	05	06	07	08	09	10

BURGER KING

01	02	03	04	05	06	07	08	09	10

WENDY'S

01	02	03	04	05	06	07	08	09	10

ARBY'S

01	02	03	04	05	06	07	08	09	10

TACO BELL

01	02	03	04	05	06	07	08	09	10

Aren't you ashamed at all that you were able to rattle those off so quickly?

THE INDIE CRED TEST

MATCH

THE INDIE CRED TEST

MATCH COLUMN A WITH COLUMN B.
DO NOT SCREW THIS PART UP.
GOD IS WATCHING YOU.

I. Match the band that's staying at your house to the "cool" place you'll drag them for breakfast in the morning

01. The Mantles ....   A. Barbeque Barfy's

02. Wolves in the Throne Room ....   B. Your apartment garden

03. Daniel Higgs ....   C. The Druid's Rejoinder

04. Ween ....   D. Dream Salad

05. Souls of Mischief...   E. The soul food place

06. Dan Deacon ....   F. The place where you have to try their amazing pancakes, oh my god seriously

07. The Depreciation Guild ....   G. The closest supermarket dumpster

Answers: 1.F, 2.C, 3.B, 4.E, 5.A, 6.D, 7.G

II. Match the following musicians with the comestible they are best known for, or the one that best matches their professed diet

01. Ted Nugent ....   A. Fatburger

02. Steve Albini ....   B. O'Douls

03. Morrissey ....   C. Vegan BLT (tempeh bacon)

04. Justin Timberlake...   D. Slim Jims

05. Hasil Adkins ....   E. Cheesecake

06. Darius Rucker ....   F. Dirt and worms

07. Queen Latifah........   G. Tender Crisp Bacon Cheddar Ranch sandwich

08. Ian MacKaye ....   H. Venison that he done killed hisself

09. P. Diddy ....   I. Memphis BBQ

10. Moby ....   J. Seafood Pan Roast

Answers: 1.H, 2.D, 3.E, 4.I, 5.F, 6.G, 7.A, 8.B, 9.J, 10.C

SECTION II

JUSTIFIED & ANCIENT:
GETTING PAID.
GETTING LAID.
GETTING OLD.

CHAPTER 5

EMPLOYMENT ACCREDITATION

WHAT YOU DO MAY NOT DEFINE YOU, but it definitely defines what you can afford to do. A powerful job bestows power on the individual, and we all know power is sexy. Therefore your man muscle will probably only love you as much as she loves your money. But here at Chunklet Industries, we're not shallow, gold digging hoochies. So even if your rate of pay is so pitiful that you can only afford one shoe, half a pair of pants, three meals a month, a cardboard box in a ditch and a flat tired unicycle, we love you just as much as if your compensation level were stratospherically ridiculous while your actual "duties" consist of golfing, coffee pisses and enthusiastic parrotings of various hackneyed business-isms, like, "Absolutely sir, our integrated network solutions are shovel-ready and reflect our ongoing commitment to market flexibility. Hail Satan!" Besides, your reading this is evidence that you found a way to afford this book, so you're okay with us no matter what. Unless you're a professional shoplifter.

YES/NO

THE INDIE CRED TEST

COMPLETE THE FOLLOWING QUESTIONS WITH A YES/NO ANSWER OR SUFFER THE CONSEQUENCES.

01. Do you call the primary source of your income your "day job"?
02. Did you get your job by clicking on a banner ad on an Internet porn site?
03. Does your job have flextime?
04. Do you think "flextime" sounds a little gay?
05. Does your employer pay you enough to *actually care* or simply to *act like you care*?
06. Do you get irrationally angry when you see improper kerning?
07. Have you ever had to explain the difference between "italic" and "oblique"?
08. Do you judge a day at work as being good or bad by the number of coupons customers redeem?
09. Do you judge a day at work as being good or bad by the number of customers who lived?
10. Do you spend the majority of your paycheck at your place of employment?
11. Is there a tip jar anywhere on the premises of where you work?
12. Did your current employment come about as the result of your losing a bet?
13. Are you allowed to wear headphones at your job?
14. Are you forced to wear headphones at your job?
15. Does your job get a new set of employees each semester, with you being the only full timer?
16. Do you have to pretend to love Jesus in order to get along with your co-workers?
17. Do you have to pretend to think Rush Limbaugh is entertaining in order to get along with your co-workers?
18. Do you have to hide your tattoos in the workplace?
19. Does your company have a softball, bowling, chess or boxing team?
20. Do color forecasts give you a boner (fashion, cosmetic, skin)?

21. Do you clean up mystery juices in jerk booths or jack shacks for monetary compensation?
22. Do you characterize "working for a temp agency" as "freelancing"?
23. Does the phrase "action items list" fill you with irrational rage?
24. Do you describe yourself as a professional writer even though you do all your work for free?
25. Did you list PowerPoint on your resumé as a "skill"?
26. Are you required to answer the phone with a catch phrase?
27. If so, does it change daily, based on whatever crap the company is pushing?
28. Do you actually know who you'd have to piss off in order to get fired?
29. If you park in the employee of the month's parking space, and you're not the employee of the month, will there really be hell to pay?

JOB REQUIREMENTS

30. Does your job require full disclosure as it pertains to relationships if you're gay?
31. Does your job require a drug test using a Scantron? That's fucking awesome.
32. Does your employer insist that you freeze to death because it's good for the computers?
33. Does your job require you to hide your political affiliations?
34. Does your job require having sex for money?
34A. What about for a promotion?
34B. What about for charity?
35. Does your job require you to live in New Jersey?
36. Does your job require you to live under water?
37. Does your employer require that you purchase a plastic see-through purse to use while on the job to cut down on employee shoplifting?
38. Does your employer require that you purchase plastic see-through clothing to wear while on the job to cut down on employee shoplifting?

THE INDIE CRED TEST

WARDROBE

YES NO

39. Does "dress professionally" at your office mean "wear a shirt with at least two buttons"?

40. At your job, does the "dress code" require sleeve tattoos?

41. Does your chosen vocation require you to wear a name tag? If so, isn't it about time you "choose" something else?

42. If you're required to "dress up" at work, were you stupid enough to buy more than one pair of black pants? Because, y'know, you could wear those everyday and no one would notice. And if they do, they're assholes.

43. If your job allows you to dress casually, do you have tape over the word "dick" on your Chunklet shirt?

DRUGS/ALCOHOL

44. Did you ever accept a job based on its proximity to your favorite bar or strip club?

45. Have you ever been required to take a drug test at work?

46. If "yes", was a positive result considered a positive result?

47. Is on-the-job drinking acceptable?

47A. Mandatory?

TRAVEL

48. Does your job require you to travel?

49. If so, does it require you to strap a plastic car topper with a logo on it on the roof?

50. Does your "job" require you to cram controlled substances up various body cavities and quickly run across international borders?

51. Are you on a first name basis with INS agents due to this profession?

52. Do your customers consume the goods you produce from a pipe or a syringe?

THE BOSS

53. Have you ever seen your boss eat a bowl of money?

54. Do you have pizza lunches every other month as a way for your boss to ensure everyone will be there so he can tell you what a shitty job you've all been doing on a collective level?

55. Do you ever go to great lengths to explain why the person at your job who tells you what to do is not, technically, your boss?

YES NO

56. Do you get two (and only two) days off only if your mom or dad dies? One day for grandparents?

56A. Do you have to use "vacation days" to go to your friend's funerals?

57. Do you get your wife to call in sick for you hoping to convince them that you really are dead?

58. Is your boss aware that if he/she were bleeding to death you would lift up their legs and squeeze really hard?

59. Does anyone in the world know when boss appreciation day is?

60. Does your boss' breath smell like the inside of a cancerous lung?

61. Have you ever gotten drunk with your boss, thought for a while he was an okay guy, woke up the next day realizing the mistake you made, filmed yourself killing yourself, burned it to DVD, and put it in your 5 year old daughter's DVD player so she can see whata failure you are?

THE OFFICE

62. Are titty posters allowed in your cube?

63. What about band posters?

64. Do you often field dumb questions all day regarding said bands?

65. Do you work near a guy whose cubicle is filled with action figures and who you only recently discovered hasn't been on the phone the whole time, but was in fact just talking to the toys?

66. Do you describe yourself as "kinda the office cool guy"?

67. Does anyone else describe you in such a manner?

68. Do you take the whole box of your favorite pencil/pen from the supply area, to be a dick?

69. Do you use your e-mail signature to inspire others?

70. Do you use your e-mail signature to promote your blog, book, band, or your bad taste in blogs, books, and bands?

71. Do you provide your own headset for your job to avoid dealing with less-than-sanitary co-workers?

72. Do you get a kick out of listening to other people's fights with their wives in the cube next to you?

73. Do you also pretend that a two-inch-thick cube wall made of foam will keep other employees from hearing *your* poopie-pants fights on the phone?

YES NO

74. Do you often get away with doing absolutely nothing but dick around on the Internet in your cube? ☐ ☐

75. Have you ever snorted a drug out of your desk drawer? ☐ ☐

76. Is your cubicle bigger than your apartment? ☐ ☐

77. Are there vintage Frank Kozik posters in it? ☐ ☐

78. Do you get suckered into doing everything music related at work because you're known as the band guy? ☐ ☐

79. Let's say an email goes around with music from some bullshit band like Korn or whatever attached to it. Does everyone look at you and say, "Yeah, that's *his* kind of music" just because it's loud and has heavy guitars? But they're so fucking wrong! Aren't they? ☐ ☐

MUSIC/RADIO

80. Are you in "the biz"? ☐ ☐

80A. If so, do you make more money from selling promos than you do in salary? ☐ ☐

81. Have you ever gotten laid for making a band's MySpace Music page? ☐ ☐

82. Have you ever donated to the radio station that you used to steal CDs from? ☐ ☐

83. Do you feel guilty that the radio station you interned for is now a top 40 station, thinking, "What if I had just told them about Fugazi?" ☐ ☐

YES NO

84. Have you ever interviewed someone famous on the air and kept the windscreen that collected their spittle? ☐ ☐

85. Did Howard Stern make it cool for you to admit and joke about your below-average sized penis? ☐ ☐

BURGER MASHIN'

86. Is it acceptable in your job to pull food from the garbage can? ☐ ☐

87. What if the chef left it there for you, for your break time? ☐ ☐

88. Is there a sign in the employee restroom giving detailed instructions on how to properly wash your hands? ☐ ☐

89. Do you wash your hands *only* if someone else is in there with you? ☐ ☐

90. Do you not wash your hands as an act of rebellion? ☐ ☐

91. Do you have any idea what "no fucking onions" means? ☐ ☐

92. Are you one of the four billion burger slingers who interpret "no mayo" as "mo' mayo"? ☐ ☐

93. Do you pound beef, beans, or whatever kind of burger you're making into its appropriate shape to the beat of "Am I Evil"? ☐ ☐

THE INDIE CRED TEST

MULTIPLE CHOICE

THE INDIE CRED TEST

CHOOSE OR LOSE. DICK.

01. Your working environment consists of:
A. Corner office in a swank downtown building with a view.
B. Interior office with a door but no view.
C. Cubicle in a cube farm.
D. Leg space of boss' desk.

02. A "good week" at your job means:
A. New clients and revenue streams.
B. Making your boss happy.
C. Never having to say you're sober.
D. You didn't buy a replacement squid.

03. After ten years of working at your company you receive:
A. A promotion and the respect of your co-workers.
B. The respect of your co-workers and a personalized mug.
C. A demotion and a number of extremely personalized insults.
D. A severance package.
E. A restraining order from the woman in the cubicle next to you.

04. Your job and your personal life overlap:
A. In a comfortable, organic way.
B. At times, but not often.
C. Less than they used to now that you're not blowing your boss.
D. Constantly and without any particular reason.

---

05. In the "power chart" associated with your organization, you would be:
A. At the top.
B. Second-tier.
C. Bottom of the pyramid.
D. Basement sub-section that rest of pyramid pretends doesn't really exist.

06. You are:
A. Working hard but hardly working.
B. Working to live, not living to work.
C. Working smarter as opposed to harder.
D. Neither working smart nor particularly hard.
E. Not working out, but it's not personal.

07. A typical "working lunch" might be:
A. Meal at downtown steak/seafood chain on the company credit card.
B. Applebee's two-for-one lunch special.
C. Dollar-menu items from fast food restaurants.
D. Mad Dog 20/20 gulped behind a cardboard sign that says "I wouldn't lie to you...I just want a beer."

08. The most famous person you've ever been able to meet through your position is:
A. Patti Smith
B. Patrick Stewart
C. William Hung
D. Wavy Gravy

09. Which of the following best describes your current employment?
A. Gainful
B. Baneful
C. Painful
D. Shameful

10. Which of the following best describes the flavor and/or consistency of the coffee in your office?
A. Tar in turd sauce
B. Turds in tar sauce
C. French vanilla bong resin
D. Maxwell House of the Dead

11. Which of the following do you consider to be the primary "perk" of your job?
A. Bonin' bitches.
B. Shoplifting.
C. Beating up shoplifters.
D. Getting beaten up by shoplifters.
E. Blowing your paycheck in less than 24 hours on whores and Old Milwaukee (and old Milwaukee whores).

12. What kind of music do you say you listen to when the work crowd asks?
A. Alternative.
B. Indie rock ("you've never heard of any of them" acceptable too).
C. Underground bands.
D. Rock/Classic Rock (to avoid the conversation but save face somewhat).
E. Everything, so they'll just go away.

13. "Good news" at your job is:
A. Getting a client to sign off on a three-week location shoot in Australia.
B. A nominal bonus when productivity is up for the quarter.
C. A night when nobody clogs the backstage toilet with vomit and a used rubber.
D. When the test comes back "negative."

14. Which skill set is most closely associated with your job?
A. Proficiency in Photoshop, Avid, QuarkXpress.
B. Experience with ProTools, Melodyne, software and physical preamps/compressors.
C. Knowledge of macros and formulas in Excel.
D. "Fluffing," lack of a gag reflex, ability to stifle tears.

15. When can you expect a promotion?
A. The next time Rudy calls in sick.
B. After a year or so of good solid work.
C. After three to five years of showing up on time.
D. When Dad dies.

16. What do 'benefits' mean to you?
A. Good health insurance, pension plan & 401(k).
B. Lots of sick time, vacation time, and holidays.
C. All the previous day's food you can eat.
D. Maybe standing a chance with that girl who works Wednesdays and weekends.

17. What are the first words you look for in a want ad?
A. "Generous salary"
B. "Lots of room for advancement"
C. "Entry level; no experience necessary"
D. "No drug test required"

18. What is your title?
A. Senior Vice President of Artist Management
B. Assistant to the Regional Manager
C. Bucket Squad Lead (Graveyard Shift)
D. Larry

19. How far would you stretch a claim that you're in the music industry?
A. You work for a big record label, albeit not in a "creative" job.
B. You're in a band, even though you're not signed and have no paying gigs.
C. You get to listen to whatever you want on your headphones while doing data entry at an insurance company.
D. Part of your job as a mailman is to deliver copies of Rolling Stone to peoples' houses.
E. You frequently sell off your dwindling CD and vinyl collection to pay the rent.

ACCEPTABLE REASONS TO
GET A DIVORCE

You asked for a frittata and the bitch made you a quiche.

You have battered wife syndrome but you're a dude.

She repeatedly files your 4Skins records under "F," rather than numerically.

The only one that didn't spend any time in her mouth was yours.

Your wife's much hotter sister became available.

Because your spouse adopted a full-blown Satanic Black Metal persona, corpse paint and all.

You just don't feel like being married anymore after you found out "she" was packing a 9 inch dong.

You're white, she's Asian... but the baby came out Mexican.

The bitch ate the last Pop-Tart.

It's the damn playoffs and she *still* won't shut the fuck up.

She said she needed to "find herself"... at the bottom of a man-pile, apparently.

She said MC Ren was the best rapper in N.W.A.

Marriage is like electroclash, here one minute, wait, that wasn't even a minute...15 seconds, maybe?

She traded in the Mac for a PC.

That crazy ass whore thinks Interpol is better than Joy Division.

We only got married because she had a nice comfy couch that I liked to sleep on. But then she donated it to Salvation Army.

She slept with somebody from Dredg, and those assholes eat meat.

She thought SST was an STD.

She won't respect your action figure collection as a legitimate comment on the aesthetic commodification of nostalgia. Also: She eats her own shit.

Your children aren't sufficiently emotionally devastated to become artistic, creative types.

The kids are *already* fucked up.

2 words. Face tattoo.

Your spouse uses the kid as a "wingman."

They're in some kooky improv dance troupe, and that's *always* an recipe for disaster mixed with failure.

Your record collection had to go while the mountainous collection of throw pillows stayed.

On a quiet night, you can hear his sores.

Your spouse's latest album received less than an 8.0 from Pitchfork, resulting in their being dropped from Matador.

She got drunk and blew Ben Gibbard behind a post office because she thought you'd find it clever.

You've got a lawyer buddy that I want to give a test run.

She joined a metal band as a melodic lead vocalist, and we all know how embarrassing that is.

She took my drum shells out in the front yard and planted daisies in them.

You keep finding another woman's lipstick on your husband's penis.

You went in with one condom on and came back out with two.

Her porn collection is *way* bigger than yours. So is her dick.

She can burp "Don't Know Much" by Linda Ronstadt and Aaron Neville in its entirety.

She claims to know what J. Robbins is talking about, and I can't help but believe her because I have no fucking idea.

She's often heard using the phrase "big tittied bitches."

When she goes to shows, she goes to see, not be seen.

You bought too many records and now can't afford to send your 5-year-old daughter to the Schlitz Technical Institute to learn to drive the big rigs.

Your spouse is Tony Brummel.

Her enticing collection of vintage '80s metal tees all prove to be recent remakes from Hot Topic.

You've just won the Lotto.

You quit drinking.

S/he reads *Chunklet*.

AN INDIE CRED TEST SUPPLEMENT

ONLINE MUSIC JOURNALIST APPLICATION FORM

SUPPLEMENTAL STAFF

Henry H. Owings..Publisher
Aaron James Draplin ....Production Artist
Bun E. Carlos .... Australian Labradoodle I
David Lee Roth .... Australian Labradoodle II

CHUNKLET CHARTER

We here at Chunklet Industries believe in only the highest standards in music journalism. That is why we make everyone take this test. You think yourself a purveyor of taste, an aesthete, or otherwise some form of music "journalist"? Then we suggest you take this test to see how you stack up.

WRITING

EDITORIAL

YES NO

01. Have you ever had a writer who plagiarized entire paragraphs from another article and then got defensive and self-righteous when you called him on it? ☐ ☐

02. Have you ever had to tell a writer, "Sorry about how your piece got edited. There was nothing I could do"? ☐ ☐

03. Do you spend more time on YouTube than you do selling ads or generating content? ☐ ☐

04. Have you ever had a writer who regularly adds paragraphs (sometimes entire pages) of irrelevant autobiographical sidebars to their articles and then gets mad when you keep editing them out? ☐ ☐

05. Have you ever had a writer who hands off articles he's originally written for you to other publications without telling you or crediting your publication? ☐ ☐

06. Have you ever had a writer who fakes their death, gets their friends to lie about it to you, and then has the nerve to ask for a job reference before you found out it was all a hoax? ☐ ☐

07. Do you demand exclusives on your site? ☐ ☐

08. Have you ever had a writer send you an article that's already been available elsewhere but neglects to tell you that? ☐ ☐

09. Have you ever asked staff writers to send in letters to the editor or post comments on your site to generate content? ☐ ☐

10. Do you think giving your unsolicited opinions to the coat-check girl qualifies as a "tip"? ☐ ☐

11. Which is more important: recycling garbage or recycling material? *(Please submit one.)* ☐

12. Have you ever passed off a mass email as an article in a magazine or blog? ☐ ☐

13. Do you refer to yourself in first-person plural even though it is evident you are the sole writer and editor of the site? ☐ ☐

14. Have you ever let a publicist do your work for you? ☐ ☐

15. Have you ever thought, "Maybe I should fact-check that?" and then answer yourself by saying "Eh, fuck it"? ☐ ☐

DEALING WITH EDITORS/MAGAZINES

16. Does your blog/website exist so you can avoid the hassle of "editors" who demand you write using frivolous concepts such as "grammar" and "syntax" and actually want you to have "something interesting to say" about music? ☐ ☐

17. Have you ever had an editor totally rewrite your intro to an interview without telling you, which resulted in you getting an angry call from the publicist about the crap you supposedly wrote there? ☐ ☐

18. Have you ever had an assignment where your instructions for a blurb were longer than the word count you were given? ☐ ☐

YES NO

19. Have you ever asked an editor what a "pitch" is after asking if you could write about some random band? ☐ ☐

20. Have you ever had a magazine ask you to write something in the middle of your lawsuit against them? ☐ ☐

21. Have you ever been told by an editor that the first draft you turned in was "killer," only to have it savaged by the top editor who had scrawled, "This is as unpleasant to read as it is incomprehensible" across it? ☐ ☐

22. Have you ever had an editor assign you an article on a genre in which at least half the bands to be interviewed had only a vague association with said genre? ☐ ☐

23. Have you ever submitted an excellent draft filled with pertinent quotes by interesting and relevant individuals only to be told that the quoted individuals aren't famous enough and you should spend the next three weeks trying to get Christina Aguilera on the phone for thirty seconds? ☐ ☐

24. Have you ever spent $150 on phone calls and had to sue the magazine that assigned you the article for reimbursement? ☐ ☐

25. Does your most blissful dream involve the day you finally get a response from Pitchfork for your unsolicited but totally awesome review of the new Spoon record? ☐ ☐

26. Have you ever thought an editor's command of "And no first-person crap" to be unfair to your art? ☐ ☐

INTERVIEWS

27. When a band calls for an interview, are your first words "I got it, Mom. Hang up"? ☐ ☐

28. Is the first topic of conversation with any interview subject inevitably a recap of the last time you saw, met, or were at the same show with the interview subject? ☐ ☐

29. On what medium do you record your interviews? *(Please list your medium of choice.)*

30. Have you conducted interviews via iChat, AOL Instant Messenger or some other form of IRC (Internet Relay Chat)? ☐ ☐

31. Have you broken press-release protocol and asked relevant questions? ☐ ☐

32. Do you think anyone besides you remembers that interview you landed with that artistically brilliant and commercially successful band with whom you were unfamiliar the day before? ☐ ☐

33. Have you ever agreed to an interview with an artist whose music you don't like but whom you find physically attractive? ☐ ☐

34. Have you ever conducted a really good interview, only to find out you never hit the record button? ☐ ☐

YES NO

35. Have people told you that you ask tough questions? ☐ ☐

36. Do you secretly feel proud when your subject responds to something you ask by saying, "That's a good question"? ☐ ☐

WRITING

37. Do you try to avoid ending sentences with prepositions, or just employ your own distinct, devil-may-care "voice"? ☐ ☐

38. How many times a day do you refer to "my readers"? ☐ ☐

39. Do you think you have a following? ☐ ☐

40. Do you write on your PDA? ☐ ☐

41. Have you ever described another writer as being "tragically ill-informed"? ☐ ☐

42. Do you consider your writing to be in the stream of consciousness vein? ☐ ☐

43. Have you ever used the phrase "seminal" to describe a record that has been out for less than a year? ☐ ☐

44. Do you use Microsoft Word's thesaurus to find alternate words for "angular"? ☐ ☐

45. Does reporting about a band's stool qualify as real journalism? ☐ ☐

46. Have you ever passed off writing in the comments section on your website as your own? ☐ ☐

47. Do you consider rewriting a one-sheet a hard day's work? ☐ ☐

48. Has anyone ever co-wrote a piece with you and turned it in to a publication without telling you? ☐ ☐

49. Do you refer to yourself regularly in any article you write? ☐ ☐

50. Have you ever compared a band's music to a personal childhood memory? ☐ ☐

51. Have you used the phrase "sophomore slump" in reference to anything other than a band's second album? ☐ ☐

52. Do you know what the word "deadline" means? ☐ ☐

RECORD REVIEWS

53. How many records have you reviewed? ☐

54. Do you rate records on a scale of one to ten? ☐ ☐

55. Have you ever complained about having too much music to listen to and/or review? ☐ ☐

56. Has a fan ever threatened you with bodily harm over a review? ☐ ☐

57. Do you misuse sports metaphors ("hits a touchdown") to try to appeal to a wider audience? ☐ ☐

58. Have you ever had a cease-and-desist order placed on you by the publishers of the $33^{1}/_{3}$ book series because of your repeated unsolicited submissions of your short stories about various albums? ☐ ☐

59. Have you ever compared a new band to some older, historically important band whose music you haven't actually heard? ☐ ☐

60. Have you ever gotten an idea from an industry newsgroup you are subscribed to and rewritten it as a feature article? ☐ ☐

YES NO

61. Do you think taking a band's name and adding "–esque" at the end of it adequately functions as criticism? ☐ ☐

62. Do you own at least 10 albums for every year you've been alive? ☐ ☐

MUSICIANS HATING YOU

63. Have you ever had a musician send someone out to let you know that they were going to give you a beatdown over a review that you wrote, while referring to you as another critic? ☐ ☐

64. Has a musician ever taken time out during a show to complain about a review you wrote? ☐ ☐

65. Have you ever written back to a band just to start a flame war? ☐ ☐

66. Has a band member ever threatened you via email over a review you wrote? ☐ ☐

67. Have you ever had a musician glue your mailbox shut for selling his promo CD? ☐ ☐

LIVE SHOW REVIEWS

68. When writing a live review, have you ever used the phrases "tight" or "locked-in" to describe the rhythm section upon realizing that you'd spent the rest of the review talking about the guitarist and singer? ☐ ☐

69. Do your press credentials allow you to not feel like the chaperone/creepy old guy at the club? ☐ ☐

70. Do you choose a vantage point at a concert depending on whether the lighting will overly accentuate your balding? ☐ ☐

71. Do you write about the show while you're at the show? ☐ ☐

72. Do you own a $200 digital camera so that you can take blurry live shots of the show you're on the paid reserve list for? ☐ ☐

73. Do you consider going to shows your "work"? ☐ ☐

PUBLICIST REQUESTS

74. Have you ever requested a CD from a label three months after it hit stores? ☐ ☐

75. Have you ever had a label offer to send you a promo copy after the release date for a review you're doing and months after you made the original request? ☐ ☐

76. Have you ever had a publicist tell your editor that the artist has informed her/him that your interview was the worst one s/he ever had to do? ☐ ☐

77. Have you ever spent 45 minutes trying to get a publicist off the phone, only to be informed that s/he thought s/he was speaking to someone else? ☐ ☐

78. Has a publicist called your home phone several times a week trying to work a record you've had absolutely no interest in, even after expressing said lack of interest? ☐ ☐

79. Is your favorite pastime kvetching about how all of the bands whose shows you couldn't get into at South By Southwest really suck, even though you waited in line to try to see them? ☐ ☐

RESUMÉ

CHUNKLET REMINDS YOU TO "ANSWER HONESTLY."

WPM

01. How many words per minute do you type?

02. Do you write for as many magazines as possible to fill out your writer's resumé?   YES / NO

03. What magazines have you written for? _____

_____

04. Have you ever written a band's bio?

05. Has your name appeared in a print publication?

06. Do you have a radio show?

07. When asked, do you say your profession is "music journalist," even though you've never made one red cent doing it?

YES / NO

08. Have you ever had to sue a magazine to get paid?

09. Do you need to be paid to write?

10. Did you get a passing grade in a high-school creative-writing class?

11. Have you been kicked out of a band due to your complete and utter lack of talent?

12. Do you actually think most people notice the author of an article?

13. Have you rode in a van with a band?

14. Have you ever played golf with a rock band?

LIFESTYLE

SOCIAL

01. What percentage of your friends are white? Black? Asian? Hispanic? Other? *(Please fill in percentages.)*

WHITE	BLACK	ASIAN	HISPANIC	OTHER
%	%	%	%	%

YES / NO

02. Would you continue the pretense of being a "journalist" if you had a girlfriend/boyfriend to attend shows with?

03. Are you on a first-name basis with all the people that work at your neighborhood coffee shop?

04. Have you ever chosen an apartment based on its proximity to the cool club in town?

BODY

05. If you don't eat meat, do you still wear leather products?

06. Have you come to terms with your balding, or do you still think of your hair as "thinning"?

07. Do the majority of your meals come from meet-and-greets for bands you "don't even really like"?

MIND

08. Are you on antidepressants? *(If yes, please list.)*

_____

_____

_____

_____

09. Do you experience depression when the only comments you receive involve boner drugs?

10. Do you believe in God?

11. Are you easily shamed?

WORK

YES / NO

12. Do you sell coffee to yuppies for a living when you're not writing?

13. Do you refer to your full-time, health-benefits-providing employer whom you have no intention of leaving as your "day job"?

14. Do you look down your nose at record-store clerks while handing them your application to work at their store?

LIFE

15. Are you still a music critic at the age of forty?

16. Would you still be a rock writer if there were no access to backstage, the band and their drugs?

17. Have you ever chosen to move to a city because an influential source called it a "scene" or "the next Athens"?

MONEY

18. What percentage of your annual income is comprised of selling promo CDs to second-hand stores?   %

19. How many thousands of dollars do you still owe on your student loan?   K

20. Has almost every item of clothing you own somehow been obtained freely?

21. Have you ever tried to write off your new iPad as a "business expense" on your taxes?

22. Are you poor enough to be eligible for food stamps?

23. Do you rack up tremendous credit card debt trying to support your rock'n'roll lifestyle?

24. Do you have experience in any of the following:
    A. Public relations?
    B. Concert promotions?
    C. Indie marketing?

THE INDIE
CRED TEST

THE INDIE
CRED TEST

01. What was the first show you ever saw? *(Please list.)*

WHO: _____

WHERE: _____

WHEN: _____

02. What was the last show you attended? *(Please list.)*

WHO: _____

WHERE: _____

WHEN: _____

03. What are the top five hip-hop recordings of all time, excluding Public Enemy, Grandmaster Flash and Run-DMC. *(Please list.)*

I. _____

II. _____

III. _____

IV. _____

V. _____

04. Have you ever felt indifferent about certain bands?
(If yes, please list.)

_____

_____

_____

_____

_____

05. Why do you think anybody would be interested in your analysis of or opinion about anything? *(Please explain.)*
(Bonus points: use of the phrase "unique perspective.")

_____

_____

_____

_____

_____

_____

_____

		YES	NO
06.	Do you only write about music that you like?	☐	☐
07.	Do you actually still like rock music?	☐	☐
08.	Do you write about bands you're friends with?	☐	☐
09.	Do you have any musicians' phone numbers in your cell phone?	☐	☐
10.	Do you only go to shows where you get in for free?	☐	☐
11.	Have you ever refused to sell the "cool" CDs you're supposed to like because you were afraid of negative judgment at the record store?	☐	☐
12.	Is your greatest hero and personal idol Rob Gordon from *High Fidelity*?	☐	☐
13.	Is your stock reply to any spin-off band, "I liked his first band better"?	☐	☐
14.	Have you ever rolled your eyes when one of your friends mentions a news article from last week's music blog headlines?	☐	☐
15.	Do you consider the phrase, "I really just like their older stuff," a legitimate line of aesthetic defense?	☐	☐
16.	Have you ever claimed to be at an iconic show but, when pressed, say you really can't remember it because it was too boring?	☐	☐
17.	Have you ever bad-mouthed prog rock?	☐	☐
18.	Have you ever bad-mouthed hip-hop?	☐	☐
19.	Do you mostly learn about new bands from the college-aged intern at your office or the salon where you get your hair cut?	☐	☐
20.	Is a band already too big for you if another writer has already written about them?	☐	☐
21.	Do you self-reference your bad musical taste from your teenage years but misrepresent the genres you liked?	☐	☐
22.	Have you ever hidden records that you really like when people come over to your house because you're embarrassed by them? *(If yes, please list.)*	☐	☐

_____

_____

| 23. | When people you want to impress are coming over, do you intentionally place albums or CDs of obscure bands at the front of your stacks of records? | ☐ | ☐ |
| 24. | Do you have a large selection of David Foster Wallace-type neo-fiction just to prove to the rare house guest that you are "well-read"? | ☐ | ☐ |

THE INDIE CRED TEST

COLLECTING HABITS

THE INDIE
CRED TEST

THE INDIE
CRED TEST

YES NO

01. Do you have boxes of unopened promo CDs in your room? ☐ ☐

02. Has anyone ever described your record collection as being obsessive? ☐ ☐

03. Do you mock people who merely alphabetize their collection as opposed to some other complex filing system involving genres, labels, years, and producers? ☐ ☐

04. Do you tell people you were in New York shopping your unauthorized Arcade Fire biography when you were really just hitting street sales and dollar bins praying for another copy of that Velvet Underground acetate? ☐ ☐

05. Do you have an extensive concert T-shirt collection? ☐ ☐

06. Have you ever paid more than $40 for a vintage band T-shirt on eBay? ☐ ☐

07. Do you own a Peter Max tie? ☐ ☐

08. Have you ever collected autographs or music memorabilia? ☐ ☐

09. Does the name "The Melvins" make you salivate? ☐ ☐

10. Have you ever traded a record for furniture? ☐ ☐

YES NO

11. Do you sell your CDs for rent money? ☐ ☐

12. Have you ever realized that you have accumulated five or more CDs from a band you don't really like, and you keep them just in case you change your mind some day? ☐ ☐

13. Has a majority of your collection been relegated to a garage, attic, basement or some form of a "geek room" by your spouse? ☐ ☐

14. You have gone on at length about the superiority of:
(Please check all that apply.)

☐ CDs to MP3s
☐ LPs to CDs
☐ 78s to 33-$\frac{1}{3}$s
☐ Masturbating to having real sex

15. You shop at: *(Please check all that apply.)*

☐ Amoeba
☐ Amazon
☐ Best Buy
☐ Fusetron
☐ Insound
☐ ForcedExposure.com
☐ Other Music

☐ Blogs that post entire rare or obscure psych, garage, punk or noise records.
☐ A record store that opens only when called ahead of time.
☐ Some website distro nobody knows about.

ONLINE HABITS

THE INDIE
CRED TEST

THE INDIE
CRED TEST

01. List the websites you check daily:

_____

_____

_____

_____

_____

YES NO

02. Do you have your own website? ☐ ☐

03. Do you have a personal blog on Tumblr? ☐ ☐

04. Do you consider the Internet a viable form of legitimate journalism? ☐ ☐

05. Have you ever uploaded a particularly great performance on YouTube? ☐ ☐

06. Have you ever uploaded something on YouTube that was taken down? ☐ ☐

07. Is your fact-checking done via the Wikipedia? ☐ ☐

08. Do you leak albums? ☐ ☐

09. When you get watermarked albums, regardless of the repercussions, do you still give them to friends? ☐ ☐

10. Is your web browser's home page Google? ☐ ☐

11. Do you link to other people's website entries and call it journalism? ☐ ☐

YES NO

12. Do you consider getting an early advance or finding a pre-release MP3 on the Internet to be part of your involvement in the music industry? ☐ ☐

13. Have you ever loudly proclaimed that print is a dead medium while actively shopping for a book deal or a job with a print magazine? ☐ ☐

14. Have you ever used the word "bittorrent" or any derivation of it in a social setting? ☐ ☐

15. Do you have a long-winded opinion on streaming versus downloadable promos? ☐ ☐

16. Do you consider doing a podcast that's heard by three of your friends "getting your voice out there"? ☐ ☐

17. Are you an active fixture on your own site's message boards? ☐ ☐

18. Do you judge how successful you are as a writer by how many comments one of your posts has gotten? ☐ ☐

19. How many times a day do you check your stat counter? ☐ ☐

20. Have you ever started a blog as a joke, then have it blown all out of proportion by a few well-meaning sites? ☐ ☐

21. Have you ever requested contact info for a musician or band's management through a listserv using a variation of the subject line, "_____-dex" or "rolo-_____"? ☐ ☐

22. Was the first time your work was the subject of a thread the proudest day of your life? ☐ ☐

23. Have you ever been inwardly proud of how many posts you have on a message board as compared to other members of the same board? YES ☐ NO ☐

24. When you Google yourself, do you put your name in quotation marks? YES ☐ NO ☐

25. Do you think anyone remembers a piece you've written, and if so, could they actually cite you as the writer? YES ☐ NO ☐

26. Are you able to do research online 24/7, or just when your neighbor's wireless connection is open? YES ☐ NO ☐

27. Is your sense of entitlement indirectly proportional to the importance of your medium? YES ☐ NO ☐

28. Has something you wrote ever become a thread on a band's forum? YES ☐ NO ☐

29. Have you ever written a band or album biography for Wikipedia and cited yourself in that entry? YES ☐ NO ☐

30. Have you ever checked All Music Guide more than once in a 24-hour period? YES ☐ NO ☐

31. Have your "memes" been poached by other, more widely read websites repeatedly, despite your protests? YES ☐ NO ☐

THE INDIE CRED TEST

TEST YOUR KNOWLEDGE

THE INDIE CRED TEST

---

01. What part of the country do you find Waffle Houses? In-N-Out Burger? Del Taco? Steak 'n Shake?

WAFFLE HOUSE

DEL TACO

IN-N-OUT BURGER

STEAK 'N SHAKE

02. Explain the difference between the Louisville and Gainesville sounds.

_____

_____

03. When you first heard the Wilco song "The Late Greats," did you actively try to find copies of the song "Turpentine" because you didn't get the joke? YES ☐ NO ☐

04. Have you ever found yourself on FlyingNun.co.nz just agonizing over the "reissues" section? YES ☐ NO ☐

05. Have you ever thought something like, "IMHO, this album will go down as their *Hot Charity*," and not felt the least twinge of pretension? YES ☐ NO ☐

06. Have you ever smugly quoted Mark E. Smith in a *faux*-Mancunian accent (that sounds more akin to Groundskeeper Willie) and feigned a "disbelief shock" when no one got the reference or even cared what "whinging, ephemeral" meant. YES ☐ NO ☐

07. Have you gone back and changed *Hot Charity* to *Hallelujah! All The Way Home* after spending $106 on Flying Nun reissues? YES ☐ NO ☐

08. Are you prone to loudly declaring, mid-show, to no one in particular, that "I bet they don't even know they're ripping off Scratch Acid?" YES ☐ NO ☐

09. How did you handle your unexpected total disinterest in Fugazi after loving them for so long?

_____

_____

10. Would you admit to not actually being that familiar with your frequent points of reference you name-drop (e.g., Captain Beefheart or Gang of Four)? YES ☐ NO ☐

11. When did you realize that Greil Marcus and Robert Christgau are total flatulent shitbird poofs?

_____

12. My "journalism" appears on *(please check all that apply)*:
☐ Pitchfork ☐ Stereogum ☐ Gawker
☐ A new Web 2.0 venture...that hasn't launched yet

13. Define the following in both the textbook and colloquial usages of the term:

A. Cascading Dylanesque melodies

_____

B. Caterwauling Karen O yelps and wails

_____

C. Gang-of-Fourisms

_____

Please fill in the blanks:

Beirut's _____ mix of Gypsy melodies and _____ wails of caterwauling dynamics are in stark contrast to the _____ of today's blog-friendly MP3 generation. To say they are anything but the _____ to Gogol Bordello's _____ would be an understatement.

Their _____ mix of _____ garageisms, brash Lazy Cowgirls _____, and 13th _____ Elevators psychedelia have let _____ carve out their own little niche in the world of _____ of the proletariat. The bass _____ when it should, _____ but this untested _____ proves to be a _____ success juxtaposed against _____ electronics and a mini-malist's _____ aesthetic of synth and _____ of distorted licks.

(This sounds like the most awful record ever.)

THE INDIE CRED TEST

JOURNALIST JARGON

THE INDIE CRED TEST   THE INDIE CRED TEST

HAVE YOU EVER DESCRIBED A BAND OR THEIR RECORD AS...

Please check all that apply.

NUMERICAL:
- [ ] 101
- [ ] '20s
- [ ] '30s
- [ ] '40s
- [ ] '50s
- [ ] '60s
- [ ] '70s
- [ ] '80s
- [ ] '90s

A:
- [ ] a dummy's guide to...
- [ ] a return to form
- [ ] A to Z
- [ ] abetted
- [ ] -abilly
- [ ] -able
- [ ] abruptly
- [ ] abusive
- [ ] achingly
- [ ] acid
- [ ] actual
- [ ] acuity
- [ ] addictive
- [ ] admirable feat
- [ ] adulation
- [ ] aesthetic
- [ ] affable
- [ ] aforementioned
- [ ] African-American
- [ ] aggro
- [ ] airbrush-wielding
- [ ] album length
- [ ] alcoholic
- [ ] all-
- [ ] all purpose
- [ ] all the way
- [ ] all-female
- [ ] all-star lineup
- [ ] alongside
- [ ] alpha
- [ ] alt-
- [ ] altered states
- [ ] alterna-
- [ ] alternative music
- [ ] amateur
- [ ] ambient
- [ ] ambitious
- [ ] Americana
- [ ] anal
- [ ] analog
- [ ] Anglo-
- [ ] angular
- [ ] anthem
- [ ] anthemic
- [ ] anti-
- [ ] anxiously
- [ ] apex
- [ ] Appalachian
- [ ] appalling
- [ ] approach
- [ ] apropos
- [ ] architects
- [ ] arena rock
- [ ] armageddon
- [ ] art house
- [ ] artifice
- [ ] ascent
- [ ] assaultive
- [ ] audiophile
- [ ] augmented
- [ ] avant

B:
- [ ] average
- [ ] axe-wielding
- [ ] axis
- [ ] balladeer
- [ ] balladry
- [ ] bamboozled
- [ ] banal
- [ ] banjo pickin'
- [ ] -based
- [ ] bastard child
- [ ] battered
- [ ] beaten-down
- [ ] beats
- [ ] becoming
- [ ] bedlam
- [ ] bedraggled
- [ ] bedrock
- [ ] beginnings
- [ ] belatedly
- [ ] bespectacled
- [ ] better known for...
- [ ] bi-
- [ ] big-beat
- [ ] bile
- [ ] bitch goddess
- [ ] biting
- [ ] bitter
- [ ] black arts
- [ ] black power
- [ ] blackout
- [ ] blanket
- [ ] blast beat
- [ ] blood-splattered
- [ ] bloody-faced
- [ ] blown out
- [ ] bluegrass
- [ ] blurry
- [ ] blurt
- [ ] bona fide
- [ ] bonus cut
- [ ] bootleg
- [ ] border radio
- [ ] braided
- [ ] brain child
- [ ] brain dead
- [ ] bravado
- [ ] breakdown
- [ ] breakout
- [ ] breathy
- [ ] brevity
- [ ] bright
- [ ] Brit
- [ ] bro-
- [ ] brooding
- [ ] brown note
- [ ] bro-zone
- [ ] bruised
- [ ] brutal
- [ ] bubble gummy
- [ ] bucketed
- [ ] buck eyed
- [ ] bulky
- [ ] buried vocals
- [ ] burst
- [ ] bury the needle
- [ ] bush league
- [ ] butcher
- [ ] buzz
- [ ] by the grace of god

C:
- [ ] caffeine-fueled
- [ ] cage-heat
- [ ] call and response
- [ ] called in
- [ ] candor
- [ ] cannon
- [ ] canonized
- [ ] career
- [ ] catalog
- [ ] catchy
- [ ] cathartic
- [ ] cauldron
- [ ] cello-like
- [ ] chalky
- [ ] challenging
- [ ] championed
- [ ] chanteuse
- [ ] charades
- [ ] charge the hill
- [ ] charted
- [ ] cheeky
- [ ] cheese ball
- [ ] cherry picked
- [ ] chest bangin'
- [ ] chirpy
- [ ] churning
- [ ] civilian
- [ ] clandestine
- [ ] classic
- [ ] cleaned-up
- [ ] clearer
- [ ] clever
- [ ] club music
- [ ] club trashing
- [ ] coast-straddling
- [ ] coda
- [ ] codified
- [ ] collective
- [ ] combo
- [ ] comeback
- [ ] comfortable
- [ ] comically
- [ ] commend
- [ ] comparison
- [ ] composer
- [ ] computerized
- [ ] conceptual
- [ ] concoction
- [ ] confessional
- [ ] consequently
- [ ] contemporary
- [ ] contribution
- [ ] -core
- [ ] corkscrew
- [ ] cornerstone
- [ ] corn-fed
- [ ] coruscating
- [ ] cosmic
- [ ] countrified
- [ ] country bumpkin
- [ ] cover-
- [ ] covered
- [ ] cow punk
- [ ] co-writer
- [ ] coy
- [ ] crack smokin'
- [ ] crash course
- [ ] cred police
- [ ] crisp
- [ ] critical darling
- [ ] Cro-Mag
- [ ] crossover
- [ ] crumpled
- [ ] crunchy
- [ ] crunk
- [ ] crusty
- [ ] culled
- [ ] cult
- [ ] culture bearer
- [ ] cumbersome
- [ ] curious
- [ ] current
- [ ] curve
- [ ] cutoff

D:
- [ ] dabbling
- [ ] dance floor
- [ ] dank
- [ ] dark
- [ ] day job
- [ ] de facto
- [ ] de rigueur
- [ ] dead
- [ ] deals with
- [ ] death
- [ ] debut
- [ ] decade-long
- [ ] decorum
- [ ] deep focus
- [ ] deep love
- [ ] deep-fried
- [ ] default
- [ ] deflowered
- [ ] deformed
- [ ] deft
- [ ] -defying
- [ ] delicate
- [ ] deluxe
- [ ] demented
- [ ] densely harmonic
- [ ] denuded
- [ ] depression era
- [ ] depressive
- [ ] derivative
- [ ] destroy
- [ ] detox
- [ ] detritus
- [ ] diabetic
- [ ] diced
- [ ] different direction
- [ ] digital
- [ ] dire
- [ ] disbanded
- [ ] disc
- [ ] discordant
- [ ] disgrace
- [ ] dismal
- [ ] disorienting
- [ ] distinct
- [ ] distinguishing
- [ ] divine
- [ ] dogma
- [ ] -dom
- [ ] dominating
- [ ] dope-
- [ ] double-
- [ ] dour
- [ ] down home
- [ ] downbeat
- [ ] drab
- [ ] dramatic effect
- [ ] dread
- [ ] dread locked
- [ ] dreamy
- [ ] -drenched
- [ ] driving
- [ ] drool
- [ ] droopily
- [ ] drowning
- [ ] drop tuned
- [ ] drug addled
- [ ] drug-damaged
- [ ] druggy
- [ ] dud
- [ ] dumbed down
- [ ] duo
- [ ] dust off

- [ ] -dusted
- [ ] dynasty
- [ ] dyspeptic

E:
- [ ] early days
- [ ] earnestly
- [ ] earsplitting
- [ ] earthy grainy
- [ ] easy listening
- [ ] ebb and flow
- [ ] econo
- [ ] edge of 30
- [ ] edgy
- [ ] edifying
- [ ] effin'
- [ ] effort
- [ ] egghead
- [ ] electric
- [ ] elements
- [ ] elfin
- [ ] emotive
- [ ] enchanting
- [ ] encyclopedic
- [ ] -endorsed
- [ ] endorsement
- [ ] enhanced
- [ ] enigmatic
- [ ] ennui
- [ ] epic
- [ ] eponymous
- [ ] equity
- [ ] -era
- [ ] -esque
- [ ] essential
- [ ] eternal struggle
- [ ] ethnic
- [ ] European
- [ ] ever chipper
- [ ] ex-
- [ ] exalt
- [ ] exasperating
- [ ] excessive
- [ ] exciting
- [ ] ex-girlfriend
- [ ] expansive
- [ ] expresses
- [ ] extraneous
- [ ] extreme-
- [ ] exuberance
- [ ] eye-popping

F:
- [ ] faded
- [ ] fanboy
- [ ] fanciful
- [ ] far reaching
- [ ] far-fetched
- [ ] father and son
- [ ] featuring
- [ ] fevered
- [ ] fey
- [ ] fiddling
- [ ] fiery
- [ ] fight of their life
- [ ] -filled
- [ ] find themselves
- [ ] finest hour
- [ ] fireworks
- [ ] fivesome
- [ ] -fix
- [ ] flanger
- [ ] flatulent
- [ ] fleeing
- [ ] flighty
- [ ] floor pounding
- [ ] florid

flourishes
- [ ] flourishes
- [ ] flow
- [ ] flurry
- [ ] flutter
- [ ] folky
- [ ] foofery
- [ ] fooled
- [ ] foppish
- [ ] foray
- [ ] forces
- [ ] formerly
- [ ] four-track
- [ ] frankly
- [ ] frantic
- [ ] fraught
- [ ] -free
- [ ] French
- [ ] frenetic
- [ ] frequent flyer miles
- [ ] frequently photographed
- [ ] -fried
- [ ] friendly
- [ ] from hell
- [ ] front man
- [ ] -ful
- [ ] fully dispensed
- [ ] fuming
- [ ] funky
- [ ] fused
- [ ] future
- [ ] futuristic
- [ ] fuzz

G:
- [ ] gadget
- [ ] gamble
- [ ] gaping
- [ ] garage
- [ ] gargoyle
- [ ] garish
- [ ] gasping
- [ ] gathered
- [ ] generation of
- [ ] genial
- [ ] genius
- [ ] genre
- [ ] genre-bending
- [ ] genuinely
- [ ] get
- [ ] gherricurled
- [ ] giant
- [ ] give a nod to
- [ ] glitter
- [ ] glossy
- [ ] gnome
- [ ] God
- [ ] goddamned
- [ ] going through the motions
- [ ] golf ball
- [ ] gooey
- [ ] gothic
- [ ] gormandizer
- [ ] grave
- [ ] gregarious
- [ ] grinding
- [ ] grief
- [ ] grievous
- [ ] grind
- [ ] ground zero
- [ ] grrrl rock
- [ ] grunge
- [ ] guest
- [ ] gulch-filling
- [ ] gut wrenching
- [ ] guttural

H:
- [ ] haggard
- [ ] haiku-length
- [ ] hails from
- [ ] hairy
- [ ] half hearted
- [ ] ham-fisted
- [ ] hammer of Thor
- [ ] hammers
- [ ] handed
- [ ] handsome
- [ ] hard luck
- [ ] hardcore
- [ ] harkens back
- [ ] hashed out
- [ ] hatchet-faced
- [ ] head tripping
- [ ] heady
- [ ] hearkens back
- [ ] heartwarming
- [ ] heavily effected
- [ ] heavy
- [ ] hefty
- [ ] Herculean
- [ ] here to stay
- [ ] heretofore
- [ ] heritage
- [ ] herky jerky
- [ ] heyday
- [ ] hideously
- [ ] hi-fidelity
- [ ] high-five
- [ ] high-
- [ ] high end
- [ ] high-cheekboned
- [ ] highly anticipated
- [ ] hillbilly
- [ ] hip hop
- [ ] hirsute
- [ ] histrionic
- [ ] hokey
- [ ] hold
- [ ] hollow-bodied
- [ ] Hollywood
- [ ] home recorded
- [ ] honorary fifth member
- [ ] hooks
- [ ] hope
- [ ] horn-driven
- [ ] horny
- [ ] huge
- [ ] husky
- [ ] hustle

I:
- [ ] iconic
- [ ] idiosyncratic
- [ ] idly
- [ ] ill-
- [ ] immortalized
- [ ] impact
- [ ] implausible
- [ ] imposing
- [ ] imprimatur
- [ ] in association with
- [ ] in the pocket
- [ ] incarnation
- [ ] incomparable
- [ ] increasing levels
- [ ] incumbent
- [ ] indie
- [ ] indifference
- [ ] indigo-worn
- [ ] indubitable
- [ ] industrial
- [ ] infamous

JOURNALIST JARGON

- infectious
- -infused
- ingenious
- inherent
- initial
- innate
- inner nerd
- inner workings
- insistence
- instant
- instrumenstrual
- insular
- integer
- interludes
- intoxicating
- intriguing
- intro-
- introspective
- inverted
- involuntary
- irony
- -ish
- -ism
- -ist

J:
- jangle
- jazzbo
- jazzy
- jet engine
- Jewish
- Jihad
- jittery
- joie de vivre
- journey
- jubilant
- juggernaut

K:
- kaleidoscope
- killer
- kingpin
- kitchen sink
- kitsch-loving
- Kiwi
- knowingly
- knuckle dragging
- kudos

L:
- late-blooming
- latest victims
- latter
- lavish
- layered
- legend
- legendary
- -less
- less fat
- less-than-sudden
- leveled
- lexicon
- lighthearted
- lightweight
- -like
- limp-wristed
- lionized
- literally
- live
- lives up to its name
- lodestar
- lofty
- logo
- long ignored
- longest
- long-serving
- loses the point
- lossy
- lounge
- love letters
- low rent
- loyal fanbase
- Luddite

- lurking
- lyrical content

M:
- machismo
- maestro
- mainstay
- mainstream
- makeover
- maniacs
- mantra
- mastering
- masturbatory
- -math
- mature work
- maverick
- mellow
- members of
- memorabilia
- memory
- mensch
- mercurial
- messy
- meta-
- -metal
- meth-fueled
- metrically
- micro-
- mid-
- midget-like
- mid tempo
- mild-mannered
- minimal
- mission statement
- modular
- mogul
- mono-
- monolithic
- Moog
- moppish
- moralist
- motherfunkin'
- mother lode
- mountainous
- mouthy
- movement
- mudslinging
- multi-
- multitude
- musician-producer
- myopic

N:
- nadir
- narrative
- narrow-minded
- natty
- nay-saying
- neglectful
- neo-
- Neolithic
- nerd
- nerdy
- new
- new age
- new wave
- nexus
- no wave
- noise
- noisemaker
- noisy
- nom-de-band
- Norwegian
- nosebleed
- not
- n-th

O:
- obedient
- OCD
- -octane
- octet

- oeuvre
- off-
- off Broadway
- off limits
- off roading
- oft-sarcastic
- old fashioned
- old school
- olé
- omega
- on a trip
- on acid
- on par
- one-hit wonder
- one-second
- online
- opens
- optimal
- opulent
- orchestral
- orgiastic
- original
- originators
- ornate
- outlandish
- outsider
- outing
- over-rated
- ozone

P:
- pariah
- part-
- part of their sound
- past their prime
- pastiche
- pasty
- pathetic
- pedal activated
- perpetrator
- -phile
- philosophical
- phoning it in
- pink noise
- pioneer
- plaid
- plaintive
- plangent
- playful
- playing off
- pleading
- politicized
- polyrhythms
- poor quality
- pop
- poppy
- popularity contest
- populate
- positive
- post-
- posthumous
- post-production
- posturing
- potential
- pothead
- powerful
- pranksters
- pre-
- precious
- precipice
- predating
- predictable
- premature
- presage
- pre-taped
- primal
- primary
- primeval
- pristine
- producer
- production value

- prolonged
- prominence
- promise
- proper
- protest
- psych-
- psychedelic
- pub rock
- pummels
- punchy
- punctuate
- punk
- purist
- putting

Q:
- quartet
- queer
- quench
- quintet
- quirky
- quixotic

R:
- raconteur
- raffish
- raisin-dried
- rank and file
- rarity
- raucous
- raunchy
- raven
- raw
- rawk
- re-
- Reagan-era
- real treat
- recently cut
- reckless abandon
- red-lined
- redonkulous
- reenact
- refutation
- rehabilitated
- reissue
- remixed
- renegade
- resonate
- restrained
- restraint
- retox
- retro-
- retrospective
- reunion
- reveal
- revelating
- reverb
- reviled
- revisionist
- revisiting
- revival
- rewind
- rigid
- rise to the occasion
- rock-
- rock influenced
- rock steady
- rocker
- rocket
- rock slide
- romanticized
- romp
- roots
- Rosetta Stone
- rough hewn
- rusty

S:
- Saccharine
- saffron
- salvo
- samba

- same
- sample
- sandscapes
- satanic
- scattered
- scene point
- schadenfreude
- screamo
- scribblings
- secret weapon
- seizure
- self-written
- sentimental
- serenity
- serotonin
- session musician
- sexaholic
- sexual
- shallow
- shambolic
- sharp
- shines
- shiny
- shirtless
- shitstorm
- shoegaze
- short-
- shortest
- shotgun
- show tunes
- shred of emotion
- shrill
- sibilant
- sibling
- side career
- side project
- signature
- similar sense
- simultaneously
- singer-songwriter
- single-digit
- -sized
- sizzle
- sketchy
- skronk
- slam dancing
- slam dunk
- slamming
- slang
- slaughterhouse
- sleepwalk
- slick
- slummin' it
- smothered
- snarl
- snobbery
- -soaked
- soaring
- SoCal
- socialist
- soft pop
- softer
- solo-
- somewhere back in the swamps
- somnambulant
- songwriting
- soon-to-be-classic
- sophomore effort
- sophomore slump
- sore throat
- soul-draining
- source material
- southern
- southern fried
- special edition
- specialized
- splayed
- sprawling
- sprinkled
- square-jawed
- squeaky clean

- squeal
- stakes
- stalwart
- stamp of approval
- standard
- star-crossed
- starry-eyed
- static
- steeped in
- stock
- stomp
- stone cold
- straight-ahead
- strain
- stranded
- street punk
- striking
- string
- stunning
- stripped down
- -style
- sub-
- subgenre
- subscribe
- subsequent effort
- subtle
- successfully
- succinctly
- sucked
- suited
- sultry
- summer
- sun-
- sundry
- super fly
- superseded
- swagger
- swirling
- switched on
- symphony
- syndicated

T:
- tarnished
- -tastic
- tattooed
- tawdry
- technically
- tempo
- tense
- tenuous
- tepid
- territory
- -tet
- Teutonic
- Texas-based
- the boot
- the depths of
- thematically
- then-reviled
- thesis
- thrashing
- three-legged
- throwback
- thumping
- tight
- timbre
- timely
- tinny
- tinted
- tired hearted
- tool
- top of the head
- top shelf
- topped
- topple
- totally
- toxic
- trad
- trademark
- trailblazer
- transformation

- transmission
- trenches
- trend
- tribute
- tricked out
- tricky
- trio
- trip
- triple-
- trippy
- tsunami
- tumultuous
- tuneful
- turbulent
- tussled
- twang
- twee
- twelve-stringed
- twilight

U:
- über-
- ultra-
- unabashed
- unaccountably
- undeniable
- understandable
- unequivocal
- unfolding
- unforgiving
- unique
- unlike
- unparalleled
- unquestionably
- unreleased
- upscale
- up-tempo
- urban
- user-friendly

V:
- vampire
- vaudevillian
- vehicle for...
- varicose-veined
- vintage
- violent
- virtuosity
- virulent
- visceral
- visionary
- vocal
- vogue
- volatile

W:
- watershed
- weekend warrior
- weighty
- weirdness
- well-traveled
- whimsical
- white collar
- white hot
- white noise
- whiz
- whole cloth
- winking
- wintry
- with baited breath
- woody
- world music
- world weary
- worship
- wrecking crew

Y:
- -y
- youthful

Z:
- Zen

CHAPTER 6

ELDER AUTHENTICATION

GRAB YOUR SCROLL, SHARPEN YOUR LEADED No. 2 pencil and turn up your hearing aid, you decayed old bastard, it's time to show us snot-nosed shitheels how they used to do it. If ever there were a group of ruffians with actual cred, it'd be the older sect who knows that "pickin' up change" is for pussies — "pickin' up bonds" is where it's at. These people actually had to work for cred. It wasn't just handed to them by some dumb book. Goddamned kids these days...

YES/NO

THE INDIE CRED TEST

COMPLETE THE FOLLOWING QUESTIONS WITH A YES/NO ANSWER OR SUFFER THE CONSEQUENCES.

YES NO

01. Do you spend a lot of time trying to figure out if the word "hipster" is a compliment or an insult? ☐ ☐

02. Does rap music still sound aggressive and/or threatening to you? ☐ ☐

03. Do you fondly remember Quaaludes? ☐ ☐

04. Have any of your favorite musicians ever OD'd on Metamucil? ☐ ☐

05. Do you know any Revolutionary War protest songs? ☐ ☐

06. Do you think current music lacks the quality songcraft of the old IWW labor songs? ☐ ☐

07. Do you think of music genres in terms of "pre" and "post" electricity? ☐ ☐

08. Do you have to check with your significant other to see if it's alright to let a band stay at your place? ☐ ☐

09. Do you make them sign a guest book? ☐ ☐

10. Have any of your favorite musicians ever been tried for heresy or witchcraft? ☐ ☐

11. When you're hitting on someone at a club, is your default line, "I remember when this place used to be called..."? ☐ ☐

12. Is your favorite band sponsored by Ensure? ☐ ☐

13. Did you give up on your dream of owning a bar, not because you couldn't afford it, but because you can't imagine staying up until 3AM every night? ☐ ☐

14. Has your city had at least three "scenes" come and go? ☐ ☐

15. Do you only smoke pot when your college friends are in town? ☐ ☐

15A. Is it good pot? ☐ ☐

15B. Can you even tell the difference? ☐ ☐

16. Have Indian attacks ever made your locomotive so tardy that you missed an entire hootenanny? ☐ ☐

17. Have you gotten an email from an almost completely forgotten college friend who thinks the time is right to get the band back together? ☐ ☐

TECHNOLOGY

YES NO

18. Do you still try to flip CDs over to play "side B"? ☐ ☐

19. Would you legally buy MP3s if only you knew how? ☐ ☐

20. Do you think your car stereo is awesomely high-tech because it gets both AM and FM? ☐ ☐

21. Do you worry that your 8-track converter will start eating your cassettes any day now? ☐ ☐

22. Do you miss the superior fidelity of reel-to-reel? ☐ ☐

23. Do you still refer to your stereo as "the hi-fi"? ☐ ☐

24. Do you think the Victrola will make a comeback any day now? ☐ ☐

25. Do you lecture people about fire safety when you overhear them talking about "burning a CD"? ☐ ☐

26. Do you think an iPod is something you plant in dirt and water twice a week? ☐ ☐

27. Do you run your iPod/iTunes through your work computer because your wife forbids you from using the one at home after you "accidentally" bought the deluxe subscription to maturemamas.com? ☐ ☐

28. Did you sell your vinyl when 8-tracks hit the scene? ☐ ☐

29. Did you feel like an idiot? ☐ ☐

30. Did you buy it all back at inflated prices? ☐ ☐

31. Did you feel like an idiot? ☐ ☐

32. Do you avoid putting an accurate-looking photo of yourself on your Facebook profile because you look like Sean Connery's granduncle? ☐ ☐

OLDER MUSICIANS

YES NO

33. Have you ever needed a nap after playing? ☐ ☐

34. Do soundmen regularly call you "sir"? ☐ ☐

35. Have you ever checked your blood sugar between songs? ☐ ☐

36. Have you ever cancelled a gig because you couldn't get a babysitter? ☐ ☐

37. Do you have a guitar that was an anniversary gift from your spouse? ☐ ☐

YES NO

38. Have you ever opened for a band, then tried to sell them life insurance? ☐ ☐

39. Did you rationalize purchase of a minivan because it could double as more fuel-efficient transportation for your band? ☐ ☐

40. Have you ever had to move a baby seat in your minivan to make room for your bass amp? ☐ ☐

41. Have you ever picked up groceries on the way home from a gig? ☐ ☐

42. Have you ever tried to schedule a visit with your in-laws during a tour? ☐ ☐

CHILDREN

43. Would you ever consider buying a clean version of a record because the kids are around? ☐ ☐

44. Have you learned to love Kidz Bop? ☐ ☐

45. Do you still accidentally refer to the nursery as your studio? ☐ ☐

46. Did you name your kids after your favorite musicians, but not a common or popular name that serves a dual purpose (Dylan, Lennon, etc.), opting instead to name your son or daughter something like Westerberg, Bun E. or Beefcake the Mighty? ☐ ☐

47. Have you purchased a T-shirt or onesie with a now-defunct (and highly inappropriate) band's logo on it for your child? ☐ ☐

48. Are you excited to find out that artists from the '80s have made a kid's record (Jason Ringenberg, They Might Be Giants, Metallica—and yeah, *St. Anger* was totally made for eight year olds)? ☐ ☐

49. Were any of your children conceived in the parking lot or restroom of a local club or bar? ☐ ☐

50. Do you own rock magazines that are older than your children? ☐ ☐

51. Are you pushing the drums on your kids? ☐ ☐

52. When digging through a bag of your old music T-shirts with your son, did you embarrassingly shove the "Frankie Says" shirt to the bottom of the bag and quickly hand over your prize Guns 'n' Roses T-shirt? ☐ ☐

53. Have you ever run into one of your kids at an all-ages show? ☐ ☐

54. Have you run into a former bandmate's son/daughter at an all-ages show? If so, did you buy them beer? ☐ ☐

55. Have you gotten rid of any band tees because their graphics/slogans weren't kid-friendly? ☐ ☐

56. Do the majority of your movies not play on your DVD player because of how high the parental controls are set? ☐ ☐

SHOWS

YES NO

57. Have you ever had to ask the band to turn their amps up so you can hear? ☐ ☐

58. Have you started taking a full range of snacks and hard candy to shows? ☐ ☐

59. Do you ever rush home after a concert to watch the Golden Girls? ☐ ☐

60. Have you ever told the people in front of you at a concert to keep their voices down? ☐ ☐

61. Did they obey you or merely mock you for the rest of the show? ☐ ☐

62. Have you ever seen a vocalist perform with a speaking trumpet? ☐ ☐

63. And if so, did you think to yourself, "What in tarnation is that fancy new technology"? ☐ ☐

64. Have you ever seen a show in the Louisiana Territory? ☐ ☐

65. Have you ever ridden a horse to a concert? ☐ ☐

66. Would you lie about going to a show and brag about how great it was from the review in the paper? ☐ ☐

67. Have you finally stopped complaining about ticket surcharges? ☐ ☐

68. At basement punk shows, do you check for foundation cracks and other structural flaws that would require repair or remediation before the basement could be finished into a kickass home theater/rec room? ☐ ☐

69. How long does it take you to convince the doorman that you're not a cop? ☐ ☐

70. When a pit forms, do you find yourself concerned for the safety of its participants? ☐ ☐

71. Has a band you liked ever had to cancel a show because of an impending Redcoat attack? ☐ ☐

72. Have you ever gotten your teeth knocked out at show, and then picked them up and put them right back in? ☐ ☐

73. Has your stagecoach ever been stolen outside of a show in a bad neighborhood? ☐ ☐

74. Have you ever been to a Yellow Fever benefit show? ☐ ☐

75. After a set by a band you were unfamiliar with, do you often say either to yourself or the person standing next to you, "That was just weird"? ☐ ☐

76. Do you feel terribly out of place until someone passes a "J" your way? ☐ ☐

YES NO

77. While attending shows in Virginia, Maryland, or Pennsylvania, do you ever wonder if you're standing on the site of a very bloody Civil War battle? ☐ ☐

78. Have you ever been to a show where, based on your age, you could beat up the parents of most of the other people at the show? ☐ ☐

79. Did you stop going to shows because without health insurance it's just too risky? ☐ ☐

TOURING

80. While touring overseas, have you ever worried that your favorite band might sail off the edge of the Earth or be eaten by sea serpents? ☐ ☐

81. Did the Great Dust Bowl ever seriously wreck your touring plans? ☐ ☐

82. Has your band ever toured the Ottoman Empire? ☐ ☐

83. Did you take part in the California Gold Rush of 1849 to help finance a tour? ☐ ☐

84. Did you have to cut the last tour short because the drummer just had to go and get himself conscripted? ☐ ☐

FESTIVALS

85. When attending a festival/camping type show, do you constantly think about how bad you need to shower and take a nap? ☐ ☐

86. When you attend a festival, do you load your pockets with those drink mix water bottle packets to avoid the cost of buying *those outrageously priced* refreshment stand drinks? ☐ ☐

87. Did you stop going to music festivals because "the music the kids play these days sounds like just a confounded bunch of noise"? ☐ ☐

88. Do you still think brown acid jokes are funny? ☐ ☐

SHIRTS

89. Do you feel stupid buying a shirt from a band whose oldest member is at least 20 years younger than you? ☐ ☐

90. Do you still have band shirts hanging in your wardrobe from 20 years ago that will never fit you? ☐ ☐

91. Have you ever dressed your partner in your old band/gig clothes and been turned on? ☐ ☐

92. Have you ever worn a t-shirt for one of your favorite bands when you were in college, and had a teenager ask if it's the name of your old band? ☐ ☐

APPEARANCE

YES NO

93. Have you ever considered getting a complete plaid sleeve tattoo? ☐ ☐

94. Have you ever rocked a receding Mohawk? ☐ ☐

95. Does it make you feel cool that your Reeboks are 25 years older than everyone else's? ☐ ☐

96. Have you tattooed your bald spot? ☐ ☐

97. Do you ever wonder why people mistake your bald head and suspenders for a racist statement? ☐ ☐

PROFESSIONAL

98. If your job requires you to wear a suit, tie or professional attire, have you ever worn it to a show? ☐ ☐

99. Have you ever found yourself talking about your 401(k) allocations during a set change? ☐ ☐

100. Have you ever tried to replace a tie tac or clip with a "tasteful" band pin? ☐ ☐

101. When you park, do you ask the cabbie to stop a few blocks away from the club because you don't want to give off "that impression"? ☐ ☐

102. Have you ever given away your drink tickets because you need to be clear-headed for tomorrow morning's board meeting? ☐ ☐

103. Does your definition of "business attire" include Doc Martens and a sleeveless suit? ☐ ☐

104. Do you wear ties with designs or patterns you consider irreverent (e.g., tiny skulls, guitars, etc.) as your form of rebelling against the man? ☐ ☐

105. Do you keep your ticket stub collection on your office/cubicle wall? ☐ ☐

AILMENTS

106. Do you have to consult your physician before attending a show? ☐ ☐

107. Do you ever get whiplash from just *thinking* about headbanging? ☐ ☐

108. Does your walker/plastic hip/wheelchair impede your stage diving skills? ☐ ☐

109. Is tinnitus a legitimate concern? ☐ ☐

110. Do your spiked bracelets (or gauntlets) aggravate your carpel tunnel? ☐ ☐

111. Even from the front row, can you still barely see the band? ☐ ☐

112. Have you ever smuggled booze into a venue in your catheter or colostomy bag? ☐ ☐

	YES	NO
113. Have you ever brought prescription medication to a show that was actually prescribed to you?	☐	☐
114. Have you tried to pass off your medic alert bracelet as ironic?	☐	☐
115. Are your balls (if applicable) starting to get in the way of "pickin' up change"?	☐	☐
116. Do you ever sleep in after a show because you actually want to, not because your broken body commands you to?	☐	☐

ARTIST/TITLE SPECIFIC

	YES	NO
117. When someone asks you if you listen to "classic rock" do you say, "Sure, I like Fugazi"?	☐	☐
118. Did seeing the last Jesus Lizard tour make you feel young *and* old at the same time?	☐	☐
119. Do you remember when "Manowar" was still "Boyowar"?	☐	☐
120. Does Mozart owe you money?	☐	☐
121. Do your Gorgoroth-listening grandkids mock your King Diamond-listening kids while they laugh at your Alice Cooper records?	☐	☐

	YES	NO
122. Have you gone to a show alone because you just can't bring yourself to try and explain why seeing "Mogwai" would be a good thing, even to your hipper friends?	☐	☐
123. Do you actually remember firsthand when Metallica *didn't* suck major hogballs? (Bonus points if you've ever heard a version of "Seek and Destroy," "Creeping Death," or "Battery" that didn't have "Hah-hah!" "Whoah-oh," and "Yeeeah-yeauh!" at the end of every verse.)	☐	☐
124. Do you feel that your ZOSO tattoo needs a touch-up after seeing a colorful Coheed and Cambria tattoo on someone 20 years younger than you?	☐	☐
125. After any black metal show, do you laugh to yourself because Ozzy used to scare you?	☐	☐
126. As a Freudian slip, have you ever said "Engelbert Humperdinck" when you really meant "Lemmy Kilmister"?	☐	☐
127. Do you have a killer story about you and one of the Rolling Stones' roadies, but over the years, you've updated to be about a Pixies roadie and then a Strokes roadie?	☐	☐

THE INDIE CRED TEST

MULTIPLE CHOICE

THE INDIE CRED TEST

NEVER BEFORE HAS THE POWER OF SELECTION BEEN SO INDISCRIMINATE.

01. Does your back begin to ache:
   A. During the headline band's set
   B. While the support band plays its longest solo
   C. When you got into a scuffle with security for *refusing* to let them search you
   D. You woke up with a bad back

02. When looking at the new generation of kids at gigs, do you think:
   A. What a bunch of fucking pussies. I bet none of 'em could take a snow shovel to the face without bleeding.
   B. I used to look like that...only better.
   C. The whole scene is just so impossibly adorable.
   D. They've stolen my look, but to their credit, they've made it their own
   E. I hope they don't speak to me
   F. What are they laughing at?
   G. I hope they don't think I'm a pedophile

03. Where's the best place to urinate in the absence of a bathroom?
   A. Wherever I can without pissing on my shoes.
   B. Somewhere dark, but not rapey.
   C. I'm going to try to hold it until I see a combination Pizza Hut/Taco Bell.
   D. Urinate? I'm not even drunk anymore.

04. Your idea of "old school" indie rock is:
   A. The melodic bands of the 1980s post-punk scene.
   B. Sebadoh's "Gimme Indie Rock!" seven-inch.
   C. Death Cab's first four shitty albums.
   D. Jesus Jones and Jimmy Eat World.
   E. Whatever was recently canonized by several references on "Gossip Girl."

05. What do you follow beers with at a show?
   A. More beer and possibly a shot.
   B. More beer but a glass of water here and there.
   C. A glass of water, every time.
   D. A whimper and the dark realization that you have to pee again.
   E. A punch to the face of whoever's closest.

06. If someone were to judge you based solely on your Facebook profile, they would find you:
   A. As vital and active as everyone you're trying to impress.
   B. A little creepy, but connected to enough cool people to accept your friend request.
   C. Clinging desperately to a clothing style that makes you look like Will Oldham in drag.
   D. An embittered reactionary, Jesus-loving Republican douche — just like the ones you used to make fun of.
   E. About to be arrested for violating an obscure, centuries-old law involving horses and funeral pyres.
   F. Another dipshit who thinks everyone needs to read status updates about how their job sucks or how they mysteriously coughed up pubes this morning at breakfast.

ACCEPTABLE REASONS TO
COMMIT SUICIDE

Your band sucks.

You're addicted to heroin.

Everyone you idolize did it at one point or another.

Kurt Cobain, Elliott Smith, Mark Linkous, etc. all did it wrong.

It's the only way people will still be listening to your shitty music in a year.

It's better than waiting around for 40 or 50 more years.

It will teach your mom a lesson for having you.

Everybody knows about Radiohead now.

Everybody knows about PBR now.

You're married.

You're divorced.

You are 35, divorced, broke, and unsigned.

You just got your first white pube.

Your wife left you for a metal dude.

Your Mac died.

The cancer isn't fun anymore.

Gerard Cosloy personally called to tell you your demo sucks.

Weird Al's version of your song is better than your song.

Lou Reed called you out on national TV.

Laurie Anderson called you out on closed circuit TV.

You're in a faceless suburban band whose influences include Third Eye Blind and Matchbox 20.

Thrill Jockey released a Spin Doctors greatest-hits album.

You're a record industry executive.

You dropped Wilco. Then re-signed them.

As a post-modern masochist, ironic pain is your only authentic joy.

Jokingly swore you'd die the year *Chinese Democracy* came out.

All your friends found out that you're not as poor as you've been making out.

Linkin Park makes better music than you.

Jello Biafra is now dating your ex-wife (or daughter).

Found Jesus.

Two words: 72 virgins. But what if none of them are cute?

There really are no more Jimi Hendrix recordings.

The dog told you it would probably be a good idea at this point.

To vanquish that Demon/Vampire/Werewolf thing that keeps dating your mom.

To save the earth from another asshole.

To win a posthumous Oscar/Grammy.

It's either that or tell Blackwater where the bomb is.

Because you can finally do it yourself, isn't that the "in" thing to do?

The Melvins won't let you play guitar for them.

The only way you can write songs is to rip off Killing Joke solos.

You were shown in the background of a TV news report covering the opening of a new Wal-Mart.

Your favorite NPR host was demoted to Friday and Saturday nights, when no one cool is listening.

Due to obscure blue laws, Trader Joe's was permanently barred from opening a store in your state.

The day after you completed the arduous 7-year process of fully cataloging every detail of your 82,000-strong MP3 collection, your brother-in-law came over to visit with his brand new industrial-strength magnet.

After a burglary, you realized the only thing missing was your 1963 pressing of *The Freewheelin' Bob Dylan* with the four songs deleted from subsequent pressings.

You read an article in The Onion describing your sad, meaningless life more accurately than you ever could.

You're Eric Clapton's son.

Auto-erotic asphyxiation accident.

You love Nickelback's entire catalog.

You never got over Arrested Development's cancellation.

You found out Avatar was fictional.

Some band you've never heard of broke up.

Wes Anderson is *not* directing the PacMan movie.

Brenda's Thrifty Thread World moved across town.

It hurts to pee.

The plan to drop out of college and move to the mountains fell through.

You finally got a Blackberry, and now everybody's jumping ship.

Urban Outfitters had a gigantic sale... but you couldn't get off work.

The cool gay club isn't as gay as it used to be.

You think Dane Cook is any funnier than a bloody, backwoods baby raping.

No one can read your goddamned band logo.

You find yourself enjoying a Phish show for more than a few seconds (without the aid of drugs or alcohol).

You've ever driven a Hummer and weren't in the middle of a desert, dodging projectiles.

They stopped making Hot Pockets.

You invested in six seasons of Lost only to find out the island is just a snow globe being viewed by an autistic kid.

Two words: President Palin.

There's a comet returning somewhere in the neighborhood of your planet and someone offers you the opportunity to have a bunk bed and snazzy set of new sneaks.

There is an entire thread at 4chan dedicated to mocking you.

You got caught soliciting for Gary Glitter.

You are Rick Astley, and you've just been you-rolled for the 1,278th time.

Tired of that showboating Vic Chesnutt prick getting all the attention.

Hometown: Detroit.

Too big for XXXLs at Hot Topic.

You won a battle of the bands.

THE INDIE CRED TEST

07. How late is too late to consider going to a show?
A. Depending on the act, nothing is too late.
B. If I've got an 8 am meeting? 9 pm.
C. I'm only as old as I feel. 6:30.
D. Huh? Speak up son, I lost my inner cochlea protecting your sorry ass from the Emperor Hirohito and his rabid kamikaze Japs in WWII.

08. Choose the right t-shirt to portray "I was there" coolness while avoiding "geriatric territory":
A. An early '90s Guided By Voices tour
B. Handmade Hüsker Dü shirt
C. Richard Hell tank top from Urban Outfitters
D. Steely Dan anything
E. 100% wool limited edition Francis Scott Key longhandle underwear with the button-close crap flap

09. When you see somebody with a full sleeve tattoo, what do you think?
A. "Pfft, whatever."
B. "It's like outsider art that you wear forever."
C. "That must have cost more than my college education."
D. "I bet that guy winds up in lots of police lineups."

10. There hasn't been a good band since:
A. The Beatles
B. Bloodrock
C. Tears For Fears
D. Melvins
E. Animal Collective (who will probably be passé by the time you read this)
F. Falco covered Mozart's "Rock Me Amadeus."

11. I only buy albums in _____ form:
A. vinyl
B. CD
C. MP3
D. Porkskin
E. What's a fucking album?
F. What exactly do you mean by "buy"?

12. Boomers: When exactly did they wear out their welcome?
A. 1985
B. 1977
C. 1967
D. 1940
E. When their record-buying dollars financed the twin travesties that were Glenn Frey and Don Henley's solo careers.

THE INDIE CRED TEST   FILL IN THE BLANK   THE INDIE CRED TEST

YA GOTTA, Y'KNOW, LIKE QUESTION THE ANSWERS, MAN.

01. How old is too old to wear any other leather except a leather jacket?

02. How many bands from the '90s are you seeing for the first time now because you couldn't afford it first time round?

03. When did you stop picking up *Maximum RockNRoll* and start picking up *Paste* instead?

04. When was the last time you read a current music magazine?

05. When was the last time you attended a festival?

WHICH COST MORE?

06. Your record collection .... ☐
OR
Your car .... ☐

07. Your shoes .... ☐
OR
Your stereo .... ☐

08. Your last visit to Amoeba...................... ☐
OR
Your recent cosmetic dentistry .... ☐

CHAPTER 7

AREN'T YOU THAT GUY?

AN ADULT CONTEMPORARY BAND once sang, "we all wanna be big, big stars." They never made it. The key to stardom is actually a tightly-guarded recipe of surgery, luck, jackassery and payola (in that order), and even those who succeed in very minor ways can fall victim to self-puffery and delusion. As Kevin Federline might attest, had he the intellect, it's a fine line between fame and infamy. But neither are a prerequisite for developing a big head —and that's what our next chapter deals with.

YES/NO

LOCAL LUSTER

01. Did you play in one of the first bands to shape your town's scene?

02. Do you have a parking spot at the local rock club?

03. Would you think twice about moving to a different city because you'd lose your status?

04. Do you have your own section of releases you had something to do with at the local record store?

04A. Do you still have a local record store?

04B. Wait. Really?

05. Do you run a local fanzine?

05A. On a scale of slim-to-none, how gratifying is that job? *(01 is slim, 10 is none.)*

01 02 03 04 05 06 07 08 09 10

06. Did you pioneer a certain style in your town that you see getting ripped off 20 years later? Do you let them know about it?

07. Do people still talk about that one time you did that one thing somewhere a long time ago?

08. Has the local newspaper ever called you for a quote on the impending doom of record labels, record stores or failing clubs?

09. Have you ever been asked to introduce your favorite local band at a festival whose theme has something to do with a type of food? *(e.g. "Are you ready to rock Baby Boil-Off fanatics, well here they are…")*

10. When you tell people you "DJ" at a local club, do you really mean that you have a "desk job"?

11. Do people refer to you as Godfather, Forefather, Ayatollah, Boss, Sage, Kingfish, Big Money, Rug Doctor or anything guru-like?

12. Have you ever had to say anything like: "Hey look, ya get a little diarrhea while crowd surfing, people remember who you are. That's all I'm sayin'."

ENJOYING YOUR OWN FARTS

13. Is it really "notoriety" when you have to tell people why you're important?

14. When someone mentions a famous person you've met, do you play Six Degrees of Yourself for them?

15. How many of your vitriolic, pissy-pants letters to the editor have made it to print?

16. Do you routinely forego the chance to buy a record only to say, "They're sending me a copy"?

17. Do you take great pains to prominently display around your house those music releases you had a hand in?

18. Have you ever written a terribly mean-spirited review of a much-loved band's new album for Pitchfork, even though you secretly liked the album?

19. How many new fans have you forcibly made for a band due to the sheer volume of your car stereo?

20. Do you write shit about your own band on Wikipedia in an effort to take credit for pioneering a soon-to-be passé genre, upon whose coat tails you are attempting to ride?

21. Do you celebrate the anniversary of the first time you heard yourself on the radio on "Locals Only" night?

22. Do you have family pictures scattered all over your house, but an immaculately organized scrapbook of all your musical "achievements" resting in a glass case, protected by infrared lasers (that kill motherfuckers) overlooking a cloud that's overlooking the ocean?

PRESS/MEDIA

23. Have you ever been slammed on a blog or magazine?

23A. Did it hurt?

23B. Did you get revenge?

24. Have you ever received a 0.0 or similarly ass-bleedingly bad rating from Pitchfork?

25. If yes, did you mention this in your press kit?

26. How many members of the Lambgoat message board have wished you dead and/or bedridden?

27. What about People's "100 Most Beautiful People" issue?

28. Has a media appearance of yours ever gone *so* badly that it caused the press to decry your entire genre?

29. Did you or your band make Chunklet's "Pay Not to Play" issue?

30. Are you a perennial guest at the "Hacks and Flacks" dinner at South-by-Southwest?

Have you ever been interviewed in:

31. *Cat Fancy?*
32. *Circus?*
33. *Decibel?*
34. *Fangoria?*
35. *Guns and Ammo?*
36. *Highlights?*
37. *Juggs?*
38. *Maximum R&R?*
39. *Parenting?*
40. *Punk Planet?*
41. *Self?*
42. *Teen Beat?*
43. *Terrorizer?*
44. *Thrasher?*

PUBLIC OPINION

45. Are your fans mostly other musicians? YES NO

46. Are your fans mostly your parents and extended family?

47. Have you ever been accused of selling out by moving from the weekly rag to a glossy magazine even though they pay you in carpet scraps and Ramen noodles?

48. Have you ever been called "infamous" or "famous"?

49. Do people refer to you as a "music journalist," "rock critic" or "walking self-parody"?

50. Do people point to you at shows and whisper that you're "fuckin' right!" when you drunkenly heckle bands at every show?

51. Has your name ever become a "dictionary definition"? *Don't make me go all RuPaul on you.*

52. Are you known for your outlandish clothes, hairstyle and/or ever-present body odor?

53. Do you have a secret nickname like "Misfits Shirt" or "Ramones Patch" for obvious reasons?

54. Do you have phone numbers of famous people programmed into your phone that you show to people at parties but never dial—and this somehow earns you respect?

FIGHTING FOR FAME

55. Have you been involved in an on-stage melee?

55A. Did you win?

56. Do you pick fights with people of note, hoping to inflate your own name awareness?

57. Have you ever taken a swing at a member of the press?
...at another band?
...at a member of your own band?
...at one of your own grandparents?

58. Have you had your ass kicked extensively while just trying to get the fuck out of the way of a fight?

59. Have you ever released a song about being banned from performing at a club?

60. Has Courtney Love ever taken a swing at you?

61. Could you take David Bowie?

62. Could you take Eugene Robinson? YES NO

ERRONEOUS EXPERTISE

63. Have you ever been a panelist at a music conference?

64. Have you appeared on an episode of MTV's "Made" as an "expert"?

65. Have you ever been interviewed as an authority on any music-related subject?

66. Has your name ever been printed in *Record Collector* even though you've never actually appeared on a record?

MISCELLANEOUS QUERIES

67. Have you ever been denied entry to a foreign country?

68. Have you ever been denied re-entry to your home country?

69. Is your name/band/record label used as an eBay search term for records you actually had nothing to do with?

70. Has your phone number ever been etched into the run-out groove of a record (without your knowledge) preceded by "For a good time call..."?

71. Are you unnecessarily on any label's promo mailing list? *Trick question! All promo lists are unnecessary.*

72. Have you been paid to author an official bio for any artist?

73. Was payment revoked after they read your shoddy, bong-fueled work?

74. Have you ever pitched an idea to someone famous who actually seemed interested?

75. Have you ever done music "research" that didn't involve overconsumption of alcohol and air guitar?

76. Have you ever interviewed anyone famous and found out later that it is one of the more sought after clips of that celebrity on YouTube?

77. Have you ever been in a small room with famous people and said something (perhaps asking if they'd like to bang a watermelon with you) that made the actual celebrities laugh, call the cops or beat your ass?

YOU WERE GIVEN FREE WILL. USE IT OR LOSE IT.

01. Which of the following do you have in every town?
A. A booty call whose name usually escapes you
B. A comfortable bed, with coffee and breakfast
C. An arrest warrant
D. Several juvenile delinquents who bear an uncanny resemblance to you

02. Which of the following have you been a subject of?
A. A Lambgoat thread
B. An MTV News segment
C. A copyright infringement lawsuit
D. An episode of "To Catch A Predator"

03. Which of the following people have you name-dropped most in conversations?

A. Gerard Cosloy
B. Byron Coley
C. Tom Lax
D. Tony Brummel
E. Billy Mays
F. Johan Kugelberg

04. Which of the following words are usually tied to your claim to fame?
A. He's the dude who...
B. Can you believe that fucking scumbag?
C. Back before the Earth cooled, this guy was hot!!
D. Rapist.

05. Has anyone ever told you that:
A. You really have your ear to the ground?
B. You know a thing or two about a thing or two?
C. You are why I escape reality through drugs?
D. You need to get your booze soaked tongue out of my ear?

THE INDIE CRED TEST

CHAPTER 8

THE INNER CABAL OF COOL

"I'M FRIENDS WITH THOSE GUYS." Sure you are, if being tanked and fawning over one of their B-sides as they fold up the merch table qualifies as friendship. But don't fret—schmoozing is the necessary bottoming-out process committed by music fans in order to sustain the ego/sexual appetite/high of our beloved music idols. They give us so much, all we want is to give back. Usually drugs.

YES/NO

**RESPOND TO THE FOLLOWING QUESTIONS WITH A
YES/NO ANSWER OR SUFFER THE CONSEQUENCES.**

CONNECTIONS

YES NO

01. Have you ever been personally responsible for getting a band signed to a label? ☐ ☐

02. Have you ever been personally responsible for getting a band fired from a label? ☐ ☐

03. Have you ever been personally responsible for having a band's trailer stolen? ☐ ☐

04. Do people at record companies know who you are? ☐ ☐

05. If they don't, do you feel like it's their loss? ☐ ☐

06. If they do, is it because they've had to file multiple restraining orders against you for "excessive fanliness"? ☐ ☐

07. Do you find that you know more people outside your hometown than in it? ☐ ☐

08. Do waitstaff and bartenders hit on *you*? ☐ ☐

09. Do you really *need* the Blackberry? ☐ ☐

NAME-DROPPING

10. Do you refer to your friends by their band's name? *(i.e., Barry Mogwai, Nick Cutie, Ben Dirtbomb, etc.)* ☐ ☐

11. Do people refer to you by your band name? *(i.e., "Go get me a beer, Pantera!")* ☐ ☐

12. Have you ever introduced yourself to a band by telling them of all the other bands that have slept on your floor? ☐ ☐

13. Is there a mysterious stain on your carpet from when you let Mini Kiss crash on your floor? ☐ ☐

14. When talking about your "famous" friends, are you always sure to mention why they're famous? ☐ ☐

15. Has Fluss ever sat on your lap? ☐ ☐

16. Do you have an interesting Anton Newcombe or David Yow story? ☐ ☐

17. How about a G.G. Allin story involving violence, vomit and at least two cops? ☐ ☐

FREE SHIT

YES NO

18. Are there any bands that automatically give you one free copy of everything they put out? ☐ ☐

19. When you listen to the free copy, do you suddenly understand why they have to give it away? ☐ ☐

20. Do bands often give you advance copies of their records before they're released? ☐ ☐

21. Once you hear the advance copy, do you ever try to convince them to keep it unreleased? ☐ ☐

22. Do you often promise bands that you're friends with some label guy that may sign them just so they'll give you recent, unreleased recordings? ☐ ☐

23. Have you ever offered to help a band load out for free shit? ☐ ☐

IN THE WAY

24. Do you frequently travel with the band? ☐ ☐

25. Do they go out of their way to pick you up? ☐ ☐

26. Have you ever offered to pay for a band's hotel room, and then asked to sleep over? ☐ ☐

27. Have you gossiped with someone more interesting than you about someone less interesting than you? ☐ ☐

28. Do you start off conversations with band members you don't know by mentioning that you were at some show on their first tour seven years ago where they played to you, their merch guy, four empty pool tables, and a pinball machine? ☐ ☐

29. Do you think having/mentioning a friend who used to be a roadie for said band will get you beer tickets, or better yet, laid? ☐ ☐

30. Do bands only remember you by name on tour because you always give them free drugs? ☐ ☐

31. If so, do you think the fact that they remember you speaks highly or poorly of the quality of your drugs? ☐ ☐

32. Have you ever refused remittance of a debt owed you by a musician so you can continue saying "that guy still owes me twenty bucks"? ☐ ☐

THE INDIE
CRED TEST

FILL IN THE BLANK

THE INDIE
CRED TEST

IF YOU SEE A HOLE, YOU FILL IT. THIS AIN'T ROCKET SURGERY, KID!

01. How many signed bands have slept on your floor?
_____

02. How many unsigned bands have slept on your floor?
_____

03. How many bands got signed after sleeping on your floor or sleeping with you?
_____

04. How many band members have clogged your toilet pipes?
_____

05. How many band members have clogged your throat pipes?
_____

06. How many records have you personally been thanked on?
_____

07. Name the most famous musician to ever call you?
(Returning your call does not count.)

08. Name the five most famous musicians you've met who would remember you by your first name.
MUSICIAN No.01:
_____

MUSICIAN No.02:
_____

MUSICIAN No.03:
_____

MUSICIAN No.04:
_____

MUSICIAN No.05:
_____

09. Name three bands you've been in a recording studio with.
BAND No.01:
_____

BAND No.02:
_____

BAND No.03:
_____

10. Name three bands you've been in a bathroom stall with.
BAND No.01:
_____

BAND No.02:
_____

BAND No.03:
_____

11. Who is the most prestigious person who has offered you drugs? *(Isaac Brock is an immediate DQ.)*
_____
_____
_____

12. Who is the most pretentious person who has offered you drugs? *(Pete Doherty is an immediate DQ.)*
_____
_____
_____

13. What's the most fucked up thing Damon Che has ever said to you in passing?
_____
_____
_____
_____
_____
_____
_____

14. Which underground icon was the biggest prick when you met them?
_____
_____

15. Which underground icon was the biggest when you went down on them?
_____
_____

THE INDIE CRED TEST

JUPITERIMAGES/ PHOTOS.COM

The Bank of Indie Cred.®
What Can It Do For You?

Your BIC Cred Account isn't only a safe place to store the windfall of your years of name-dropping and ass-kissing. Through a host of proven services, we help you manage, cultivate, and capitalize on any cred you've already accumulated.

BIC Basic Cred Tracking®

Don't know which show to go to on an overbooked night? Can't tell when it's "über-obscure art punk" and when it's no-talents in a Spandex temper tantrum? Been confronted with a pay-to-play situation you didn't think was worth it, but wanted to know by exactly how much it wasn't?

That's where our Basic Cred Tracking can help, and all you have to do to get started is open an account with us. After that, simply do whatever you want to do — see that probably overrated band, check out that alt.porn newsgroup, buy those ironic leg warmers — and then call us for a balance check. You get the results of your actions in real time, so you're immediately aware of how badly you've screwed yourself and your reputation.

BIC Account Cred Interest®

Some say cred is unquantifiable, and that a cred account is a sham. We say those people are assholes and were probably not loved properly by their parents. At the very least, they're missing out on one of the most important features of a BIC cred account: Cred Interest. Let **Jeff Mangum** explain the benefits of this service to you:

"After Aeroplane..., my BIC rep assured me I'd never do anything better — ever. They said that with my BIC account, as long as I continue never to do anything again. I'll maintain all of my cred compounded with max Cred Interest®. That means I get emeritus "tortured artist" membership, and nobody can hold it against me that Neutral Milk Hotel is basically Toad the Wet Sprocket, or that I 'inspired' Arcade Fire."

BIC Account Perks

We offer account holders benefits at a variety of levels. Your Bank of Indie Cred Representative will help find the right match for you, or you can browse through some of the highlights below:

BRONZE LEVEL - "Bassists and It Girls" ♟

- Guest editor for MagnetMagazine.com
- Successfully self-release one (1) project per fiscal year
- Open for one (1) national touring act per fiscal year
- Slot in Daniel Johnston's backing band
- David Lovering wears your t-shirt
- Gain entry into any club or gallery in town whether or not you're on the list
- Record an EP that has "Steve Albini guitars"

- One (1) favorable review in your choice of industry periodical
- Win five (5) arguments against people that "just don't get" your art/music/etc.
- One (1) nationally promoted DJ gig per fiscal year at a hot nightclub in Portland
- Host a show on a local college radio station whether you're enrolled there or ever went to college
- Membership on up to three (3) panels at South by Southwest
- Write liner notes for a Thrill Jockey reissue

SILVER LEVEL - "Graduates of the Scene" ♟♟

- Steve Albini engineers your album
- Move to Chicago or Berlin
- Buy drugs from/make a film with Harmony Korine
- Co-own a hip coffee shop in Silver Lake
- Weekend tour with current "hot" mash-up DJ
- One (1) MySpace "Band of the Week" ad per fiscal year
- Move to a farm just to the east of BFE
- Joey Santiago contributes guitar to your project

- Release a mediocre solo album on Arts & Crafts or Peaceville
- Contribute articles to *The Believer* though you may have never written a word in your life
- Go "in a different direction" with a 15% cap on cred decline
- Obtain immunity from disparaging comments in *Vice* magazine
- One (1) critics-choice write up per fiscal year in your choice of industry periodical
- Add a pirate ship or multimedia screen to your stage show

GOLD LEVEL - "Veterans" ♟♟♟

- Subject of documentary that reveals how much of a self-serving jackass you actually are
- Reissue your back catalog
- You tour opening for Marduk
- Kim Deal shares a lid with you
- Cameo in a David Fincher movie
- Pitchfork likes you (again)
- In-store performance at Amoeba
- Product placement on "90210"
- Record Store Day exclusive release

- Steve Albini calls you "a shameless sellout"
- Favorable review in *Rolling Stone*
- Reform and tour with the band you broke up a decade ago
- Marry a model, chef and/or model/chef
- *Paste* (or some other equally shitty mag) chronicles your stint in rehab
- Be seen snorting cocaine in Park Slope with David Cross
- Receive a text message from Roger Daltrey telling you how much he liked your last project
- Buy a loft in Prague
- Name your child after an obscure writer or a member of Sonic Youth

PLATINUM LEVEL - "Dave Grohl" ♟♟♟♟

- Get attached as "Executive Producer" for whatever Focus Features is working on
- Provide the soundtrack for an Apple ad
- Get Brian Eno to produce your next album
- Steve Albini asks to record your next album
- Subject of a career retrospective at MOMA
- Your own fashion line at Target
- Limited-edition Vans
- Pitchfork claims to have discovered you first

- Publish a feature in *Interview* with Black Francis that is really all about you
- Your Record Store Day release sells out before Record Store Day and is available only on eBay
- Start a press feud with an aging British rock icon and win
- License to carry a small dog with you wherever you go
- Lend your name to a top-shelf liquor only available overseas because of its near-certain impotency risk
- Transfer cred to someone on a lower tier by having them open for you on tour
- Produce the next seven (7) bands to come out of Brooklyn

Other BIC Services

Talk to your BIC Representative about these other valuable premium services, exclusively available to BIC account holders.

Cred Coaching: Our lifestyle coordination experts will prep your primping on everything from vintage clothing to pets to that perfectly disinterested scoff.

Pseudo Soap Opera: Be confronted in a public place by an attractive young "suitor" who will loudly create a scene documenting your decision to break up with them. Play it cool amidst their tears and pleas for reconciliation.

*Having a drink and/or punches thrown at you requires an additional premium and/or waiver.

Name Drops: One of our most seasoned customers will visit a commercial establishment of your choice, engage a person(s) of your choosing, and pepper the conversation with mentions of your name. You will receive a report documenting the conversation and all public reactions.

Rumor Milling: Our most elite service. Using a team of Wayne Coyne, Dave Eggers, and the entire cast of Entourage, we will create scene wide rumors of your exploits.

Past rumors have included:

"[insert popular song] is really written about you"
"you were a member of [insert popular band] before they got big"
"your nom de plume is [insert popular film maker/photographer/poet/artist]"
"you have connections with [insert trendy Colombian cocaine cartel]"
"you used to be [insert popular/talentless socialite] before entering into witness protection"

Visit **Chunklet.com** today to see what **you** can acquire.

CHAPTER 9

ORGANIZED SPORTS

SOME PEOPLE APPROACH MUSIC CULTURE as a mere spectator's sport, while others dive in dick first in an attempt to bolster their cred and expand their horizons. Are the spectators smart in that they can be entertained while not having to get involved? Are the "Hey, Me Too! Me Too!"'s fully immersed in the music scene or just plain fucking dumb? On which side of the fence do you fall?

YES/NO

THE INDIE CRED TEST

THE INDIE CRED TEST

COMPLETE THE FOLLOWING QUESTIONS WITH A YES/NO ANSWER. BE A HERO FOR ONCE IN YOUR LIFE.

YES NO

01. Do you own an 8mm camera? ☐ ☐

02. Can I have it? ☐ ☐

03. Have you recorded other bands on your four-track so you can get "that sound" everybody's talking about? ☐ ☐

04. Have you ever hosted a record stuffing party? ☐ ☐

05. Have you ever hosted a Stove Top Stuffing party? ☐ ☐

06. Have you ever gone on tour and you're not in the band? ☐ ☐

06A. Is your name Henry? ☐ ☐

07. Did you know that millions of crappy bands are rich? ☐ ☐

08. Does that make you want to go start a crappy band right now? ☐ ☐

09. Have you ever played or been featured as a guest on a 311 record? ☐ ☐

10. Do you run a distro to do your part to back the scene? ☐ ☐

11. Do you only use your TV to watch DVDs and stream Netflix? ☐ ☐

12. Did you just lie and say yes when you know you watch whatever new fat show Kirstie Alley will be hocking at the time of this publication? ☐ ☐

13. Do you consider video games to be an "activity"? ☐ ☐

14. Do you consider masturbation to be an "activity"? ☐ ☐

15. Have you ever smoked pot for more than eight hours in a row? ☐ ☐

16. Have you ever worn a home-made t-shirt of an obscure band, hoping to find other fans of said band? ☐ ☐

17. Have you ever worn a homemade t-shirt of a local band hoping to score brownie points with said local band and their inner circle? ☐ ☐

18. Have you ever moved to a city because the scene was starting to take off? ☐ ☐

19. Have you ever moved away from a city because the scene blew up? ☐ ☐

20. Have you ever quit your job, sold your house, and moved away from a city because the scene was being taken over by posers? ☐ ☐

YES NO

21. Does a group of friends hanging out in a house playing music together in various one-off "projects" constitute a scene? ☐ ☐

21A. How about if they all bang each other too? ☐ ☐

22. Have you ever lived in the best venue/house in your particular scene? ☐ ☐

23. Do you only drink water that 50 Cent had a hand in (not literally)? ☐ ☐

23A. How about literally? ☐ ☐

24. Do you do the Dew? ☐ ☐

24A. Is it extreme? ☐ ☐

RADIO

25. Are you still a college radio DJ even though you haven't been a college student for over a decade? ☐ ☐

26. Did you put your band's album into your college station's rotation? ☐ ☐

27. Did the records you charted to *CMJ* actually get played? ☐ ☐

28. Do you know what that means? ☐ ☐

28. Did you listen to other shows on the station or only your own? ☐ ☐

30. Do you find that your radio show helps you meet eligible sophomores? ☐ ☐

31. Did you land a job after college thanks to connections made at the station? ☐ ☐

32. Do you prefer listening to your aircheck tapes instead of making mix tapes for your car? ☐ ☐

33. Did you steal stuff while working at the station? *No, seriously. We won't tell.* ☐ ☐

LABEL SCUM

34. Do you own a record or tape label? ☐ ☐

34A. Are you retarded? ☐ ☐

35. Do you whine about illegal file sharing? ☐ ☐

36. Have you ever said the phrase, "As soon as I get my label going..."? ☐ ☐

37. Have you ever paid for an advertisement in any zine? ☐ ☐

37A. Do you feel it paid off? ☐ ☐

37B. At all? ☐ ☐

YES NO

38. Have you ever paid a publicist to do anything more than get you a cup of coffee? ☐ ☐

39. Have you ever kissed the ass of a zine editor (or music director) so that they will feature your band? ☐ ☐

40. Did you know bands "make it" on this premise alone? ☐ ☐

41. Do you have anybody famous on your label? *(Compilation appearances do not count.)* ☐ ☐

42. Did you leave a managerial/directing position at your college radio station to focus on your label? ☐ ☐

42A. In retrospect, was that a smart move? ☐ ☐

43. Have you ever been an intern at a record label? ☐ ☐

44. Have you had a "label" for years now only to release your own stuff? ☐ ☐

45. Is your garage full of cassettes still in shrink-wrap because you thought 1,000 copies of your band's first release would move in no time? ☐ ☐

46. Do your parents call often to ask when you're coming to get all that label shit you left there 10 years ago? ☐ ☐

ZINES

47. Do/did you put out a zine? ☐ ☐

48. Do you still think somewhere down the line you may put out another issue? ☐ ☐

YES NO

49. Do you think people, after waiting years, will still care? ☐ ☐

50. Do you think people have actually been waiting? ☐ ☐

51. Were you a zine publisher/contributor for the sole purpose of getting free stuff? ☐ ☐

52. Have you ever kept a pretentious, nihilistic road journal to publish in your zine? ☐ ☐

53. Did you stop reading *MRR* because it turns your fingers black? ☐ ☐

54. Do you have a lifetime subscription to any music magazine? ☐ ☐

55. Do you give up on reading a zine if the general grammar and design flat-out suck? ☐ ☐

56. Did you start a high school-styled slam book based on bands you used to love but now hate because their personal interest in you seems to have waned over the years? ☐ ☐

Which of these old zines do you have displayed in your home for guests to admire?

57. ☐ *ANSWER Me!*
58. ☐ *Bomp!*
59. ☐ *Bunnyhop*
60. ☐ *Cometbus*
61. ☐ *Conflict*
62. ☐ *Crunch Factory*
63. ☐ *Disaster*
64. ☐ *Forced Exposure*
65. ☐ *Gearhead*
66. ☐ *Killer*
67. ☐ *Matter*
68. ☐ *Motorbooty*
69. ☐ *RE/Search*
70. ☐ *Slash*
71. ☐ *Subversive Workshop*

THE INDIE CRED TEST

FILL IN THE BLANK

THE INDIE CRED TEST

01. At what age did you stop listening to commercial radio?

02. How many band or record label mailing lists are you on?

03. What does "No Depression" mean to you?

04. When was the last time you reminded someone that Fugazi charged only five dollars for their shows?

05. How many editions of the *Trouser Press Record Guide* do you own?

06. How many zines can you name?

07. How many publications do you subscribe to and/or regularly purchase?

08. You've been taking note of this for years, dork. So tell us, after "Free Bird," "_____" is the second most likely thing you'll hear a drunk yell.

09. If _____ is not on tap, you're fucking out of there because a successful night depends on it, whatever that means.

CRED PROXIMITY

Some might argue that location isn't everything, but we'd like to invite those people to kindly suck it. Cred doesn't travel down dirt roads. If it takes more than an hour to get to anything that's not a yard sale, you're entirely too far from where the magic happens. You brain-dead suburban zombies aren't in the clear either. How many times have you introduced yourselves as being from the larger, cooler city closest to the boilerplate shithole in which you reside? Don't lie, you poser! Whether your surrounding digs include the choicest of bully, boss, radical or a godawful slipshod mess of squalid wildebeest shit, or any of the passably undistinguished locales atwunst, we've got to know. Like, now.

ARE YOU CLOSER TO...

A. A good house for basement shows
B. A good theater for Off-Broadway shows
C. A good alley for hip toothless hobos doin' it

A. $1 PBRs
B. $12 Heinekens
C. $5 speedballs

A. Good Lebanese food
B. A raw bar
C. A soup kitchen (featuring cream of E-Coli and broccoli head cheese soup)

A. A community garden
B. A Whole Foods
C. The dirty dumpster behind a Fuddruckers

A. A cool dive bar where they save you your usual table
B. A martini bar that does "under the table" service
C. An Applebee's where the bartender will give you customers' leftover drinks for free

A. The corner liquor store that always has a good selection of cheap brews
B. A vineyard that hosts the most delightful annual Beaujolais tastings
C. A guy who knows a guy who knows a dealer that only occasionally mixes rat poison and bullshark jizz with the blow

A. A well-stocked public library
B. Barnes & Noble
C. The Christian Science Reading Room

ARE YOU CLOSER TO...

A. An indie record store with a great used section
B. A chain store that doesn't sell a CD for less than $12
C. A street corner where you can get hookers, crack, and bootleg top-40 discs for under a buck

A. A comic book shop that'll hold issues for you
B. A cigar bar that always saves the new stock for you
C. A Yankee Candle outlet that has frequent "Buy One, Get One For Double Price" sales

A. A cheap vintage clothing store
B. A tailor who used to do a lot of work in Hollywood before everyone found out he wasn't gay
C. A Salvation Army donation box with a busted lock

A. Urban Outfitters
B. Prada
C. The run-off chutes from the local tannery

A. A space that hosts local artists' showings
B. A high-end art gallery
C. A gas station with a bathroom stall that usually has some good graffiti

A. A coffee shop where you always get in on a lively debate
B. Your yacht club, where you always get good investment advice
C. A free clinic where you can always get the latest tips for Hep-C prevention

ARE YOU CLOSER TO...

A. A free public wi-fi hotspot
B. One of the six wireless N+ routers in your summer home that may or may not be slowly doing something horrible to your insides
C. Neighbors who don't password-protect their network

A. A public transit stop
B. Your limousine driver
C. Your Honda Spree

A. A decent-sized green space to run or bicycle through
B. Your personal trainer's home studio
C. The neighborhood pit bull that's never on a leash and always wants to eat your torso

A. An underground club with great DJs
B. A velvet-roped club where you can rub jeweled elbows with celebrities
C. The local Single Square Dancers, USA chapter

A. House parties with underage girls
B. High-society functions with underage girls
C. Fraternity hazings with overripe dudes

A. A culturally-mixed neighborhood, parish, or borough
B. A gated, exclusive (i.e. "white") community
C. A correctional facility

A. The home of the local scene kingpin
B. The home of a celebrity
C. The home of a registered sex offender

If you answered mostly "A"s, you've got a
Strong Cred Proximity Effect

You're right in the middle of everything, and your cred reflects it. It's surprising you even took the time to finish this quiz — don't you have dinner plans at the underground vegan deli? Or was tonight the private screening at the art-house theater above the Antiguan organic glassblower's market? Must be tough. The only downfall to your charmed existence is that, well, can they still be considered friends if they only like you for your convenient concert parking? Do you even care?

If you answered mostly "B"s, you've got a
Weak Cred Proximity Effect

We say "studio apartment," you say "hip district loft." We say "guest list at The Black Cat," you say "backstage at Coachella." We say "you're a lowly vice-chancellor of douchedom," you say "but aren't you enjoying your ride on these silky coat-tails?" It's tough to say which is worse — the fact that your trust fund bought you your cred, or the fact that we'll all buy into it to ensure there's enough room on your coke spoon for us.

If you answered mostly "C"s, you've got
No Cred Proximity Effect

Have you ever wondered why, even with the lure of tickets to a kick-ass show or a pony-keg of limited-edition micro brew, your friends are always meeting with their sponsors or are donating their third kidney for the month? Perhaps you've failed to notice the pack of unleashed, unfed, and uncircumcised pit bulls around the corner from your hovel, or the peculiar chemical smells emanating from your neighbor's double-bolted door? Face it: you're so far away from anything cool that it's surprising people even humor you with excuses. Maybe tonight will be the night the fumes from your neighbor's bathtub still finally catch a spark...

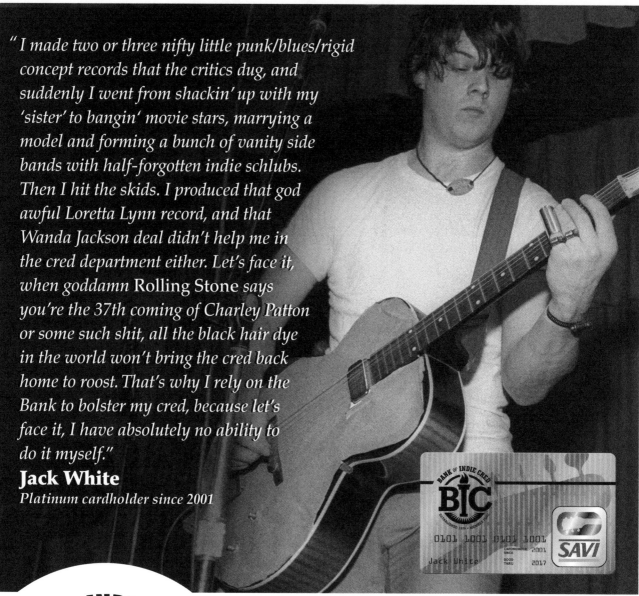

"I made two or three nifty little punk/blues/rigid concept records that the critics dug, and suddenly I went from shackin' up with my 'sister' to bangin' movie stars, marrying a model and forming a bunch of vanity side bands with half-forgotten indie schlubs. Then I hit the skids. I produced that god awful Loretta Lynn record, and that Wanda Jackson deal didn't help me in the cred department either. Let's face it, when goddamn Rolling Stone says you're the 37th coming of Charley Patton or some such shit, all the black hair dye in the world won't bring the cred back home to roost. That's why I rely on the Bank to bolster my cred, because let's face it, I have absolutely no ability to do it myself."

Jack White
Platinum cardholder since 2001

DON'T PLAY A NOTE WITHOUT IT. ™

LET US HANDLE YOUR CRED. YOU JUST TRY TO KEEP UP WITH THE REST.

It's the secret that no self-respecting cred-seeker wants exposed, but it's the one that every one of them shares: under that reckless, unwashed, and meticulously-calculated exterior beats the heart of a toddler that just wants to be loved, hand-fed, and protected from themselves. The cred maintenance and security programs we provide will help assure you that even though you can't step out of the way of a single, miraculously bad idea that's coming to torpedo your rep, there is at least one thing that will protect you from yourself. Now, get back on that stage and try not to tongue-kiss your "sibling."

Visit **chunklet.com** today to see what **you** can acquire.

SECTION III

FORGET HIGH SCHOOL. REMEMBER THE SCENE. IT'S ALL ABOUT THE MUSIC.

CHAPTER 10

FANBOY (OR GIRL) PROCLIVITIES

FANATICISM IS A FORM OF DEDICATION. It's also incredibly annoying. Deeply, music has touched us, and deeply, we are hyper-anal, know-it-all, obscurity-seeking, completist jerks for it. Take a simple question like, "what are you listening to lately?" The sane can answer in a few words. The rest of us...well, you got a minute? You'll need a bit of background on mid-era Flamenco-Tech first. Maybe the guy or gal who "just listens to everything!" has it right. Enter the rabbit hole.

THE INDIE
CRED TEST

YES/NO

THE INDIE
CRED TEST

COMPLETE THE FOLLOWING QUESTIONS WITH A YES/NO ANSWER OR SUFFER THE CONSEQUENCES.

YES NO

01. Do you know what a sycophant is? ☐ ☐

02. Do you consider yourself a "fan" of anything that would be widely considered a "franchise"? ☐ ☐

03. Do you maintain a band's official (or unofficial) web page or fan club even though you're not in the band? ☐ ☐

04. Have you ever joined a fan club just to get access to tickets and/or special shows? ☐ ☐

05. Is there any other non-asskickable reason to be in a "fan club"? ☐ ☐

06. Are you often heard saying, "Yeah, but it's not as good as their earlier stuff"? ☐ ☐

07. Do you like to describe guitar tones as "frenetic" or "miasmic" in casual conversation? ☐ ☐

08. Do you own more than 20 versions of one song? ☐ ☐

09. When a friend or co-worker plays you something by a new band, do you give it a full verse before saying, "Pfft...This just sounds like a shitty version of [insert band]"? ☐ ☐

10. In conversations, do you confuse bands that have similar names? ☐ ☐

11. Have you ever described a band as being "quirky" or "lo-fi"? ☐ ☐

12. Do you brag about seeing a band "back when they were playing VFWs and fire halls"? ☐ ☐

13. Do you always bring up production value in an obnoxious, bellowing manner when discussing records? ☐ ☐

14. Do you only listen to the local college station, even though you didn't go there and you haven't been in school for 25 years? ☐ ☐

15. Are you a Hobbitron who is secretly obsessed with the Lord of the Rings trilogy? ☐ ☐

16. Do you want to be known as the first Hobbitron? ☐ ☐

17. Do you know any of the catalog numbers of release by heart and you *don't* work for the label in question? ☐ ☐

18. Are you on the Mishpucha, Indie-Pop, or Drone-On mailing lists? ☐ ☐

19. Have you ever recognized a star and drunkenly repeated their name until they had to seek shelter or stomp your guts out? ☐ ☐

YES NO

20. Have you ever been in the position of serving a famous musician and couldn't help continually whistling the tunes to all of his/her hits? ☐ ☐

ERAS & GENRES

21. Have you ever drafted a firmly written, notarized statement that you have stopped listening to any music after a designated cut-off year? ☐ ☐

22. Do you enjoy any music made prior to 1955? *(Robert Johnson and Hank Williams don't count.)* ☐ ☐

23. Do you enjoy any music made prior to 1988? *(The Velvet Underground, Joy Division, Slayer, Metallica, and Krautrock don't count.)* ☐ ☐

24. Do you enjoy prog but you don't play a musical instrument? ☐ ☐

25. Did you stop reading the previous question when you saw the word "prog"? ☐ ☐

26. Have you ever used the phrase "Kiwi-pop" or "jangle-twee" because you didn't already know what a horrendous blowhard it would make you sound like? ☐ ☐

27. Have you come up with a description for a particular genre of music that has become widely used? ☐ ☐

28. Is Jazz the music made for morons? ☐ ☐

29. Are you a moron for even considering that? ☐ ☐

30. Improv: Total bullshit, right? ☐ ☐

MERCH TABLE

31. Do you flirt with the merch girl/guy even if you know they're a band member's significant other? ☐ ☐

32. Would you buy a record you already own just to get it signed? ☐ ☐

33. Do you compare prices of records at the merch table if a record store is close by? ☐ ☐

34. Do you have the urge to punch people who buy the band's t-shirt at the show and have the gall to actually put it on right away? ☐ ☐

AUTOGRAPHS

35. Have you ever gotten an autograph from a band or member of a band? ☐ ☐

36. What about a local news anchor or minor league baseball mascot? ☐ ☐

37. Have you ever faked an autograph to get more money on eBay? ☐ ☐

YES NO

38. Have you ever suspiciously lurked near a van or tour bus for an autograph? ☐ ☐

39. Has a musician refused to give you fourteen copies of an autograph because they somehow seemed to know you're going to sell it later? ☐ ☐

40. Have you ever attempted to find a band at a restaurant, hotel, or bathhouse to get an autograph? ☐ ☐

41. Do you become upset when you find out someone who wasn't on the record you brought has fucked it up by signing his Johnny-come-lately name all over it? ☐ ☐

42. Have you ever Frankensteined an autograph? ☐ ☐
    (Frankenstein, verb: To collect a band's autograph after said band's dissolution or hiatus by getting individual members to sign the band's album or poster at their solo or side-band gigs.)

43. In the process of getting a Frankensteined autograph, have you ever tracked down a band member outside of their musical career? ☐ ☐
    (Example: Getting Greg Norton to sign a Hüsker Dü record by sneaking into his Minneapolis restaurant disguised as a delicious rack of lamb.)

44. Do you carry your own multi-colored Sharpie pack for autographs or the occasional gay pride graffiti? ☐ ☐

MOMENTOS & GIMCRACKS

45. Have you ever elbowed aside a five-foot-tall girl to snatch up a hand-written set list? ☐ ☐

46. Have you ever received a swift, vicious, and highly embarrassing beatdown by a five-foot-tall girl you attempted to elbow aside to snatch up a hand-written set list? ☐ ☐

47. Do you lose sleep over lost ticket stubs, posters or autographs? ☐ ☐

48. Do you keep old set lists, backstage passes and/or tour laminates stuffed in your sock drawer? ☐ ☐

49. Have you ever taken a piece of equipment, after it's been destroyed on stage, by someone famous? ☐ ☐

50. Have you ever had your picture taken with Lydia Lunch and thought it was cool? ☐ ☐

51. Have you ever had your picture taken with David Allen Coe because you thought it was funny because he's a douche and you're, like, so totally not? ☐ ☐

52. Have you ever purchased a poster for a concert you did not attend? ☐ ☐

NAME

53. Do you only own jazz records by performers with three names? ☐ ☐

54. Have you ever tried to count all the bands with "Wolf" in their names? Were you high? If you

YES NO

answered "No," congratulations! You're just stupid.

55. Can a band be taken seriously if their name has more than two words and an article in it? What if it's the indefinite article? ☐ ☐

56. Do you get upset when people don't capitalize "the" in band names? ☐ ☐

BAND SPECIFIC

57. Die Kreuzen: One of the key links between punk and metal or nickname for Hitler's penis? ☐ ☐

58. Did you only find out about Squirrel Bait after the records got re-released by Drag City? ☐ ☐

59. Are you more partial to Half Japanese with David Fair? ☐ ☐

60. Did you avoid Nirvana until Kurt died, upon which you suddenly became their biggest fan? ☐ ☐

61. Were you fascinated by the ideas of Gwar, Lisa Suckdog and Costes but were too scared to see their shows? ☐ ☐

62. Were you into Steve Martin before he un-ironically played the banjo on stage? ☐ ☐

63. Did you actually listen to all of Robert Pollard's post-GBV output before decrying it, or was that not even necessary? ☐ ☐

64. Do you wish Joanna Newsom was more of a shameless porn star and less of a mealy-mouthed cartoon? ☐ ☐

65. What about Devendra Banhart? ☐ ☐

66. Should Mac McCaughan be sainted or knighted? Or perhaps simply flogged? ☐ ☐

67. Have the Mountain Goats just not been the same to you since John Darnielle stopped recording with a condenser mic? ☐ ☐

68. Would Ian MacKaye leave a found suitcase full of money in the woods if it had a note attached reading: "If you take this it means you like BBQ ribs and commercials"? ☐ ☐

69. Did you hate keyboards on principle until Stereolab? ☐ ☐

70. Did you hate skateboards on principle until the Skatenigs? ☐ ☐

71. Had you heard of Sonic Youth prior to their signing to DGC? ☐ ☐

72. Were you even born before Sonic Youth's signing to DGC? ☐ ☐

73. Had you heard of Jon Spencer prior to the Blues Explosion? ☐ ☐

74. Would you support a band called "The John Denver Pants Explosion"? ☐ ☐

	YES	NO

75. Did you used to make fun of country until Palace, or will you *always* make fun of country?

76. Have the Ramones put out a bad record?

77. Have the Ramones put out a good record?

78. Have you turned on Saturday Night Live at some point in the past few years and been shocked to discover that the drummer of Trenchmouth is a cast member?

79. Have you gone through an über-misanthrope Jim Goad/Boyd Rice phase?

79A. Follow up: have you ever made it through a Whitehouse LP in its entirety?

80. Is Phil Spector really in prison because of Paul McCartney's dislike of the mix on *Let It Be*?

81. Is anything by Mötley Crüe worth owning besides their autobiography or Vince Neil's leftover face meat from plastic surgery?

82. Were you annoyed when Big Star's "In The Street" was covered by Cheap Trick for the theme song to That '70s Show?

83. Has Henry Rollins spit on you more than once?

84. Is pre-Rollins Black Flag the *only* Black Flag?

85. Were you aware that there was a pre-Rollins Black Flag?

86. Have you ever exchanged personal emails with Henry Rollins?

87. Have you ever exchanged personal blows with Henry Rollins?

88. Have you ever bought a glow in the dark Bob Marley poster?

89. Did you think Spinal Tap was a real band?

90. Have you ever taken a proactive role in trying to impress Steve Albini on the Electrical Audio forum?

91. Does the commercial use of "Lust for Life" annoy the shit out of you?

92. Have you ever gone to a laser light show to see Pink Floyd's *The Wall*?

93. Do you "get" Loren Mazzacane-Connors?

94. Do you "get" the Shaggs?

95. Do you "get" Shat?

96. Have you ever tried to convince someone that you've heard a record by Buddy Bolden?

97. Not counting Paul Westerberg, do you own any solo records by members of the Replacements?

98. Has steadfastly adhering to a specific genre resulted in buying albums by really mediocre bands like John Cafferty & the Beaver Brown Band, Tommy Conwell & the Young Rumblers or Richie Sweetoes & the Bumblefuck Orchestra?

99. Have you ever chased all of the members of the Polyphonic Spree (who had changed out of their silly cult robes) for several miles to complete a full autograph set?

MULTIPLE CHOICE

THE INDIE CRED TEST

YOU WERE GIVEN FREE WILL. USE IT.

01. When you hear the name Moonshake, what first comes to mind?
A. A failed 1960s McDonalds ice cream treat
B. A Can song
C. A '90s shoegaze/postrock band
D. Lunar seismic activity

02. What wave of bands do you think of when the term "emo" is mentioned?
A. Revolution Summer DC bands (Embrace, Rites of Spring, etc.)
B. Braid, Cap 'n Jazz, Joan of Arc, etc.
C. Sensefield, Texas is the Reason, Promise Ring, etc.
D. Anything not Gorgoroth

03. In your opinion, the "band signing" that did the most permanent damage to SST Records in the period between 1986-1988 was:
A. Sonic Youth.
B. Trotsky Icepick.
C. Zoogz Rift.
D. SWA.

04. Irony plays a huge part in my enjoyment of:
A. Whitehouse.
B. Manowar.
C. Steely Dan.
D. Black metal.

05. When did you start listening to "noise rock"?
    A. 1990
    B. 1998
    C. About a month after Pissed Jean's
       Hope For Men came out.

06. For how long can you talk about your
    favorite Black Flag permutation?
    A. 30 seconds
    B. 30 minutes
    C. How long have you got?

07. How long did you cut your hair like Thurston Moore?
    A. 1-2 years
    B. 3-5 years
    C. Since 1992
    D. Never. That poseur cuts *his* hair like *mine!*

08. What was your initial reaction to news
    of the Slint reformation?
    A. Unbridled glee
    B. Lip-curling cynicism
    C. Nervous collapse at the tarnishing of yet another
       fond memory
    D. "Whatever."

09. Have you ever made your own t-shirt for
    one of the following bands?
    A. The Wipers
    B. Labradford
    C. Chronic Sick
    D. Squirrel Bait
    E. Krokus

10. Your love of this band/artist helped deliver a death blow
    to one (or more) committed relationships in your life:
    A. The Jesus Lizard
    B. Melvins
    C. The Lemonheads/Evan Dando
    D. Ryan Adams
    E. Abba

11. Which band/artist do you claim to like, but, truthfully,
    you're only into them so that you're more likely to meet/
    attract members of the opposite sex?
    A. Cocteau Twins
    B. The Smiths/Morrissey
    C. Sunn O)))
    D. Poison Idea
    E. Neutral Milk Hotel
    F. The J. Giles Band

12. The day Kurt Cobain killed himself, you were:
    A. Just a twinkle in my father's milky eye.
    B. Too young/old to care.
    C. A pizza-faced malcontent riveted
       and shocked by the news.
    D. Wait, wasn't he in Pearl Jam?
    E. Hoping he was trying to shoot his wife instead.

13. How much would you pay for a limited edition tour
    poster that looks like it was designed in the van
    on the way to the gig and hastily Xeroxed at Kinko's?
    A. It's hand numbered by my idol. $75.
    B. If it'll help them pay for gas to the next town,
       $25, I suppose.
    C. It's late and I want to drink more. $10.
    D. Which way is up? $0.

14. Do you get autographs with the intent of selling
    it later? If yes, was it on:
    A. Some item of detritus you found at the show
       (napkin, cigarette pack, scrap paper, ticket stub)
    B. An item you purchased from the band at the show
       (CD, t-shirt, vinyl)
    C. An item you brought from home to have signed
       at the show
    D. A *rare* or collectible item that impressed the artist
    E. More than one of the above

15. My next poster purchase/score will be because:
    A. I really like the band.
    B. I might be able to sell it on eBay for twice what I paid.
    C. I want something for the walls of my
       office/practice space.
    D. There's room at the back of my closet for at least
       one more cardboard poster tube.
    E. Whoever dies with the most posters wins.

16. If you brought items from home, did you:
    A. Bring them into the club, jammed in your pockets,
       at the start of the show?
    B. Race out to the car between the end of the set
       and the encore?
    C. Comfortably walk to the car after the show ended,
       knowing the band would be at the merch table
       when you got back?
    D. Tote all of them (including rare vinyl and
       out-of-print CDs) in your aging messenger
       bag which reeks of club smoke and old beer?

17. The art for the majority of my posters is by:
    A. Derek Hess
    B. Aaron Turner
    C. Coop
    D. Frank Kozik
    E. Lindsey Kuhn
    F. Art Chantry
    G. Seldon Hunt

18. The majority of my posters are:
    A. Stolen.
    B. Ripped off the wall at a show.
    C. Purchased off their web site.
    D. Purchased during a frenzied and/or drunk
       eBay bidding war.
    E. Given to me by the band as payment for weed.
    F. Felt blacklight posters featuring panthers, pythons,
       skulls, flames and/or flying V guitars purchased
       from Spencer's Gifts in the mall.

19. Which record did your girlfriend/boyfriend make
    you turn off while in the middle of sex?
    A. The Birthday Party, *Prayers on Fire*
    B. Public Image Limited, *First Issue*
    C. Can, *Tago Mago* (the second disc)
    D. Sonic Youth, *Bad Moon Rising*
    E. Big Black, *Songs About Fucking*
    F. W.A.S.P., "Animal (Fuck Like A Beast)"
    G. Foghat, "Slow Ride"

UNBLANKIFY THE EMPTY SPOTS.

01. Complete this lyric/song title...
"Morrissey rides a _____" *(Hint: it's not "cock-cycle.")*

02. "I Hate the Bait" refers to what band?

03. Which illegal drug did Hüsker Dü consume the most while recording Zen Arcade? _____

04. Who replaced Chris Mars in the Replacements?

05. What is the total body count on Nick Cave & the Bad Seeds' *Murder Ballads*? _____

06. What is Yukki Gipe's real name?

07. Please properly pronounce and define the phrase "Les Rallizes Dénudés." *(Sucker. It's made up...and Japanese too. You lose.)*

08. ESSAY: Why do people keep giving Courtney Love money to do things?

09. In the space provided, please write one good thing about Merzbow.

10. In minutes, what is the most amount of time you've waited outside the backstage area in hopes of scoring an autograph or ingesting some DNA? _____

11. Which band do you claim you were into before your peers?

12. List five justifications you've made to hang onto your cassette collection.

13. How long will you consider thumbing through crap on the merch table in hopes of speaking to the band with no intention of buying anything whatsoever?

14. Favorite song by The Vines. *(Caught you. Trick question.)*

WHEN

15. When was the last time you asked a musician for their autograph?

16. When did Pavement start sucking?

17. When did you purchase *Spiderland*?

18. When did you discover Thalia Zedek?

19. When did your teenage idols start sucking?

20. When did punk "break" for you? _____

21. When did Urge Overkill stop being a great rock band?

22. Wait, did Urge Overkill ever start being a great rock band?

23. When did *Alternative Press* hit the shitter?

24. When was the last time you remember being excited by hearing a band that was dubbed "no-wave"?

25. When did you decide that you were completely sick of "metalgaze"?

26. When did you accept reality and start referring to Touch & Go in the past tense?

27. When did you decide Animal Collective was overhyped?

28. When did you stop listening to Sunny Day Real Estate?

29. When did you first feel intimated by New York/L.A./Chicago music hipsters?

30. When did you write off Bob Mould's solo catalog?

31. When did you see your first Brian Jonestown Massacre breakup?

32. When did The Last Great Indie Rock album come out?

33. When did Lou Barlow become grating and over earnest?

34. When did John Lydon become a fucking joke?

35. When did Metallica become the Beverly Hillbillies?

LIST

36. Name eight bands whose post-reunion output is better than their first time around.

37. Name three bands (that aren't The Melvins) on Boner Records.

38. Name nine bands that Bob Bert has been in.

39. Name 15 bands that Robert Pollard has been in.

_____

_____

_____

_____

40. Name five bands that Chris Thomson has played in.

_____

_____

41. Name four bands that Penn Rollings has been in.

_____

42. In one breath, quickly name all the bands and side-projects that all the current and past members of Napalm Death have been in before losing consciousness.

43. Name a band whose major label release(s) were better than their indie label releases.

_____

44. Name all of the members of Rocket From the Tombs and the bands they formed afterwards.

_____

45. Name two of the five bassists (excluding Joan Jett) for the Runaways.

_____

46. Name all four members of Bauhaus. Then, name two of the side projects of Bauhaus members NOT including Love and Rockets.

_____

_____

47. Name five tolerable bands on Saddle Creek. *(Bonus points for non-shared members.)*

_____

_____

48. Name all 36 guys Dave Mustaine has kicked out of Megadeth over the years.

_____

_____

_____

49. Name the last 10 records you bought by non-white artists.

_____

_____

50. Name the ill-fated label that Madness started.

_____

51. Name the punk bands from the 1990s which are permissible to like.

_____

_____

52. If time machines existed, name one band whose inception and early career you'd choose to witness.

_____

53. Now name one you'd choose to witness only to drive a preemptive car bomb into.

_____

54. Name the three most overlooked and under appreciated bands ever.

OVERLOOKED No.01: _____

OVERLOOKED No.02: _____

OVERLOOKED No.03: _____

55. Name two bands that deserve a tribute record in their honor, but as of yet, don't have one.

TRIBUTE No.01: _____

TRIBUTE No.02: _____

56. Name five vocalists who are shorter than Ronnie James Dio.

LILLIPUTIAN No.01: _____

LILLIPUTIAN No.02: _____

LILLIPUTIAN No.03: _____

LILLIPUTIAN No.04: _____

LILLIPUTIAN No.05: _____

57. Name three dweebs nerdy enough to answer more than four of the above questions (then go take their lunch money).

DWEEB No.01: _____

DWEEB No.02: _____

DWEEB No.03: _____

AMOUNT

58. How many Ipecac Records (in)action figures do you own?

59. How many bands that recorded for the Two-Tone label can you name?

_____

60. How many fingers do The Konks have? _____

61. How many New Order side-projects can you name? How many do you own?

62. How many times will you ask an artist to take a photo with you, insist that it's a bad photo and request another one?

63. How many AmRep bands have you seen perform? *(Note: must have been on the AmRep roster at the time. Seeing Helmet or Today Is The Day at a CMJ showcase last year doesn't count.)*

64. How many band lighters do you own? Foam fingers? Neck braces? Colostomy bags?

65. Without doing laundry, how many consecutive days could you wear a clean band shirt?

66. How many different Melvins line-ups have you seen perform?

67. How many years total have you said that "roots rock" is going to be the next big thing?

68. How many ska revivals have you lived through?

69. How many label's blogs are on your RSS feed?

CHECK ALL THAT APPLY

01. I have traveled to a different city for the sole purpose of:

☐ Going to record stores.
☐ Going to a legendary club.
☐ Stalking a famous musician who lives there.
☐ Escaping the clutches of Dawg the Bounty Hunter.
☐ Going to a show of a band I hate, and picking fights with all of their fans.
☐ Witnessing the ol' Tijuana banana trick.
☐ Eating a McRib.

02. When you see the word "peel," what comes to mind?

☐ That one Donovan song
☐ The instructions that go with the Warhol banana on the cover of the first VU record
David Peel and the Lower East Side
☐ The quick acceleration of your vehicle out of the parking lot, and the accompanying scream of tires that shows the rest of those seniors who's boss
"Shake Appeal" by The Stooges
☐ The magazine/online forum concerning sticker/stencil street art
☐ John Peel and his Peel sessions
☐ The Futurama Message Board
☐ all of the above
☐ none of the above

04. Which of the following bands/artists have you stated that you really like, but deep down can't listen to sober?

☐ Flipper   ☐ Pylon
☐ Gram Parsons   ☐ The Pogues
☐ The Replacements   ☐ Ween

05. Which of the following chronological genre hot spots are you familiar with?

(Krautrock does not count)
☐ 1950/60s One Hit Wonders
☐ '60s Rock Steady
☐ Early '60s Garage Rock
☐ Late '60s New York Loft Scene
☐ Late '60s Bubblegum Pop
☐ '70s Power Pop
☐ '70s Yacht Rock
☐ Mid '70s Dub
☐ Late '70s Cleveland Punk Rock
☐ Late '70s British Art Punk
☐ Early '80s Hardcore
☐ '80s New Zealand Rock
☐ Late 80's Hardcore
☐ Early '90s "This Basement Smells Like BO"-core
☐ Early-mid '90s "Patch on Your Back Pack"-core
☐ Mid '90s Guilt-core
☐ Mid '90s Office Rock
☐ Mid-to-late '90s "We Finally Learned How to Play Our Instruments"-core
☐ '90s Complaint Rock
☐ Ought-tens "Country" *(as played by heavily tatted dudes who used to be on Fat Wreck Chords)*
☐ D.C. Go-Go funk
☐ Dreampop
☐ Mod Revival
☐ Shoegaze
☐ other

06. Which of the following bands have you radically changed your opinion over during the course of a lifetime? *(check all that apply)*

☐ AC/DC
☐ Animal Collective
☐ The Apples (In Stereo)
☐ The Beach Boys
☐ The Beatles
☐ Bonnie Prince Billy
☐ Captain Beefheart
☐ Devo
☐ Guided By Voices
☐ The Frogs
☐ Jack Logan
☐ Jandek
☐ Motörhead
☐ Pavement
☐ Royal Trux
☐ Scritti Politti
☐ Sonic Youth
☐ The Strokes
☐ all of the above
☐ none of the above

07. If radio was a formative part of your "active listening" development, which of the following radio formats were you exposed to early on?

☐ Major-market rock blocks and shock jocks
☐ Dr. Demento
☐ Left-of-the-dial college radio fuzz rock
☐ AM rightwing yammering
☐ NPR's smoothly infuriating liberalese/Garrison Keillor
Old-time radio reruns with vintage ads via the Internet
☐ all of the above
☐ none of the above

08. If there is a hell and you ended up there, which band(s) would you be forced to listen to 24/7, for eternity?

☐ .38 Special
☐ 4 Non Blondes
☐ Beastie Boys
☐ Blink 182
☐ Bob Seger and the Silver Bullet Band
☐ Cake
☐ Citizen Cope
☐ Crash Test Dummies
☐ Creed
☐ Guns N' Roses
☐ Jane's Addiction
☐ Kid Rock
☐ Nickleback
☐ No Doubt
☐ Phish
☐ Puddle of Mudd
☐ Smashing Pumpkins
☐ Smashmouth
☐ Staind
☐ Stevie Ray Vaughn and Double Trouble
☐ Sublime
☐ Third Eye Blind
☐ Tom Petty
(But not Aerosmith. Even Satan wouldn't be that cruel.)

03.   Which of the following bands have you stated that you really like but deep down can't really listen to by yourself?

☐ 13th Floor Elevators	☐ The Decemberists	☐ Lemonheads	☐ Shonen Knife
☐ A Place To Bury Strangers	☐ Deerhoof	☐ Lightning Bolt	☐ Sigur Rós
☐ AC/DC	☐ The Descendents	☐ Love	☐ Nina Simone
☐ Anal Cunt	☐ Die Kreuzen	☐ Magik Markers	☐ Skrewdriver
☐ Andrew Bird	☐ Dillinger Escape Plan	☐ Man Is The Bastard	☐ Skullflower
☐ Andrew W. K.	☐ Dirty Projectors	☐ Man...or Astro-Man?	☐ Slayer
☐ Angry Aryans	☐ Dolomite	☐ Mayyors	☐ Sleep
☐ anyone you know personally	☐ Drive Like Jehu	☐ Mecca Normal	☐ Elliott Smith
☐ anything from France	☐ Bob Dylan	☐ Melt Banana	☐ The Smiths
☐ The B-52's	☐ Earth	☐ Melvins	☐ The Smithsonian Anthology
☐ The Bad Seeds	☐ Eleventh Dream Day	☐ Merzbow	of American Folk Music
☐ Devandra Banhart	☐ Brian Eno	☐ Metallica	☐ Sonic Youth
☐ Baroness	☐ The Fall	☐ MGMT	☐ Sore Throat
☐ Bastro	☐ Felt	☐ The Minutemen	☐ Spacemen 3
☐ The Beach Boys	☐ Flipper	☐ Mission Of Burma	☐ Spazz
☐ The Beastie Boys	☐ Flying Luttenbachers	☐ Joni Mitchell	☐ Spin Doctors
☐ Big Black	☐ Flying Saucer Attack	☐ Mogwai	☐ Spiritualized
☐ Big Business	☐ Frank Zappa	☐ most of the crap on the	☐ Steely Dan
☐ The Birthday Party	☐ Charlotte Gainsbourg	*Nuggets* box sets	☐ The Stranglers
☐ Black Flag	☐ Serge Gainsbourg	☐ Motorhead	☐ Suicide
☐ Black Keys	☐ Diamanda Galas	☐ Naked City/John Zorn	☐ Sunn O)))
☐ black metal *(any)*	☐ Galaxie 500	☐ Naked Raygun	☐ Superchunk
☐ Blue Cheer	☐ Gang Of Four	☐ Napalm Death	☐ Swans
☐ The Boredoms	☐ Marvin Gaye *(after 1970)*	☐ Negative Approach	☐ Teenage Jesus and the Jerks
☐ Boris	☐ Girl Talk	☐ Neu!	☐ Television
☐ David Bowie	☐ Guided By Voices	☐ Neurosis	☐ This Heat
☐ Braid	☐ Woody Guthrie	☐ New Pornographers	☐ Throbbing Gristle
☐ Brainbombs	☐ Half Japanese	☐ Nickelback	☐ Tortoise
☐ Glenn Branca	☐ Neil Hamburger	☐ Nirvana	☐ U.S. Maple
☐ Brutal Attack	☐ Happy Mondays	☐ Mike Patton	☐ Van Halen
☐ C&C Music Factory	☐ Harry Pussy	☐ Pavement	☐ The Velvet Underground
☐ Cabaret Voltaire	☐ Harvey Milk	☐ Pissed Jeans	☐ The Virgin Prunes
☐ Can	☐ Helmet	☐ Pixies	☐ Tom Waits
☐ Captain Beefheart	☐ Jimi Hendrix	☐ Portishead	☐ Kanye West
☐ Chrome	☐ Dan Higgs	☐ Prince	☐ the WFMU webstream
☐ The Clash	☐ High On Fire	☐ Public Image Ltd.	☐ Barry White
☐ The Clean	☐ hip hop *(any)*	☐ R.E.M.	☐ Whitehouse
☐ Clinic	☐ Hüsker Dü	☐ Radiohead	☐ Wilco
☐ Cocksparrer	☐ Iron Maiden	☐ The Ramones	☐ The Wipers
☐ Leonard Cohen	☐ Jandek	☐ Rapeman	☐ Wire
☐ Coil	☐ Jay-Z	☐ Residents	☐ world music *(any)*
☐ John Coltrane	☐ jazz *(any)*	☐ Rolling Stones	☐ Wu Tang Clan
☐ Converge	☐ The Jesus Lizard	☐ Roxy Music	☐ Geza X
☐ Helios Creed	☐ Joan of Arc	☐ Saint Vitus	☐ XTC
☐ The Cure	☐ Daniel Johnston	☐ Scratch Acid	☐ "Weird" Al Yankovic
☐ D.R.I.	☐ Joy Division	☐ Scream	☐ The Yeah Yeah Yeahs
☐ Miles Davis	☐ later NOFX	☐ Pete Seeger	☐ Young Marble Giants
☐ Dead Moon	☐ Le Tigre	☐ Shellac	☐ your own stupid shit *(any)*

"I never had a problem with my indie cred. Y'ever heard of the F*CKIN' STOOGES, man? But no amount of slicin' up yer ripplin' abs will save you from a Top 40 duet with Kate Pierson or an album produced by Don Was. That's when the Bank of Indie Cred came bustin' in like a street walkin' cheetah with a heart full of napalm. They've earned their keep for sure, particularly since my most recent record was based on a French novel. I may have given up stage diving, but my abs still look great, and my card protected me from the Rock and Roll Hall of Fame backlash."

Iggy Pop
Member since 1990

SHIELDING YOU FROM YOUR CRED-MURDERIN' FLUBS SINCE 1979.

Whether it's old age, wrongly-inflated senses of self-worth, poor advice, or years of drug abuse, it seems that everyone hits the wall at some point and starts to chip away at their own cred. Everyone, that is, except BIC members. This card entitles its holder to a level of cred protection that's unprecedented by any others in the cred preservation services industry. Before you accept the invitation to cut some tracks with Fred Schneider, call one of our representatives to discuss exactly what we can do to protect you. It may be the only thing you do right this year.

Visit **chunklet.com** today to see what **you** can acquire.

BANK OF INDIE CRED

CELEBRATING GENERATIONS OF INVESTING IN YOUR CREDIBILITY FOR OUR FUTURE

DON'T PLAY A NOTE WITHOUT IT. ™

CRED TEST FOR GIRLS

Cred is an equal-opportunity concept. It shall not discriminate on the basis of race, age, orientation, health, wealth, IQ, or as you're about to witness in this single page we've generously devoted to it, gender. And for good reason — some of music and culture's greatest icons possess the X chromosome by the billions. Because females (girls, chicks, wymyn, broads, grrrls, petunias, Darias) serve so many unique roles in the cred universe (artist, manager, wife, financier, hanger-on, stylist, equipment transporter), it's critical to identify coolness metrics specific to the fairer sex. Think of the following quiz as a ruler: one designed to empower all the ladies in the house to measure where it counts.

01. Your favorite musician is:
    a. Bjork
    b. PJ Harvey
    c. Kathleen Hanna
    d. Chan Marshall
    e. Joanna Newsom

02. Your actual favorite musician is:
    a. Lou Reed
    b. Brian Eno
    c. Leonard Cohen
    d. Bob Dylan
    e. Alex Chilton

03. You would most like to "sis out" on a lost weekend with:
    a. Kim Deal
    b. Patti Smith
    c. Mo Tucker
    d. Kim Gordon
    e. Kate Bush

04. You "got into music" through:
    a. Riot Grrrl/zines
    b. Hardcore
    c. Some guy you liked
    d. A cool older girl
    e. You just enjoy listening to music, learning about bands, and going to shows. What the fuck else would it be?

05. When you were fourteen you were a:
    a. Punk
    b. Hippie
    c. Mod
    d. Raver
    e. Rockabilly
    f. Normie

06. Your favorite Joni Mitchell album is:
    a. *Blue*
    b. *Ladies Of The Canyon*
    c. *Court And Spark*
    d. *Hejira*
    e. *Don Juan's Reckless Daughter*

07. Your mom's favorite musician is:
    a. Carly Simon
    b. Carole King
    c. Stevie Nicks
    d. Joni Mitchell
    e. Annie Lennox

08. Your guilty pleasure is:
    a. Twee
    b. Pop punk
    c. Trance
    d. Tween pop
    e. Folk rock

09. Genre you hate but pretend not to dislike so as not to reinforce sexist notions about what genres girls are into:
    a. Prog
    b. Noise
    c. Grindcore
    d. Math rock
    e. Drone
    f. Jazz

10. Your dream boyfriend is:
    a. Stephen Malkmus
    b. Ian Svenonius
    c. Jim O'Rourke
    d. David Byrne
    e. Lou Barlow
    f. Jandek

CHECK ALL THAT APPLY

YOU GENERALLY DATE GUYS WHO HAVE:

- [ ] beards [ ] glasses [ ] shaggy hair [ ] great record collections
- [ ] a sense of entitlement about their taste in everything [ ] beer guts
- [ ] complicated emotional issues that you don't find out about until halfway through the relationship [ ] neck tattoos [ ] face tattoos
- [ ] their own place, even if it's a corner in the basement of the local collective squat [ ] a subscription to Vice or Clash
- [ ] borrowed your pants and worn them regularly in public
- [ ] only played in the coolest band in town at the moment
- [ ] ironic ties to counter their otherwise disheveled appearance
- [ ] the ability to quote entire pages from Che Guevara's biography
- [ ] one Republican friend

AT SOME POINT IN YOUR LIFE, YOU HAVE HAD:

- [ ] piercings [ ] a white belt [ ] jet black dyed hair [ ] combat boots
- [ ] band pins [ ] worn out Chuck Taylors [ ] nerd glasses [ ] bad posture
- [ ] An ex's record collection *(later sold)* [ ] crippling marijuana addiction
- [ ] a bedazzled iPhone case [ ] naked pictures of you posted online
- [ ] your grandfather's sweater [ ] a stash of European cigarettes
- [ ] ironic metal shirts of bands you've never heard [ ] your ass kicked

YOUR MUSIC NERD BUCKET LIST INCLUDES:

- [ ] alienating boys by being more knowledgeable about music than they are
- [ ] have pretended to know less about music than you really do just to hook up with some dude using the patriarchal paradigm inherent in the music scene that results in no one taking your opinion on bands seriously
- [ ] punching a boy in the dink for rolling his eyes at you when you use the phrase "patriarchal paradigm"

YOUR LIFE GOALS INCLUDE:

- [ ] touring in a band with an ex-boyfriend [ ] running an all ages venue
- [ ] starting a message board for female bassists [ ] arts degree
- [ ] getting the fuck out of this town someday [ ] breaking up that shit band
- [ ] being the biggest promoter in town...and *then* they'll all be sorry
- [ ] coming up with the perfect band name so you can finally learn to play guitar and start...a band [ ] getting your own Wikipedia page
- [ ] updating "girl power" with a more modern catch phrase

YOU HAVE HABITUALLY DATED:

- [ ] bassists [ ] lead guitarists [ ] lead singers [ ] drummers [ ] sound techs

GENRE TEST

Just like fake gold has fake value, so too does your knowledge of real vs. fake music genres.
So drop everything immediately and take this test to determine if you are of Righteous
Deuteronomy or a gullible, walking self-parody who should go back to reading Sawdust
Digest and watching American Gladiators.

01. Which of the following are NOT real ROCK genres?

- ☐ Classic Rock
- ☐ Surf Rock
- ☐ Garage Rock
- ☐ Stoner Rock/Cosmic Rock
- ☐ Spock Rock
- ☐ Butt Rock
- ☐ Dad Rock
- ☐ Noise Rock
- ☐ Rape Rock
- ☐ NPR Rock
- ☐ Effects Pedal Rock
- ☐ Math Rock
- ☐ College Rock
- ☐ Puppet Rock
- ☐ Yacht Rock
- ☐ Rocksteady
- ☐ Rockabilly

02. Which of the following are NOT real POP MUSIC genres?

- ☐ Power Pop
- ☐ Dreampop
- ☐ Noise Pop
- ☐ Agri-Pop
- ☐ Brit Pop
- ☐ Shit Pop
- ☐ Clit Pop
- ☐ Jailbait Pop
- ☐ Pop Trip
- ☐ Mop Pop
- ☐ Nook Pop
- ☐ Doom Pop
- ☐ Safety Pop
- ☐ Soda Pop

03. Which of the following are NOT real HIP HOP genres?

- ☐ Trip Hop
- ☐ Dirty Souf Crunk
- ☐ Emo Hop
- ☐ Hebrew Hop
- ☐ Basketbeat
- ☐ Hip Hopera
- ☐ Hate Hop
- ☐ Prog Hop
- ☐ Lilly White Honky Hop
- ☐ Hip Stop
- ☐ Old School Rap
- ☐ Preschool Rap
- ☐ Dirty Christmas Rap
- ☐ New Age Ninja Rap
- ☐ Portuguese Kraut Rap

04. Which of the following are NOT real METAL genres?

- ☐ Glam Metal
- ☐ Thrash Metal
- ☐ Death Metal
- ☐ Doom Metal
- ☐ Black Metal
- ☐ National Socialist Black Metal (NSBM)
- ☐ Power Metal
- ☐ Fantasy Metal
- ☐ Funk Metal
- ☐ Folk Metal
- ☐ Golf Metal
- ☐ Vagina Metalogue
- ☐ Blackened Surf Metal
- ☐ I-cant-believe-it's-not Metal
- ☐ Jew Metal
- ☐ Nu Metal
- ☐ Nu-nobettencourt Metal

05. Which of the following are NOT real PUNK genres?

- ☐ Gutter Punk
- ☐ Anarcho Punk
- ☐ Art Punk
- ☐ Steam Punk
- ☐ Black Crust Punk
- ☐ Straightedge Punk
- ☐ Ska Punk
- ☐ House Punk
- ☐ Bunny Punk
- ☐ Granny Punk
- ☐ Grand Punk Railroad
- ☐ Funk Punk
- ☐ AIDS Punk

06. Which of the following are NOT real EMO genres?

- ☐ Emo
- ☐ Screamo
- ☐ Emoviolence
- ☐ Crunk Emo
- ☐ Emo Hop
- ☐ MTVmo
- ☐ R&Bmo
- ☐ Viking Emo
- ☐ Finding nEmo
- ☐ Yelpy Bullshit
- ☐ Re: gay
- ☐ Straight Vag
- ☐ Dude, Where's My Eyeliner?

07. Which of the following are NOT real CORE genres?

- ☐ Hardcore
- ☐ Grindcore
- ☐ Metalcore
- ☐ Deathcore
- ☐ Slowcore
- ☐ Noisecore
- ☐ Horrorcore
- ☐ Crunkcore
- ☐ Artcore
- ☐ Nerdcore
- ☐ Nintendo/Casiocore
- ☐ NAScore
- ☐ Crabcore
- ☐ Fashioncore
- ☐ 401Kore
- ☐ Cashcore
- ☐ 'Tardcore
- ☐ Lardcore
- ☐ Retro Postmodern Core
- ☐ Manticore
- ☐ Mexicore
- ☐ Marine Corps.
- ☐ Trancecore
- ☐ Softcore
- ☐ Apple Core
- ☐ Fiddlecore
- ☐ Discore
- ☐ Albicore
- ☐ Nardcore
- ☐ Rapecore
- ☐ Chick Flick Moshcore
- ☐ Abortioncore
- ☐ Hatecore

09. Which of the following are NOT real POST genres:

- ☐ Post Rock
- ☐ Post Metal
- ☐ Post Punk
- ☐ Post-It
- ☐ Post Swans
- ☐ Post Office
- ☐ Post Apartheid
- ☐ Neo Trance
- ☐ Post Toasties
- ☐ Pre-Future Past Post

09. Which of the following are NOT real FUNK genres?

- ☐ Funk Rock
- ☐ Afrobeat
- ☐ Funk Core
- ☐ Funk Metal
- ☐ G-Funk
- ☐ Pitchfunk
- ☐ Hot Funk
- ☐ Handi-funk
- ☐ Whitey Funk
- ☐ Christian Funk
- ☐ Calypsphunk
- ☐ Motherfunker
- ☐ Slam Funk Contest
- ☐ Shaolin Monk Funk
- ☐ Thrash Funk
- ☐ Badonkafunk
- ☐ Tit Swing

10. Which of the following are NOT real CRUST genres?

- ☐ Crust Punk
- ☐ Crust Pop
- ☐ Black Crust Punk
- ☐ Melodic Crust
- ☐ Lust Crust
- ☐ Chicago Deep Dish Crust

11. Which of the following are NOT real DUB genres?

- ☐ Dubstep
- ☐ Power Dub
- ☐ Dub Punk
- ☐ Roots Dub
- ☐ Tourette's Dub
- ☐ Pub Dub
- ☐ Rub-a-dub Dub
- ☐ Frat Reggae
- ☐ Dub-ya

DEATH METAL

Death Metal has never been much of a girl's sport. It's ugly music, made for ugly dudes, by ugly dudes. Skirts aren't exactly flocking to the gauntleted guy stabbing his angry, stubby fingers into a fretboard, slinging spit and sweat while his bullet belt creates semi-permanent pinhole dimples in the undersides of his jiggly love handles. Yes, Death Metal may even rival LARPing as the most effective pussy repellent known to man, therefore, most women and all hippies can skip this section right now. But if you get wood when you see entrails, wax philosophic about bile n' maggots or own more than 12 meat cleavers, guess what? You can also skip this section, cuz you get a perfect score by default. As for the rest of you, proceed with extreme vigilance.

BLACK JEANS OR BLACK JEANS? MAKE THE CALL, CREATURE OF THE NIGHT...

01. You're trying to impress a young female cadaver with your musical taste. Do you play:

A. Melodic Death Metal (Carcass, At the Gates)
B. Death Doom (Disembowelment, My Dying Bride)
C. Classic Death Metal (Death, Morbid Angel)
D. Gore Grind (Regurgitate, Torsofuck)

02. Cannibal Corpse's music may not be all that great, but I respect any band who names a song:

A. Fucked with a Knife
B. Rotted Body Landslide
C. Severed Head Stoning
D. Entrails Ripped from a Virgin's Cunt

03. Which of the following is the typical drug of choice for death metallers?

A. Speed
B. Hash
C. Spray paint
D. Goofballs
E. Jenkum

04. Which of the following is the most brutally metal name for poo-poo and boo-boos?

A. Fecal Hemorrhage
B. Excrement Ecchymosis
C. Poo Petechia
D. Caca Contusion
E. Doodie Bruise

05. You decide to form a death metal band. Which of the following would serve as the best name:

A. Narcoleptic Decapitation
B. Pustulent Uglification
C. Stagnant Fountains of Colostomy
D. Intense Dislike

06. Mmmmmmmph! Mmmmmuuuurrrmmmph?!?

A. Yieeeeeearrrrrrrgggggh!
B. Uoooooooouh!
C. Raaaaaaarrrr!!!
D. Pbbbtt!

07. On band name alone, I'm interested in checking out:

A. Pig Destroyer
B. Decrepit Birth
C. Prostitute Disfigurement
D. Goatwhore

08. The most homoerotic name I've ever heard for a death metal band is:

A. Job For A Cowboy
B. Anal Blast
C. Face Down
D. Assück
E. Autumn Leaves

WHICH ONE IS REAL? CHOOSE ONE, AND CHOOSE WISELY, OH GREAT DISEMBOWLER OF THE DARK PAGE...

☐ Coffins
OR
☐ Box Of Elders

☐ Disfear
OR
☐ Datpain

☐ Deeds Of Flesh
OR
☐ Surge Of Mung

☐ The County Medical Examiners
OR
☐ Funeral Of Piss

☐ Cattle Decapitation
OR
☐ Hematoma Helper

☐ Fuck, I'm Dead
OR
☐ Curses, I Surmise That I Have Recently Ceased Primary Respiratory Function

☐ Raunchy
OR
☐ Randy

☐ Shrieking Clot
OR
☐ World Under Blood

☐ Eternal Tears Of Sorrow
OR
☐ Burning Lake Of Gore

CHAPTER 11

MUSIC PERFORMANCE INTAKE

DO YOU GO TO SHOWS TO BE ENTERTAINED and witness a live performance of music you so thoroughly enjoy, or do you go to shows with the sole purpose of drawing every ounce of attention off of the band people paid to see and placing it directly onto your cursive, angel-winged chest piece? Do you merrily bounce off of your sweaty pitmates in a joyous bout of unity, or do you take pit time as an opportunity to kick and flail at invisible assailants whilst managing to piss off everyone in eyeshot? Have you ever been so overwhelmed with energy that your clothes just could not contain your perspiry tenement? Ever get a friend of the same sex involved? This is the type of shit Chunklet wants (make that *needs*) to know.

YES/NO

COMPLETE THE FOLLOWING QUESTIONS WITH A YES/NO ANSWER. THE SHOW STARTS NOW.

YES　NO

01. Is going to a loud, smelly, windowless dive for a concert your idea of a "night out"? ☐ ☐

02. If someone uses the word "concert" to describe a "show," do you immediately know they don't *really* get it? ☐ ☐

03. Do you show up early in hopes of finding a non-adhesive/feculent/retched-upon place you can sit down? ☐ ☐

04. Do you only ever leave shows before they're over because you "got it" after the second song or, more preferably, only when a security thug throws you out? ☐ ☐

05. Have you ever attended shows at more than two venues in the same night? ☐ ☐

06. Do you have a precise "club math" formula to calculate what time bands will be hitting the stage so you can miss shitty opening acts? ☐ ☐

07. Do you prefer to leave the ball and chain at home so their bitching won't harsh your buzz? ☐ ☐

08. Do you ever wax poetic about some poorly attended show ten years ago by some now famous band? ☐ ☐

09. If yes, has anyone ever done permanent damage to their optic nerves from the furious eye-rolling that ensued? ☐ ☐

10. Is eye-rolling your equivalent to applauding a performance? ☐ ☐

11. Have you ever claimed that you saw 17 bands at 6 separate shows in one night, just to prove that there was, in fact, "something to do around here"? ☐ ☐

12. Have you ever gone to what later turned out to be a famously bad or great show written about in a book? ☐ ☐

13. Were *you* the central reason that such a show turned out to be "famously bad"? ☐ ☐

14. Have you seen a now popular band during their early start in a completely embarrassing genre? (i.e., back when they were "third-wave ska" or "rapera")? ☐ ☐

15. Do you rattle off lists of the legendary bands you saw and qualify each one with "yeah, but they weren't that great"? ☐ ☐

16. Do you go to shows with the sole intention of requesting obscure material the band has forgotten long ago? ☐ ☐

17. Has a band ever personally addressed you from stage during their set? ☐ ☐

18. If yes, did they refer to you as "hey shit bag" or something similarly derogatory? ☐ ☐

YES　NO

19. Have you ever actually seen a real "final" show of a band or artist? (Bonus points if the artist dies shortly after. Extra bonus points if the artist dies on stage AT the show. Ultra-extra bonus points if you killed the artist.) ☐ ☐

20. Do you make a big obnoxious show of lip-synching to your favorite songs just so people are aware you're a bigger fan of the band than they are? ☐ ☐

21. Have you ever tripped balls so hard at a Kiss cover band show that you lost track of reality and thought it really was Paul and Gene playing the tiny stage at "Roper's Rockin' Country"? ☐ ☐

22. Do you record shows? ☐ ☐

23. Does the term "bootleg" make you cringe, while the word "lossless" gets you hard? ☐ ☐

24. Have you sworn you saw a Suicide Girl at a show, and then realized it was just another barely hot chick with shit all in her face and a couple of corny flash tattoos? ☐ ☐

25. Have you ever seen a dude at a show who was so wasted he thought that Foghat was really playing when some hipster ironically played "Slow Ride" on the house system prior to sound check? ☐ ☐

26. Have you ever masturbated at a show? ☐ ☐

27. Have you ever fallen asleep at a show and snored so loud that the band stopped playing to ask you to "keep it down"? ☐ ☐

28. Have you ever ignored the band and instead propped yourself up on a stool with a stack of quarters and fed the Galaga machine for an hour? ☐ ☐

29. If yes, did you ever achieve a top ten score and enter your initials as a dirty word? ☐ ☐

30. Have you ever had Wesley Willis headbutt you? ☐ ☐

31. Have you ever had to out-run skinheads after a show let out? ☐ ☐

Which of the following have come into contact with you or your clothes while watching a show (and not while in the bathroom)?

YES　NO

32. baby batter ☐ ☐
33. hydrochloric acid ☐ ☐
34. piss ☐ ☐
35. potassium nitrate ☐ ☐
36. shit ☐ ☐
37. snot ☐ ☐
38. vomit ☐ ☐
39. whey ☐ ☐
40. yellow no. 5 ☐ ☐

PROMOTIONAL PROCEEDINGS

YES   NO

41. Have you ever put on a show at your house? ☐ ☐

42. Have you promoted anyone you didn't like personally? ☐ ☐

43. Have you ever promoted a benefit show where the primary beneficiary wasn't your wallet? ☐ ☐

44. Have you ever paid a band in booze? ☐ ☐

45. Have you ever purposefully under-promoted a show because of your petty grievances with the headlining band? ☐ ☐

46. Have the shows ever showcased obscure experimental (and/or excremental) noise bands? ☐ ☐

47. Is putting on shows just a prelude to starting what you're sure will be the greatest independent record label ever? ☐ ☐

48. Have you ever plugged a show at an inappropriate time or place, such as a funeral or retirement home? ☐ ☐

49. Due to a poor turnout, have you ever paid a band "sympathy money" out of your own pocket only to have them shit talk you as you walk out of the club? ☐ ☐

50. Has anybody involved with organized crime ever approached you for protection money at a gig you're promoting? ☐ ☐

51. Are you suddenly *not* "the guy in charge" when the cops show up? ☐ ☐

52. Have you ever promoted an underage show to get your "creepy ol' dude" on? ☐ ☐

53. Has a booking agent ever screamed at you over a "minor detail" that the band never brought to your attention, such as that they only play 5-minute sets or they perform exclusively in the nude? ☐ ☐

ACCOUTREMENTS

54. Do you have special clothing you wear to shows? ☐ ☐

55. Do you dress like you're headed to a fishing rodeo when attending a show? ☐ ☐

56. Are Converse okay on Friday night? ☐ ☐

56A. How about steel-toed Hush Puppies? ☐ ☐

57. Do you wear your earbuds even while the band you're there to see is performing? ☐ ☐

58. Do you carry a backpack to a show even though you have no intention of documenting the performance in any way? ☐ ☐

TRAVELS

59. Have you ever flown to another country for a festival? ☐ ☐

YES   NO

60. Do you not go to shows because they're on the other side of town? ☐ ☐

61. Have you ever been on a trip and changed your itinerary in order to see a band that happened to be playing at a nearby club? ☐ ☐

62. Have you gone on road trips to see a local band play out of town? ☐ ☐

63. Do your vacations center on out-of-town shows? ☐ ☐

64. Have you ever bought plane tickets solely for the purpose of seeing a concert? ☐ ☐

TICKETS/GUEST LIST

65. Do you buy advance tickets for shows? ☐ ☐

66. Do you buy advance tickets for shows that you know have no chance of selling out just so you'll have the ticket stub? ☐ ☐

67. Have you paid double for a ticket to see the same band you saw less than a year ago? ☐ ☐

68. Have you ever bought tickets from a ticket broker? ☐ ☐

69. Have you ever bought tickets from a ticket broker to a show at a small club (200 capacity or less)? ☐ ☐

70. Do you even need tickets, or does the phrase "I'm Chester fuckin' Blompkins, mortal. Outta my way!" get you into most places? ☐ ☐

71. Have you ever sold your guest list spot to a scalper? ☐ ☐

72. Have you ever given some random fan the thrill of their life by getting them in to a sold-out show with your extra guest pass? ☐ ☐

73. Have you ever said "If I wasn't on the guest list for all these shows, there's no way I could afford them all"? ☐ ☐

74. Do you bet your friends in pizzas and high fives that certain bands will have you on their guest list at shows? ☐ ☐

VENUE

75. Have you ever thought of selling bottles of that "smoky smell" you only find in clubs? ☐ ☐

76. Do you not go to shows due to a dislike for a specific venue? ☐ ☐

77. Does the phrase "art space" turn you off to a show, regardless of who's playing it? ☐ ☐

78. Do you refuse to go to certain venues if there's no smoking, and no re-entry? ☐ ☐

79. Like anyone gives a shit, but do you argue the merits of the concert venues around town? ☐ ☐

80. Do you follow up that argument with the merits of local soundmen? ☐ ☐

	YES	NO

81. If blindfolded, could you recognize certain venues just by smell? ☐ ☐

82. Do you have a favorite place to park near your favorite venue despite the fact that you've had your car broken into there? ☐ ☐

ENTRANCE

83. Do door men recognize you and let you in? ☐ ☐

84. Have you ever carried a piece of gear past the ticket taker to look like you're in one of the bands? ☐ ☐

85. Are you on a first name basis with most, if not all, staff members at any club? ☐ ☐

86. Does the door guy love you? ☐ ☐

87. Does the door guy fear you? ☐ ☐

88. Does the door guy hate you? ☐ ☐

89. Are you forbidden from entering any club? ☐ ☐

90. Do you insist on paying to get into a show? ☐ ☐

91. Do you ever brag that you never pay to get into shows? ☐ ☐

92. How many times have security confiscated your wallet chain? ☐ ☐

93. Does security ever do that triangle hand check around your groin? ☐ ☐

94. Did you start figuring out how to transfer entrance door stamps in middle school? ☐ ☐

95. Do you sneak into shows more than once a month? ☐ ☐

96. Do you ask to be put on the list for holiday shows where people bring canned food to gain admittance? ☐ ☐

97. Do you boast about your techniques to get into a club for free to all your friends? ☐ ☐

98. Has security ever made you remove your shoes before entry? ☐ ☐

99. Do you ever size up the bouncer and whisper to your friends/date "I could take that guy"? ☐ ☐

100. Have you ever spotted a club bouncer as being a retired wrestler? ☐ ☐

101. Have you ever snuck in to see a band without paying the cover and then chastised a friend for "killing the scene" by owning a burned copy of the CD instead of the original? ☐ ☐

102. Have you ever put your violent, anti-social tendencies to use by working security at a music venue? ☐ ☐

103. If so, have you ever accidentally bludgeoned a band member unconscious during load-in because you thought he was trying to sneak in or steal shit? ☐ ☐

STAKING OUT YOUR SPOT

104. Do you get to shows early just so you can stand right up against the stage? ☐ ☐

105. Do you spot locations good for taking photos? ☐ ☐

106. Do you box out your territory and refuse to let people weasel past? ☐ ☐

107. Do you weasel your way up front if you show up late despite your freakish height? ☐ ☐

HECKLING

108. Do you consider heckling its own form of performance art? ☐ ☐

109. Do people say you heckle creatively? ☐ ☐

110. Has your heckling amassed you a following? ☐ ☐

111. Have you made anyone cry? ☐ ☐

111A. On a major label? ☐ ☐

112. Have you heckled another heckler? ☐ ☐

112A. Did you win? ☐ ☐

113. Has one of your heckles ever silenced the room? ☐ ☐

114. Have you ever used a translator to better enable you to heckle a band whose native tongue isn't English? ☐ ☐

115. Have you ever gone on stage and heckled a band through their own microphone? ☐ ☐

116. Do you tailor the severity of your heckling to the scariness of the performing band? (i.e., never heckle Oxbow, sometimes heckle the Dillinger Escape Plan, always heckle Green Day...) ☐ ☐

117. Have you ever been heckled by the rest of the audience? ☐ ☐

118. Do you heckle family members at the dinner table? ☐ ☐

119. Do you only heckle a band during their performance, or do you start the moment they enter the club and don't stop until they pull out of the parking lot? ☐ ☐

120. Do you think leaving a comment on a band's YouTube video is a form of heckling? ☐ ☐

121. Have you ever yelled "Freebird!" at a show? ☐ ☐

122. Have you ever punched the asshole who yelled "Freebird!" at a show? ☐ ☐

123. Have you ever been given an oversized check for being the one-millionth asshole to yell "Freebird!" at a show? ☐ ☐

SUPPLEMENTS

124. Do you drink your own beer out in the club's parking lot before entry? (Trick question, everybody with a two-digit IQ does this.) ☐ ☐

125. Have you ever "pre-gamed" so hard that you passed out while in line to get into the venue? ☐ ☐

126. Do you bring in a flask of booze into shows and order soda to mix? ☐ ☐

127. How much ass, on a scale of "all" to "none," would you be willing to kiss for a free drink? ☐ ☐

YES NO

128. Have you ever been asked to score drugs for someone famous? ☐ ☐

129. Do you rate bands in terms of whether they're "good to drink to"? ☐ ☐

130. Can you navigate a mosh pit without spilling your wine cooler? ☐ ☐

131. Do you blow smoke in the faces of non-smokers to watch them freak out? ☐ ☐

132. Has your drunkenness ever led you to vomit on the band? ☐ ☐

133. Have you ever convinced your girlfriend to hit on random dudes for free drinks so you don't have to blow all your merch money on booze? ☐ ☐

134. Do you feel self-conscious when asking the bartender for water? ☐ ☐

135. Do you trust the "Free Water" cooler? ☐ ☐

136. Do you think drinking a PBR in public actually means anything anymore? Wait, hold on, what the hell did it ever mean in the first place? ☐ ☐

137. At a crowded show, have you ever resorted to wearing adult diapers or simply urinating where you stand so you don't lose your space or miss any of a band's performance? ☐ ☐

138. Has drinking at a gig ever led to the loss of your trousers? ☐ ☐

139. Is the only time you talk to a bartender to get a paper cup to drink water out of the bathroom sink? ☐ ☐

139A. Are you aware of how gross that is? ☐ ☐

140. Do you consider throwing up in the bathroom the end of the evening, or the beginning? ☐ ☐

MAKIN' MOVES

141. Have you ever used the line, "Are those high tops or low tops"? ☐ ☐

142. Have you ever commented on someone's tattoos as an ice breaker? ☐ ☐

143. Do you brood by the pool table hoping that women will find you intriguing? ☐ ☐

THE SHITTER

144. Have you ever passed water next to an infamous/soon-to-be hyped underground personality? ☐ ☐

145. If it's a one-holer, would you reconsider going number two? ☐ ☐

146. Have you ever seen someone getting some ass in a stall? ☐ ☐

147. If female, do you refuse to use the "facilities" unless accompanied by a friend? ☐ ☐

148. Would you drop a monster shit if the stall had no door? ☐ ☐

YES NO

149. Do you prop your beer on the urinal pipe even though your lips are going there right afterward? ☐ ☐

150. Do you think $0.75 is too much to pay for a Rough Rider condom from 1993? ☐ ☐

151. Have you ever dropped a steaming load in the opposite sex's bathroom at a gig? ☐ ☐

152. Have you ever considered using the bar of soap? ☐ ☐

153. Have you ever scratched letters on the hand dryer for the amusement of all future patrons? ☐ ☐

154. Have you ever had to pee so bad you told someone in line you'd buy them a car if they let you cut? ☐ ☐

155. Has there been a smell bad enough to force you to hold it until you got home, and if so, did you make it? ☐ ☐

156. In your experience, do you wear footwear that is most efficient at keeping your feet dry in bathrooms where standing pee water covers the floor? ☐ ☐

157. Even though every club in the United States is now smoke-free, are stalls with no doors still good places to do a bump, smoke a joint, or shoot some heroin, or drain cleaner in? ☐ ☐

BACKSTAGE

158. Do you collect backstage passes like someone's keeping score? ☐ ☐

159. Is there a club where you don't even need to slow down at security to go back and talk with the band? ☐ ☐

160. Have you ever snuck backstage to swipe the band's beer? ☐ ☐

161. Have you ever been violently escorted out of backstage? ☐ ☐

162. Have you ever banged a truly hideous bouncer to get backstage? ☐ ☐

163. Have you ever stolen a groupie? ☐ ☐

164. Have you ever found yourself blowing the bass player in an effort to get closer to the singer? ☐ ☐

165. Have you ever decapitated a pestering fanzine writer backstage? ☐ ☐

166. Has the backstage area *ever* lived up to your expectations? ☐ ☐

CUTTIN' LOOSE

167. Have you ever danced while sober? ☐ ☐

168. Does the idea of people dancing at a musical performance strike you as annoying? ☐ ☐

169. Is bobbing your head in time with the beat the pinnacle of your self-expression? ☐ ☐

170. Do you think there should be a minimum level of skill to make it okay for someone to dance on top of the P.A.? ☐ ☐

171. Is it ever okay for a straight guy to dance on top of the P.A.? ☐ ☐

172. Do you consider calling the cops if some kids form a 'Wall of Death'? ☐ ☐

MULTIPLE CHOICE

CHOOSE THE MOST APPROPRIATE ANSWER BEFITTING YOUR VACUOUS EXISTENCE.

01. The age at which you first witnessed a live musical performance (school/church choir doesn't count) without at least one parent present was:
    A. 0-6
    B. 7-11
    C. 12-14
    D. 15-18
    E. Haven't been to see live music without parents yet

02. Which of these is your preferred type of venue?
    A. Arena
    B. Bar
    C. Basement
    D. Warehouse
    E. Record store
    F. Art gallery
    G. Refugee camp
    H. Prison

03. I judge whether or not to go to a show based on:
    A. The quality and/or quantity of performing bands.
    B. How much the tickets cost.
    C. How easy it is to sneak into the venue without paying.
    D. How attractive the club staff is.
    E. What the talking soufflé who lives in my sinuses tells me to do.

04. Listening to the band you're going to see on the way to the show is:
    A. A good way to refresh yourself on the material you're about to hear
    B. A good time to expose yourself to a band you haven't heard before
    C. A good way to jinx the show, causing flat tires, equipment failures and catastrophic acts of God/Satan/Quetzalcoatl to prevent the band from performing.

05. What makes the best earplugs?
    A. Toilet paper
    B. Cigarette butts
    C. Fingers
    D. Earplugs
    E. None

06. Per your standards, acceptable merchandise at shows includes:
    A. T-shirts, CDs, and records. That's it.
    B. Maybe hats and posters, too.
    C. You name it! Panties, pins, stickers, monogrammed golf shirts, etc.
    D. Heck, why not novelty toys, custom skate decks, and special time-share package deals!
    E. Getting tasered in the neck by one of the Dropkick Murphys.

07. When you go to a show, you wear:
    A. KISS makeup
    B. the band's shirt you just bought
    C. whatever you normally wear
    D. the sluttiest thing you can find
    E. special costume/attire so that people associate you with the band

08. Seeing someone at a show in which of the following shirt(s) would make me more likely to talk to them:
    A. An ultra obscure indie rock band that you thought only you knew about
    B. A death metal band with a completely unreadable logo
    C. A home-made, marker-on-white-tee punk band shirt
    D. Some shit you've never heard of
    E. A tattered, mysteriously stained wife-beater
    F. A Dallas Cowboys football jersey
    G. No shirt, just a sweet Ninja Turtles bandana

09. Wearing the shirt of the band you're going to see is:
    A. Douchey
    B. Awesome
    C. Awesomely douchey

10. Which of these best describes your preferred show "stance"?
    A. Tight lips, arms crossed, willfully indifferent expression
    B. Same as above, but with head nodding
    C. Drunk, talking loudly during the quiet parts
    D. Metal claw held aloft, as if summoning a vast, cruel-beaked eagle of bloody steel down from the blackening skies
    E. Same as above, but in an ironic manner
    F. Sitting out back, ignoring the bands while you talk with your inner circle
    G. Bare-chested, practicing your roundhouse technique

11. When a pit forms, you:
    A. Back away, since you don't have adequate health insurance
    B. Remain on the edge and get bumped and bled on once in a while
    C. Stand on the balcony and watch the mayhem unfold
    D. Hand your jacket to your girlfriend and get sweaty
    E. Grab a friend, rip off all of your clothing, and dive in dong-first.

12. If you're not afraid of getting your ass kicked at shows, it's because:
    A. You are the baddest motherfucker in the joint.
    B. You are friends with all of the bouncers and they will protect you from harm.
    C. You hide in the back most of the time.
    D. You've gotten your ass kicked enough that it just doesn't bother you anymore.
    E. The bands you like play such pussy music that a They Might Be Giants crowd is tougher than the ones you're dealing with...
    F. I avoid shows because my fear of conflict is so crippling that I apologize to inanimate objects when I bump into them.

13. What is the greatest trauma/personal injury you have ever suffered at a show?
  A. Drink spilled on new Fred Perry shirt
  B. Recently-purchased records bent during overenthusiastic mosh section
  C. Had to have stomach pumped
  D. Broken nose/wrist/collarbone
  E. Messed-up hair
  F. Paralysis

14. Which one of the following "goes right through you," necessitating more restroom trips than the beer buzz justifies?
  A. PBR
  B. Fat Tire
  C. Newcastle Brown Ale
  D. Schell's Bock
  E. Asshouse Ice

15. The most makeshift item you've ever seen used as a stall divider in a club restroom is:
  A. Office cubicle materials
  B. Ornate carved wood screen in hinged sections
  C. Clear shower curtain
  D. Spare jumbo acoustic paneling
  E. A taxidermied bobcat

FILL IN THE BLANK

THE INDIE CRED TEST

THE INDIE CRED TEST

UNBLANKIFY THE EMPTY SPOTS.

01. What was the first show you ever attended?

02. What is the most recent show you attended?

03. What is the best show you ever attended?

04. What's the farthest distance you've traveled to see a band?

05. Do you feel that buying advance tickets is a sign of weakness?

06. What is the best heckle you've ever come up with?

07. When did you realize that nobody will ever care about your killer bootleg collection?

08. When drinking at a show, how long does it generally take for you to lose your "pee cherry"?

09. What's the cleverest thing you've ever seen written (or smeared) on a venue's bathroom wall?

10. What's the craziest color you've ever puked?

11. What's the best song you ever missed at a gig because you just had to 'release the Kraken'?

12. What is the worst injury you have ever sustained at a show?

13. Where do you hide your bag of coke so the doorman won't find it?

14. For you, how much of shows is about listening to music versus looking cool?

Please indicate the number of times you've missed each of the following for a show: (last five years only, please.)

15. Your job .... [ ]
16. Dates with significant others/spouses .... [ ]
17. Birthday parties .... [ ]
18. AA/NA meetings .... [ ]
19. Birth of child .... [ ]
20. Your girlfriend's abortion .... [ ]
21. Parole hearings .... [ ]

CHAPTER 12

YOUR OWN SHITTY BAND

"HELLO SPORT! WE ARE THAT'S ONE BIG Fucking Knife You've Got There representin' in Sugar Tit, SC. My name happens to be Elwood Dunbar Wellington IV, but my friends call me Leather Lord. I want to give you a super-fucking-special opportunity to take a minute or two of your precious time to listen to our great music. We are talking about a conceptual album, so listening to its entirety, preferably several times in a single sitting, would give a clearer view of what's all about. We are willing to be a part of your label, if not...anyways. We are looking forward for us to become one of the biggest metal bands, and, we all agree, we won't stop until we make it to the top. I was also hoping maybe you wouldn't mind sharing your list of press contacts with me, and maybe giving me a ride up to the store to buy cigarettes. I live by the airport so if wanna meet up and discuss this business, call my cousin Jimmy and he'll help you get out here."

Does the above statement sound like you? Probably. Just how much? How 'bout you just take the test, dummy?

THE INDIE
CRED TEST

YES/NO

THE INDIE
CRED TEST

COMPLETE THE FOLLOWING QUESTIONS WITH A YES/NO ANSWER. DICK.

YES NO

01. Have you ever been in a band that had at least one guitar in it?

02. Does your band's entire list of influences consist of bands you hope to open for some day?

03. Other than trying to write and play enjoyable music, does your band have a "gimmick"?

04. Is someone in the band's dad your soundguy?

05. Have your work colleagues ever mocked your music career and/or myspace page?

06. Has the life of a musician made you so broke that you'd have to take out a loan to buy dirt before you could be considered "dirt poor"?

07. Are you ashamed of your early recordings?

07A. Is anyone NOT ashamed of their early recordings?

08. Do you pass hometown clubs with your college friends and say "Yeah, we rocked that place!"?

09. Were you a music major in college? If so, was it the opposite of the music you now play?

10. Do you look for your own CDs in stores, just to see if they have them? And if so, are you disappointed if they're in the used bin?

11. When you blog about how your band is "just about to make it" do you have any idea what you mean?

12. Is your band name the surname of any of its members?

13. Do you have a rival band?

14. Do you have hundreds of copies of your band's CDs rotting in your garage?

15. Do your parents ever frame your local newspaper reviews to give to you as a present?

16. Have your parents ever come to any of your shows?

17. Does it make you uncomfortable that your mom is your biggest fan?

18. Was your band name gleaned from the lyrics of another band's song?

19. Has one of your bowel movements you wrote about on your blog been picked up as noteworthy?

20. Have you ever been beaten up for being a "sell out"?

YES NO

21. Does your band get played on satellite radio because a band member has a satellite radio show?

22. Have you made friends with a critic who once panned you?

23. Do you have a tattoo of your band's logo?

24. Ever misattributed a positive review from a friend to Pitchfork?

25. Are you working on either a Vans or Monster Energy Drink endorsement?

MUSIC

26. Have you penned an as of yet unrecorded concept album?

27. Has your band ever been solicited for a demo?

28. Do you give "shout outs" in any songs?

29. Have you ever recorded your pets making noises to put on a song?

30. Are any of your songs/albums eponymous?

31. Are any of your songs about/dedicated to Leonard Peltier, Mumia Abu-Jamal, Che Guevara or Billy "Pitchman" Mays?

WARDROBE

32. Does your band wear uniforms on stage?

33. Do your bandmates wear make-up?

34. Have you ever worn a homemade nail gauntlet on stage?

35. Has it ever resulted in injury?

36. Do you have "show clothes"?

37. Have you ever worn a leather jacket over bare skin onstage?

38. Have you ever dressed up as an animal, a monster, or a drag queen onstage?

ONSTAGE

39. Have you ever had a crowd that consisted solely of the other bands on the bill and the bartender?

40. Have you ever been too inebriated to tune your instrument?

41. Have you played a concert with one of your musical idols?

YES NO

42. Did you ever lie about your financial situation for "gas money" from the audience? ☐ ☐

43. Has your band ever carried your inebriated body to the van after a show? ☐ ☐

44. Have you ever been hit with a beer bottle/car on stage? ☐ ☐

45. Have you ever decided not to show up to your improv band's performance so it could see what real improv was all about? ☐ ☐

46. Have you ever had to restart a song in the middle of a performance? ☐ ☐

47. Have you ever asked a guy in a band that's on the same bill if he'll be your "guitar tech"? ☐ ☐

48. Have you ever played on the same bill as a straight edge band with Xs at the beginning and end of its name? ☐ ☐

49. Have you ever played an instrumental set because your singer was too drunk? ☐ ☐

50. Did you ever befriend somebody because he had a Travis Bean he let you borrow? ☐ ☐

51. Did you purchase instruments keeping in mind how they would look together on stage? ☐ ☐

52. Have you ever had to go to the hospital after a set from a "bangover"? ☐ ☐

53. Is the most meaningful relationship in your life the one you have with your sound tech? ☐ ☐

54. Is it hard being "normal" off stage? ☐ ☐

SHOWBIZ

55. Do you "roll call" band members during performances? ☐ ☐

56. Does any band member cry during performances? ☐ ☐

57. Do you perform facing away from the audience? ☐ ☐

58. Have you ever breathed fire on stage? ☐ ☐

59. Have you ever quit your band on stage in mid-song? ☐ ☐

60. Have you ever assaulted another member of your band on stage? ☐ ☐

61. Have you ever exposed yourself on stage? ☐ ☐

62. Have you ever bled on stage? ☐ ☐

63. Have you ever pissed on stage? ☐ ☐

64. Have you ever pissed blood on stage? ☐ ☐

65. Have you ever pissed off the stage and into the audience while yelling something eloquent, like: "Forecast sez RAIN muthafuckaaaas!"? ☐ ☐

YES NO

66. Do you use a fog machine unironically? ☐ ☐

67. Do you routinely make use of the word "pyro"? ☐ ☐

MUSIC BIZ

68. Do you have somebody who sells merchandise for you? ☐ ☐

69. Do you call "merchandise" "the merch"? ☐ ☐

70. Has your band printed five times as many t-shirt designs as you have recorded songs? ☐ ☐

71. Have you ever been given drinks by a promoter in lieu of payment? ☐ ☐

72. Is $25 actually a pretty good take for your band? In your hometown? ☐ ☐

73. Do your band t-shirts either come only in extra small or extra large? ☐ ☐

74. Do you have "band practices" where nothing but money is discussed? ☐ ☐

75. When the supply of your album runs out, do you just burn more copies of it on your laptop? ☐ ☐

76. Is your album's packaging printed on the singer's inkjet? ☐ ☐

77. Has your band ever received a rejection letter from a label? ☐ ☐

HIJINKS & SHENANIGANS

78. Have you ever put your band sticker on a urinal? Have you ever had someone deface your band sticker on the bathroom wall because you thought it would be funny? ☐ ☐

79. Has a record label ever let you raid their promo closet, not realizing (or maybe even not caring) that everyone in the band would be selling the unopened CDs to stores back home for rent money? ☐ ☐

80. When you've been on the road for a while, have you ever pulled on a sock that you thought was clean only to find out that your bandmate had used it to jerk off in the night before? ☐ ☐

81. Have you slept with somebody just because they had a tattoo of your band's logo? ☐ ☐

82. Has your mom, sister, or any other family member ever come to see your band and ended up hooking up with a member of the crew? ☐ ☐

GEAR

83. Ever used a ukulele/keytar/kazoo/equally 'kerazee' instrument? ☐ ☐

84. Do you own anything made by Peavey? ☐ ☐

85. Are you ashamed? ☐ ☐

YES NO

86. Would you let a stranger play or handle your guitar? ☐ ☐

87. Is your guitar worth more than your car? ☐ ☐

88. Have you ever borrowed equipment from a band you're playing with and returned it broken (or not returned it at all)? ☐ ☐

89. Do you rely on more guitar pedals than you have eyelashes for your playing "style"? ☐ ☐

VEHICLE

90. Does your car often double as a tour van? ☐ ☐

91. Does your car that doubles as a tour van also triple as your primary residence? ☐ ☐

92. Were you desperately afraid of the quality of brakes in your van when you were in San Francisco? ☐ ☐

93. Do you plan tours around days the work van is free? ☐ ☐

94. Have you ever acted on the crazy notion to convert the tour van from a reliable, fossil-fuel burning combustion engine to something at runs on liquefied Big Macs? ☐ ☐

ON THE ROAD

95. Do you purchase post cards in bulk before a tour is even booked, just to boost morale? ☐ ☐

96. Does a member of your band really "wanna get on the road" even though the rest of the band knows it's way too early? ☐ ☐

97. Have you toured Europe? ☐ ☐

98. Have you ever had to sleep on the floor of a venue you've played at? ☐ ☐

99. Does your band have a rider? ☐ ☐

100. Does your band print badges and/or backstage passes? ☐ ☐

101. Have you ever borrowed gear from another band while on tour? ☐ ☐

102. Have you driven over 500 miles to play a show? ☐ ☐

103. Have you ever been busted at a customs checkpoint? ☐ ☐

104. Are you afraid to tour because of outstanding traffic tickets? ☐ ☐

105. Have you ever stolen gas while on tour? ☐ ☐

106. During van rides, do you listen to talk/sports radio because several more hours of loud rock music before/after a concert of loud rock music doesn't sound particularly relaxing? ☐ ☐

107. Ever recorded an on-tour video diary? ☐ ☐

YES NO

108. Does a band member sleep on the pillow from inside the bass drum at the end of the night? ☐ ☐

109. Did the band you were supporting on tour ever cancel a show in order to do a TV show? ☐ ☐

110. Have you slept in your tour van overnight in order to guard your equipment? ☐ ☐

111. Have you ever played a five date west coast "tour" and decided "the road isn't for me"? ☐ ☐

112. Ever leave something (i.e. phone charger) at someone's house, and instead of having the person mail it to you, you've simply grabbed it a month later on the following tour? ☐ ☐

113. Are nightclubs and restaurants located near nightclubs the only places you have visited in most cities? ☐ ☐

114. Do you know the location of 24-hour restaurants in every large city in the continental United States? ☐ ☐

115. Do you judge an entire city based on whether or not a club owner there was a dick? ☐ ☐

116. Did you meet your current girlfriend/ boyfriend on the road? ☐ ☐

117. Have you ever made out with a young lady only to be told by a bandmate that that same young lady gave him a BJ a few hours earlier? ☐ ☐

118. Do you keep a list of people in every city who have offered to let you crash on their couch? ☐ ☐

119. When you share a room with bandmates, do you ever sleep in the nude? ☐ ☐

120. Have you ever had to wait to load into a show because the people who live there were off skateboarding? ☐ ☐

121. Have you ever arrived at a small town venue to shockingly discover that it's a front for the local Christian church? ☐ ☐

122. Did you still play the gig? ☐ ☐

123. If you're in a band, have you penned an agreement of items you will you accept in lieu of payment? This question only works if you did this in your spare time. ☐ ☐

ON THE ROAD—SPECIFICS

124. Do you have any road stories that involve Manny Theiner? ☐ ☐

125. Do you know what the "Thing in the Desert" is? ☐ ☐

126. How about the "Mystery Spot"? ☐ ☐

127. Does any band member actually prefer how the chili is in Cincinnati? ☐ ☐

128. Can you name the exact spot where White Castles become Krystals? ☐ ☐

	YES	NO

129. Can you name the point where Kroger becomes Weis? ☐ ☐

130. Can you explain the difference between a Shoney's and a Stuckey's? ☐ ☐

131. Are late-night drives actually the safest because everyone is awake and listening to "Coast to Coast AM"? ☐ ☐

132. Do you have any "I Hate Sean Carnage" stories? ☐ ☐

133. Do you think of Canada as "that place up north where the gas is more expensive"? ☐ ☐

134. Do you know Vino's in Little Rock as being the club with that really awkward door at the side of the stage that goes directly outside? ☐ ☐

135. If you've played in Baltimore, did the crazy guy in the cape who doesn't stop talking show up? ☐ ☐

136. Did you learn the hard way that A&R people don't go to SXSW to see your band like they said they were going to, but rather just to drink free booze? ☐ ☐

137. Is there a Cracker Barrel out there that has gained a special place in your heart? ☐ ☐

138. Is there a basement at the Alamo Drafthouse? ☐ ☐

139. Does Wall Drug warrant the hype? ☐ ☐

140. Did Mrs. Anita Stinson ever serve you at the Uptown Bar? ☐ ☐

141. Have you broken down near Thunder Bay? ☐ ☐

142. Did the old drunk guy get up and sing the "Batman" theme song with your band when you played Bernie's Distillery in Columbus, Ohio? ☐ ☐

143. Has your band ever played Terrastock? ☐ ☐

144. Have you ever won at Whirlyball? ☐ ☐

145. Do you actually know who Steve Lamacq is? ☐ ☐

146. Have you ever seen Cole Alexander's penis? ☐ ☐

147. Have you ever visited the Stooges Wax Museum? ☐ ☐

148. Did you get drunk and/or stoned before your Daytrotter session? ☐ ☐

149. Have you recorded a Peel Session? ☐ ☐

150. Have you met John Peel at the BBC studios? ☐ ☐

151. Is your entire knowledge of Eastern Europe limited to open fields and hockey arenas? ☐ ☐

152. Is your band's biggest aim and/or accomplishment to play All Tomorrow's Parties? ☐ ☐

THE INDIE CRED TEST

MULTIPLE CHOICE

THE INDIE CRED TEST

NEVER BEFORE HAS THE POWER OF SELECTION BEEN SO INDISCRIMINATE.

01. "Lately, our band has been influenced by a lot of..."

A. Vintage/analog tape loops.
B. Afro-beat or Dub-Step.
C. Northern Soul.
D. Bollywood soundtracks.
E. Middle-Eastern black metal.
F. '60s Peruvian garage punk.
G. Hash and whippets.

02. Claiming and/or trying to be "the loudest band ever" is:

A. Stupid.
B. Sisyphean.
C. Awesome.
D. What my band is currently doing.
E. Something for Spinal Tap and Kiss to come to blows over.
F. What? Say again? Huh?

03. Please check your preferred sports drink for on-tour 'trucker bombs':

A. Gatorade
B. Powerade
C. Vitamin Water
D. None. I just hang it out the window and let 'er fly.

04. Do you own a guitar that you are unable to play? If so, how did you acquire it?

A. A gift for a teenage birthday
B. Bought with allowance money
C. Left behind by a roommate
D. Payment for underage gay sex with some guy named Mr. Pumpkineater
E. Got a killer deal on Craigslist from a kid who had a great guitar and quickly lost interest
F. Swiped it from Christian emo band who trusted me to watch their stuff

05. The first thing you did when you got your guitar was:

    A. Turn the volume and distortion way up and made a godawful racket.
    B. Plug it in and noodle around a bit.
    C. Read the care and maintenance guide.
    D. Started a Screamo band with a name longer than John Holmes' pink claymore.

06. Your main guitar is:

    A. A vintage Fender Strat in the original case and bought in Nashville with a certificate of authenticity.
    B. An '80s heavy metal-type guitar of reputable manufacture.
    C. A Japanese Gibson knockoff that is better than a real Gibson and costs a quarter as much.
    D. An oddball brand that nobody has ever heard of and you don't know if it costs $50 or $5,000.
    E. A Frankenstein made from parts of broken guitars bought at flea markets.
    F. Whatever you call the one that comes with "Rock Band."

07. Your amp is:

    A. What else? A Marshall stack.
    B. Vintage Fender twin deluxe with matched tube set.
    C. Boutique 5 watt tube amp with only a volume knob.
    D. 300 watt Peavy with digital modeling.
    E. A distortion pedal going into a PA.
    F. Stolen.

08. When shopping for a new guitar, you first consider:

    A. How its shape and color will reflect your musical tastes.
    B. What type of wood it is and what country the wood came from.
    C. Whether it sounds and plays good.
    D. Whether it will hurt your back or give you carpal tunnel.
    E. Whether it's good for clubbing people.
    F. If you can beat up its current owner and make off with it in one piece.

09. You have customized your guitar with:

    A. Stickers of bands you've toured with.
    B. Rhinestones.
    C. The loudest electronics made.
    D. Waterproof seals to prevent shorts from bodily fluids.
    E. You sanded it down to make it look old and well worn.

10. Your view of Gibson is:

    A. They are the only "real" guitar.
    B. They are good guitars.
    C. They are way overpriced for their quality.
    D. They are trash and only sell because of their icon status.
    E. "I wish they'd give me a job."

11. Your effects chain includes:

    A. A volume and wah control pedal plus ten boutique stomp boxes.
    B. An elaborate digital effects box that still has the factory presets.
    C. Two or three Japanese stomp boxes.
    D. A 10" cable.

12. Your guitar playing is like:

    A. 20 notes a second, each one in the proper key signature for the song.
    B. A bunch of chords that have several sets of numbers in their name.
    C. About 16 chords and a few good scales that fit into most songs.
    D. One barre chord played in three different positions.
    E. You haven't gotten to chords yet

13. Your singing is like:

    A. The glorious, golden, candy-coated voices of winged supermodels serenading us from the heavens.
    B. Throaty and forced, similar to many other marginally-talented Eddie Vedder enthusiasts.
    C. The croup.
    D. A drunken aardvark with his dong stuck in a rat trap.

14. Your drumming is like:

    A. All basic rudiments and paradiddles.
    B. I have two big honey baked hams stuck on the ends of my arms.
    C. A grinding hurricane of knuckles, splinters, and sweat.
    D. A lawnmower running over a big pile of silverware.

15. Your bass playing is:

    A. Throbbing, thunderous, rumbling and whatever other generic "bassy" adjectives you can find in *Bass Player* magazine.
    B. Like my guitar playing, only less interesting.
    C. Fun, funky and completely out-of-place in my current band.
    D. Inaudible.

16. Blues guitar is:

    A. The music form of master guitarists.
    B. A basic music form that is widely versatile.
    C. Decent, but has many limitations and gets way too repetitive.
    D. A minor niche form that is now archaic.
    E. So simple a form a retarded 7 year old could be "King of the East Wyoming Slidebone Chuckbone Blues Guitar" the second time he played.
    F. Invented by Elvis Presley, mastered by Eric Clapton and perfected by John Mayer.

PLACE YOUR #2 PENCIL ON THE DESK. NO MATTER HOW YOU THINK YOU JUST SCORED, YOU FAILED.

THE INDIE CRED TEST

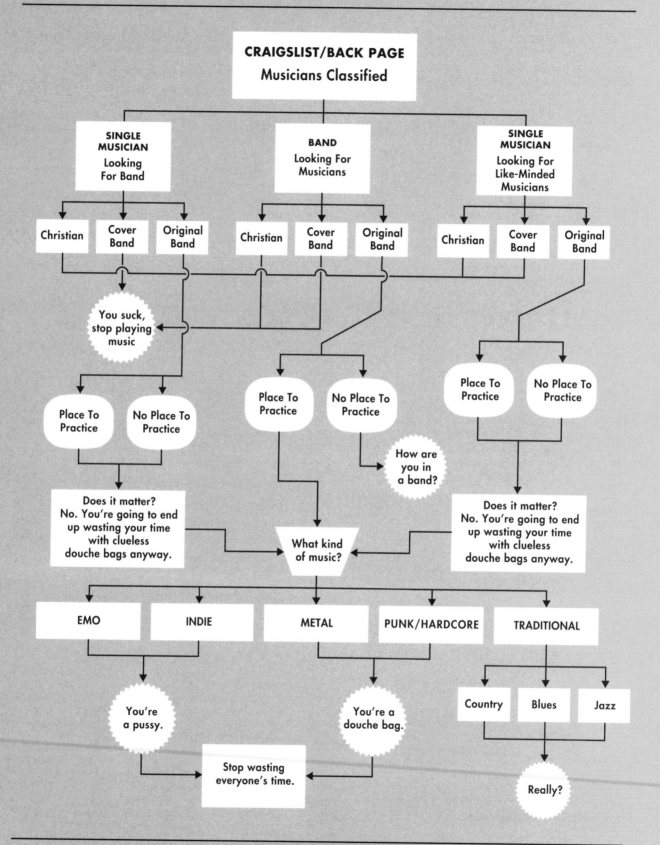

FILL IN THE BLANK

THE INDIE CRED TEST   THE INDIE CRED TEST

UNBLANKIFY THE EMPTY SPOTS.

01. What venues have you played that are completely inappropriate for full bands to play, yet seem hellbent on booking touring acts? *(i.e., a coffee joint the size of a shoebox, a Lazer Tag arena, a bar next to a house whose inhabitants demand complete silence at sunset, etc.)*

02. Fess up: Which musician's look are you ransacking?

03. What's the most wildly inappropriate bill you've ever played due to promoter mishap (i.e., a satanic stoner-grind band playing a militant straight edge twee-pop bill, electro-noise project with pop-punk bands, boozer rockabilly act with riot grrrl groups, etc.)?

04. Which band member has donated the most blood or semen to the cause? _____

05. Which band member's parent has bailed the band out most often? _____

06. Which venue that you've played had the nastiest toilet you ever had to use to drop a deuce?

07. Who's the oldest groupie you've ever bagged on the road?

08. When is the last time an A&R guy said "the problem is that the world just isn't ready for your sound"?

09. List all of your endorsements:

AMOUNT

10. How are you bankrolling your current group?

11. How many members of your band primarily wear v-neck shirts to proudly display their cursive-text chest piece tattoos?

12. What is the largest amount of people you've had in your audience? _____

13. Were more than half your friends or family?

14. How many college radio stations do you tell everyone your band has been played on?

15. How many band members have slept with your publicist? _____

16. How many times has your van been broken into? _____

17. What's the longest time you have gone without bathing on tour? _____

18. How many drumsticks/picks do you go through on a tour?

19. How many of those do you claim were taken by fans?

20. How many were actually taken by fans? _____
How much gear do you own by:
21. Electro-Harmonix? _____
22. Hasbro? _____
23. Orange? _____
24. Sunn? _____

SPECIFIC

25. Face makeup: Misfits, Kiss, Boy George or Immortal?

26. Which period of David Bowie do you claim to be inspired by?

27. Which of the three *Decline of Western Civilization* movies best represents your band?

28. Name five band stickers in the men's bathroom at the Black Cat. _____

29. What color is the green room at Red Rocks? _____

30. Why did Lounge Ax close?

31. What do the letters CBGB stand for?

32. For a West Coast tour, if you're only able to stop at one Amoeba location, which one do you choose?

33. Where is South of the Border? _____

34. Where is Mars' Cheese Castle? _____

35. Where is the Angel of the North? _____

CHECK ALL THAT APPLY.

01. If your band has ever had a song used in television commercials, were the commercials for:
☐ A department store? ☐ A car?
☐ A medication? ☐ A gun and knife show?
☐ A 3-D romantic dramedy starring Gidget, Meatloaf and a gay talking daffodil named "Butcho" (voiced by John Travolta)?
☐ Halloween candy? ☐ The US Navy?

02. The best way to describe your band's press photo is:
☐ Pensive ☐ Aloof ☐ Surly
☐ Smug ☐ Giddy ☐ Blurry
☐ Freshly blown ☐ Matronly ☐ In a factory
☐ Semi-conscious ☐ On railroad tracks ☐ Non-existent

03. If a performance by your band has ended in police intervention or arrests, was it for any of the following:
☐ Violation of a noise ordinance? ☐ Public intoxication?
☐ Public nudity? ☐ Inciting violence?
☐ Bestiality? ☐ Previous arrests?
☐ Parole violations? ☐ Sedition?
☐ Theft of intellectual property (you stole someone's brain!!)?
☐ Gross insult to the audience's intelligence?

THE LIVE CRED SCORE
AND YOUR ENTERTAINMENT DOLLAR

ARTISTS THAT HIT THE ROAD OR PERFORM LOCALLY do so for any number of reasons: to promote an existing LP or upcoming release, to hone material before recording, to capture their *Live At Leeds* or to sell the leftover merch that star500.com just can't seem to move. More popular than ever are the cash-in reunion tours, where bands make undeniable megabux playing the hits to chronologically disadvantaged fans who were in second grade the first time 'round, and their aging parents: the balding/pony-tailed, graying geysers of rock in the crowd with their lovingly-faded vintage '90s tees.

If you resemble one of these, maybe you're lucky and the acts you see play smaller clubs and theaters who charge reasonable fees. Even so, pure scum like LiveNation and Ticketbastard are right now banding together to weasel their tentacles right through the wallet chains on the security staff of (insert local indie venue of your choice). Many of us over a certain age (okay, 40) remember the cost of a show ticket as being less than the fee for the same ticket nowadays. To put it simply, the average music fan is being priced out of the game. And that's why we-with all our nascent powers of discernment-are here to help.

Deep in the underground mine shafts of ChunkLabs™, we have determined that the credibility of any act is positively correlated with the enjoyment an audience member will reap upon performances by said act. We have developed this theory with two corresponding formulas to determine both the Raw Live Cred Score (RLCS) and the Live Cred Score (LCS) of artists, and thus how much of your hard-earned salary you should feel compelled to spend to witness said live thrashings the next time they come to town.

But somehow, that just didn't take all of the factors we needed into consideration. For example, one of our senior research analysts pointed out that the replacement of various band members throughout the years had to do something to the scores, cred-wise. How to account for this? We thought on it for awhile, until a splinter research group seized upon the great notion of combining the original RLCS with a more complex equation that addressed the newer variables. Thus, the LCS was born:

Taking the formulas into consideration, it must be said that the highest RLCSs tend to be awarded to bands performing sets of quality new material with all original members. Sometimes there is a correlation with the LCS; in other instances the two are wildly divergent.

WE BEGAN WITH THE SIMPLE RAW SCORE DERIVATION:

$$D(B/A) + C/E = Y \text{ SCORE}$$

(SAME AS RLCS), WHERE:

A =	B =	C =	D =	E =
Number of years since last great record produced by the artist (or, if you will, the *Some Girls* quotient), at the time of most recent reunion,	Number of studio (not live, compilations, etc.) LPs' worth of material produced with original lineup,	Quality of performance of reunion band when compared to original band at peak on 1-10 scale (1 is worst, 10 is best),	Percentage of original members in reunion lineup, and	Amount of new material on scale of 1 (mostly new) to 10 (nothing new; total revival act).

THE MORE COMPLEX "LCS" SCORE:

$$\frac{\log(A)}{10} \times \left[B + \frac{C}{E} + \left(10 \times \frac{M_f - M_d}{M_f - M_r} \right) \right] = LCS$$

M_f = Number of founding members
M_d = Number of dead, crazy or imprisoned members
M_r = Number of replacement members

Once we have compiled our data, we'll be completing the Final Cred Correlation Calculation (FCCC), wherein we finally determine to what degree a higher Live Cred Score does result in a more enjoyable time for the consumer. We hope to peer-review and publish by the end of 2012.

In the meantime, we've prepared a table with some information you can use. For the following artists, we've given you both scores; the RLCS and the more complex LCS. Our researchers have gathered data on these acts at live shows or through the modern miracle of digitized tape; whichever is indicated after the score. Some have even provided comments on the performances, or greater insight into scoring decisions. Their judgment may be incredibly subjective, but remember: numbers don't lie.

We at Chunklet Industries are reluctant to break anyone's rice bowl for almost next to no reason. However, with the worldwide recession still in effect, our readers need a go-to resource for quick assessment of whether these Golden Oldies deserve our time, money and respect, or are simply yawning through the motions on stage to get their kids into a better school district.* We're not in the habit of doing anyone favors, but this is one from the heart.

This actually was the reason that one band on the chart got back together. Please add ten points to your lifetime score if you can name that band!

D(B/A) + C/E=Y score (same as RLCS), where:

A = Number of years since last great record produced by the artist (or, if you will, the "Some Girls" quotient), at the time of most recent reunion.

B = Number of studio (not live, compilations, etc.) LPs' worth of material produced with original lineup,

C = Quality of performance of reunion band when compared to original band at peak on 1-10 scale (1 is worst, 10 is best),

D = Percentage of original members in reunion lineup, and

E = Amount of new material on scale of 1 (mostly new) to 10 (nothing new; total revival act).

M_f = Number of founding members
M_d = Number of dead, crazy or imprisoned members
M_r = Number of replacement members

BAND/ FACTOR	A		B	C	D	M_f	M_d	M_r	E	Y SCORE RLCS	Y SCORE LCS	LIVE (L) OR TAPE (T)
Wire	23	1976	7	9	1	4	0	1	5	2.1	2.76	L(1)
The Police	28	1975	5	8	1	3	0	0	10	0.98	2.29	L(2)
Van Halen	30	1976	6	10	0.75	4	0	2	10	1.15	3.99	L/T(3)
Camper Van Beethoven	15	1985	4	10	1	5	0	0	7	1.7	1.81	L(4)
Pink Floyd	8	1965	1	8	0.75	4	1	1	6	1.43	1.11	L(5)
Meat Puppets	13	1980	10	9	0.66	3	0	1	5	2.31	2.99	L
Jane's Addiction	15	1985	3	9	1	4	0	0	10	1.1	1.63	T(6)
X	25	1977	5	10	1	4	0	0	10	1.2	2.24	L(7)
The Who	27	1964	12	8	0.5	4	2		8	1.22	2.58	L(8)
Butthole Surfers	20	1981	6	8	1	3	0	0	10	1.1	2.19	L(9)
Shelley Berman	37	1953	3	10	1	1	0	0	10	1.08	2.20	L(10))
Dinosaur Jr.	2	1982	5	10	1	3	0	0	5	7	0.51	L(11)
Public Enemy	9	1984	7	10	1	8	0	0	8	2.03	1.74	L(12)
My Bloody Valentine	17	1985	3	10	1	4	0	0	10	1.18	1.72	L(13)
Mudhoney	14	1988	6	8	1	4	0	0	8	1.43	1.95	L
The Pixies	15	1986	5	10	1	4	0	0	9	1.31	1.89	L(14)
Pavement	15	1987	5	10	0.8	2	0	0	10	1.27	1.88	L/T(15)
MC5/DTK	32	1964	2	5	0.6	5	2	1	10	0.54	1.51	L
The Fall	3	1976	7	9	0.2	4	1	29	2	4.97	0.49	L
Rolling Stones	32	1962	11	8	0.6	6	1	2	9	1	3.67	T
The Jesus Lizard	16	1987	5	10	1	4	0	0	10	1.31	1.93	L
Mission Of Burma	25	1979	3	10	0.75	4	0	1	10	3.25	2.42	L(16)
Spice Girls	14	1994	1	7	0.8	4	0	1	9	0.85	1.73	T
Doors with Ian Astbury	33	1998	6	5	0.5	4	1	2	10	0.59	3.26	T
The Stooges	34	1967	3	10	0.75	4	1	1	10	1.07	2.14	L(17)
Sex Pistols	20	1975	1	10	1	4	1	0	10	1.05	1.24	T(18)
Mort Sahl	37	1953	8	5	1	1	0	0	1	5.21	3.61	L(19)
Monkees	30	1965	6	7	0.75	4	0	0	10	0.85	2.47	T
Guns & Roses	24	1984	4	N/A	N/A	5	0	4	N/A	N/A	N/A	N/A(20)
Jackie Mason	39	1954	9	8	1	1	0	0	7	1.37	3.20	L
English Beat (U.S.)	28	1977	3	7	0.14	7	1	2	10	1.03	2.27	T
Led Zeppelin	32	1968	8	8	0.75	4	1	1	9	1.08	2.84	T(21)
"Black Flag"'03	29	1976	2	7	0.75	1	3	1	10	0.75	0.39	T
Post-Biafra DK's												L(22)
Buzzcocks	24	1986	2	9	0.5	2	1	2	10	0.94	2.47	L(23)
Naked Raygun	22	1988	4	8	0.25	3	0	3	9	0.93	-0.15	L
Black Sabbath	23	1977	4	7	1	4	0	0	10	0.87	2.00	L(24)
Primus	6	1984	4	5	1	3	0	1	8	1.29	1.53	L(25)
Iron Maiden	11	1975	1	8	0.4	1	0	4	10	0.84	-0.16	L(26)
Heaven And Hell	15	1979	4	9	1	4	0	0	7	1.56	1.80	L(27)
Coalesce	10	1995	1	9	0.5	4	0	2	5	0.6	2.28	L(28)
Homosexuals	25	1978	1	8	0.25	2	0	2	5	1.61	2.69	L(28)
Gil Scott-Heron	1	1970	16	6	1	1	0	0	4	17.5	0.00	L(29)
F.G.T.H. fake line-up	15	1982	2	1	0	5	0	5	10	0.1	0.00	L

a/ Formula. Red values indicate not equivalent to previous version

THE INDIE CRED TEST

LIVE CRED CHART

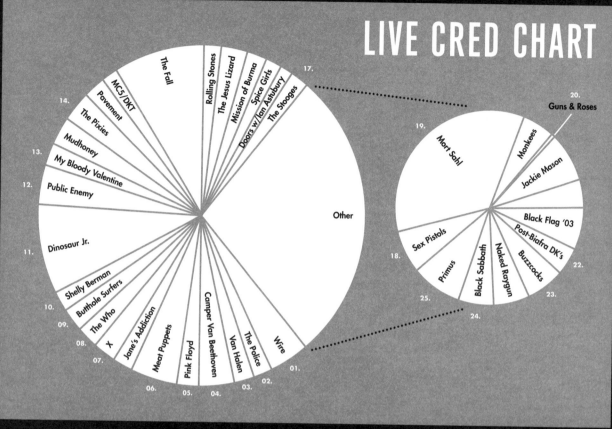

The Fall
Rolling Stones
The Jesus Lizard
Mission of Burma
Spice Girls
Doors w/Ian Astbury
The Stooges
MC5/DKT
Pavement
The Pixies
Mudhoney
My Bloody Valentine
Public Enemy
Dinosaur Jr.
Shelly Berman
Butthole Surfers
The Who
X
Jane's Addiction
Meat Puppets
Pink Floyd
Camper Van Beethoven
Van Halen
The Police
Wire
Other

17.
14.
13.
12.
11.
10.
09.
08.
07.
06.
05.
04.
03.
02.
01.

Mort Sahl
Monkees
Guns & Roses
20.
19.
Jackie Mason
Black Flag '03
Post-Biafra DK's
Sex Pistols
Primus
Black Sabbath
Naked Raygun
Buzzcocks
22.
23.
18.
25.
24.

REVIEWER COMMENTS/FOOTNOTES TO THE LIVE CRED CHART:

01. *"Played a great set with some tight renditions of new material."*

02. *"I'd add a .8 Wardrobe Credibility Multiplier to the final score if I could for Sting's stretchpants and shin-high combat boots and Stewart Copeland's ill-advised choice of a The Police t-shirt."*

03. *"Saw them in '84 and got bored by the soloing. The '07 shows seem like a better selection of material from all of the Roth years."*

04. *"Newer stuff is OK, nice to hear Jonathan Segel back with the band."*

05. *"Saw them in '87 in some Enormodome where they had room for the plane and the pig. No Roger Waters, of course."*

06. *"Anyone who heard Chris playing again and claims they didn't tear up a bit is lying. 'Lake Of Fire' molten as usual, even with Bostrom's replacement."*

07. *"Holy shit, I was too young the first time around and it's like I missed nothing–same Billy Zoom smile/stance from 'Decline'; haunted vocals still going strong."*

08. *"Townshend was great, but Daltrey succumbed to throat strain and eventually had to bow out early. Workmanlike performances from Pino Palladino and Zak Starkey carried the night but begged*

the question: How much longer can they justify calling this 'The Who'? You're better off at home with a decent copy of 'Pure Rock Theatre'."

09. *"Not half as scary and unpredictable as they used to be, but still a fearsome live unit, more so with Cabbage and King pounding away as one on stand-up kits."*

10. *"He got pissed when someone requested the 'buttermilk' bit, but went ahead and did it anyway. That's professionalism, kids."*

11. *"Saw Mascis at the local Mexican joint before the show. With the gray hair, shop-teacher glasses, and hippie wool cardigan, I felt like I was about to see a rock concert put on by my grandmother."*

12. *"I can't tell you how great this was to see in a club setting: the S1Ws crammed up on stage with Professor Griff 'out of retirement (disgrace), Terminator X and that fearsome front unit Chuck D. and Flav. Years before reality TV got the chance to ruin him, Flav was on fire, riffing extemporaneously at length and tossing fruit to the crowd periodically from the backstage area."*

13. *"Still loud and still great, even though that new record is eighteen years overdue."*

14. *"As cheesy as it sounds, the second that first snare-reverb hit from 'Bone Machine' kicked back to the crowd, we all went nuts and stayed that way. Underrated, if anything."*

15. *"Colleague in Australia says they still have it: look for further stateside feedback in the months to come."*

16. *"Played the good new stuff with conviction and killed all the hits. 'Revolver,' 'This Is Not A Photograph,' and 'Certain Fate' were standouts. Diverse crowd mix of graying baldies and curious young kids from local college town. Well worth the eight-hour drive."*

17. *"They did 'I Wanna Be Your Dog' twice. Honest to God! Iggy still tanned and pumped up."*

18. *"My favorite story related to this is Paul Cook calling Malcolm McLaren to ask if he'd be interested in road managing the reunion...then telling him he couldn't and hanging up. The band sound like the live tapes from the seventies, although much better without Sid on bass."*

19. *"Still coming up with relevant, politically/socially inspired stand-up."*

20. *(Data missing due to cancellation of concert slated for review. Where's Axl? Thanks a lot, dick!)*

21. *"More than made up for the sins of Live Aid, but not likely to be repeated in any touring capacity soon. Nice debut live version of 'For Your Life'."*

22. *(Data missing due to the fact that we can't find anyone who has admitted to seeing this lineup. Hopefully we'll find someone before this goes to print.)*

23. *"Fantastic. No new material and they tore through everything like teenage punks out to prove themselves."*

24. *"Only Ozzy records were counted in these stats. They still bring it live, consummate performers all."*

25. *"Lower rating of reunion possibly due to witnessing original line-up."*

26. *"Completely retro tour, right down to stage sets and "classic lineup" song choices. Most recent show meant no crappy new stuff, hence the elevated 'Y' score."*

27. *"Only Dio records were counted in these stats."*

28. *"They had younger guys in the band that played their balls off for a tiny half-filled club. They only had one EP, I think, but they played it all. People wanted to hear the classics. All things considered, it was an amazing show...Bruno Wizard is pushing 70!"*

29. *"No 'Lady Day,' No 'Revolution Will Not Be Televised,' No 'Washington, D.C.,' 'B Movie' or even 'Whitey On The Moon.' No, what we had was twenty-five minutes of half-assed attempts at comedy (he's no Eddie Harris, in case you were wondering) and then about sixty minutes of not-so-great music, during which none of his (excellent) new record was performed. The chart scores indicate he's either the most credible act we've reviewed or the least; given the circumstances you could make an argument either way."*

THE INDIE CRED TEST

SO, YOU GUYS WANNA JAM?

NOT ONLY ARE YOU READY TO START THE NEXT BIG THING, YOU'RE GONNA PUT YOUR REUBEN KINCAID-ESQUE MANAGERIAL
INSTINCT TO WORK AND ASSEMBLE THIS SHEBANG FROM SCRATCH. BUT WHERE DOES A PRO TURN FOR TOP-TIER TALENT?
THE CLASSIFIEDS, OF COURSE! THE INTERNET (AND TO A LESSER EXTENT, ITS GANGRENOUS, INVALID COUSIN KNOWN AS "PRINT")
PROVIDES THE PICK OF THE SOILED LITTER BOX WHEN IT COMES TO FINDING LIKE-MINDED MUSICIANS AND ARTISTS OF EVERY
CONCEIVABLE PERSUASION AND VARIANT. THE TRICK IS IN WEEDING OUT THE LUNATICS SOONER THAN LATER — *FILTERING IS YOUR FRIEND.*
DO NOT GIVE YOUR NUMBER TO THE GUY NAMED "SHELLY" WHO WANTS TO GO "NEXT LEVEL" WITH HIS FRETLESS 7-STRING.

 1

Paul Weller fan looking to put together a Jam cover band for ironic weddings and city-sponsored music festivals. Must own "In The City" and "Setting Sons" on vinyl (no reissues) and be willing to bust out the occasional Small Faces cover. I'm 40-ish, with salt and pepper beard, a priceless '70s poster collection and three pure-bred Rottweilers. We'll only meet once a week since you should have all Jam songs fucking memorized anyway. Buzzcocks and Ted Leo fans need not apply.

2

Troo kvult black metal axe player seeking guitarist to teach me guitar lessons cuz playing an actual axe is kinda limiting, musically. Also seeking: Satan. Influences: Satan. Also, windowless rooms with the lights off and chicks who cut themselves.

3

Ex-hardcore vocalist turned folkie looking for grizzled, late-30ish dudes sick of the same old punk bullshit. I'm putting together a countrified quartet for whiskey bars and indie clubs too cool for pop-country like the Avett Brothers. Must like Tom Waits, Drag the River, "Nebraska"-era Springsteen and be willing to remove (or at least cover with a flannel shirt) all Melvins and/or Danzig tattoos. Eyebrow piercings and black leather wristbands OK. Beards optional (but strongly encouraged). If interested, set ablaze your Op Ivy and Braid tapes and I'll follow the smoke trail.

 4

Male vocalist and female keyboard player in platonic relationship, but stage presence that makes you question otherwise, seek guitarist, bassist and drummer for

shoegaze/dream pop in vein of Luna, Pains of Being Pure at Heart, MBV. Already have a few 4-track demos but looking to expand. Influences: Sonic Youth, Low, Daniel Johnston, Birthday Party and Can. My brother runs Drag City so we'll have plenty of connections to get great shows even if we can't play worth shit!

 5

Who misses Kid Rock? That guy knew how to party. Let's meet and dish on some band ideas along the lines of Kid Rock, Andrew W.K., Poison, etc. The time is right for a bitchin' party-rock band that'll flatten the city and get some titties. Turn that radio up to the sweet sounds of light beer and Basic menthols, because my mom's basement just got cleaned out and I've got a month's worth of frozen White Castles in the mini-fridge. I don't play any instruments so would definitely need a guitarist, bassist, drummer, and/or bandana-wearing hype man with a name like TJ or Russ The Machine.

 6

Andy Kaufmanesque performance artist/stand-up comedian seeking audience plants for elaborate concept jokes about poop and barf. Must be able to extract and handle my feces and vomit in an efficient and professional manner, then allow them to be flung onto your face and/or person when I turn on the audience, GG Allin-style. Philosophy majors and Belle and Sebastian completists are encouraged. No prior conceptual art experience necessary.

 7

Metal/fusion guitarist with killer chops and talent to spare looking for bassist and drummer for local and out of town gigs. Own your own pro gear a must. This is no weekend warrior shit. Nothing less than total commitment. If you can sing (preferably scream) that's a plus. I'll

be holding down the lead vocals. Have a practice space in a storage shed way the hell out past the highway. Influences: Cannibal Corpse, Megadeth, Black Sabbath, Dream Theater. If you don't know who Les Claypool is don't bother replying!

 8

Heavy stoner rock band seeks bassist. We're looking for someone numb in tone, rolling in heavy, heavy licks. We want to be the band that sits on the bridge of your nose like a euphoric sneeze that never comes. Sleep's "Jerusalem" is daily dietary need. Encyclopedic knowledge of everything Sabbath, as well as worship of all bands on Hydrahead. Think Kyuss with occasional forays into Bongzilla. Long locks not required, but absolutely, positively NO DRUGS. Sorry, but we've just had some bad experiences in the past.

 9

Punk rock band needs touring guitarist. Songs are already written and recorded, due out on semi-big label in a couple of months. Tour will be heavily promoted, leading with a single to air on NBC's "Parenthood" and video rotation on Fuse. Candidate must have competent downstrokes and embody energetic stage presence. Pro-tude a must. This is a tour, NOT A PARTY. No junk gear, no whining, no nihilism. Individual will receive daily stipend and increased exposure. Waiver required (lawyer says so). For audition, please have three "punk-spirited" covers and headshot of your best grimace.

 10

Sexy but talentless vocalist seeks decent musicians to serve as his vehicle to poon and the primetime. Must not be ugly, but can't be cuter than me. Also must not care if I hit on your girlfriends repeatedly in front of you. Also, can you loan me fifty

bucks until our first gig? Influences: Mick Jagger, Vince Neil, Bob Seger.

 11

Nu Metal guitarist seeks ethnic metal dude of any persuasion to do back-up rapping. Any race welcome other than white, as we're trying to diversify our suburban flava, yo. While not required, knowing how to hook me up with some fly cornrows would be a plus, as I tried it myself once and looked like I was wearing a roadkill hat, dawg.

 12

Mechanic seeks touring musicians who know nothing about cars so I can overcharge them for routine maintenance. Must own a touring vehicle with over 150K miles and believe that some model GM's can actually suffer from demonic possession and/or infestation, both of which are, like, ungodly expensive to fix or something.

 13

Former roadie seeks prospective roadie to show the roadie ropes. Must know how to cuss, lift heavy shit and rock a wifebeater in -10 degree weather. Also, must NOT be a better musician than anyone in the band and must be willing to drive 28 hours straight and still unload everything by yourself while the band catches a pre-game buzz in the VIP room.

 14

Guitar seeks motivated player to bang out a few bad ass riffs. I've been owned by the same guy for five years and all he's ever played on me is "Row Your Boat." It's embarrassing, I was made to SHRED dammit! Influences: Gibson and/or Fender pawnshop replicas.

ATTENTION!
ALL OF THESE TERRIFYING ENTRIES REQUEST YOUR SWIFT, UNMITIGATED AND/OR UNDYING COLLABORATION!
RANK FROM MOST TO LEAST LIKELY TO GET A SHITTY RESPONSE DESPITE BEING A SHITTY AD.

CORRECT RANKING (in order from left to right): 11, 7, 4, 10, 14, 5, 8, 12, 2, 6, 13, 9, 1, 3.

THE INDIE CRED TEST

MULTIPLE CHOICE

01. If you decide to "fill in" with an existing band, they'll lose the least cred if the member you're replacing is:
    a. the drummer.
    b. joining the Peace Corps.
    c. dead.
    d. Scott Weiland.

02. Your chances of being invited to play Levi's South by Southwest day party are better with which listing?
    a. Grizzled ex-punk-turned-folkie
    b. Jam cover band — but only if we play some of Weller's less political solo stuff
    c. Both — if all band members are dressed in Levi's-brand Canadian tuxedos
    d. Neither. Levi's has already booked various Kings of Leon side projects to play all its SXSW day parties through 2020

03. Your chances of releasing a single on Secretly Jaguar are better with which listing?
    a. Heavy Trio looking for bass
    b. *"Hey, let's be famous!"*
    c. Bad ass rhythm machine – pic (pic is in fact a photo of Neil Peart)
    d. 95 Year old hippie still learning to play guitar seeks usual suspects – help me supplement the SSI check

04. You'd like to start an 'experimental' band, but your cred is more important to you than actually attracting people who share your vision. Ideally, you'd like to list as influences "bands that you've never heard of", but that seems presumptuous and also it ends a sentence with a preposition. What should you do instead?
    a. Sit in internet cafes and wait for someone to make fun of the bands you list as influences. Then hire them.
    b. Claim that your only influence is yourself.
    c. Make up a bunch of bands that you would listen to if only they were cool enough to actually exist.
    d. Just don't even bother to start the band, out of spite. That'll show 'em.

05. Your chances for cred are better with a band whose past gigs include:
    a. VFW halls
    b. Basement shows
    c. Alanon Meetings
    d. Pampered Chef parties

06. Which act is more likely to be embraced by "indie comedy" fans of Zach Galifianakis, Jon Glaser, Flight of the Conchords and Neil Hamburger?
    a. The party-rockers. Irony is a suffocating yet comforting blanket.
    b. The performance artist. Hipster sheep need to feel like they're experiencing something "real."
    c. I stopped reading at "frozen White Castles."
    d. Why not combine them into a ironic supergroup of barfing poop comedians with neon headbands?

07. You'd like to start a dynamic, multi-member hip-hop crew a la the Wu-Tang Clan, but your mom doesn't like "those people" hanging around the garage, because she's worried they'll steal her Hummel figurines. Who should you namecheck in the ad to get just the right mix of talent?
    a. Lucas
    b. Hollywood Undead
    c. Joe C.
    d. Eminem (post-"Relapse")

08. You're starting a power metal band, and you only want the purest Viking riffmongers for your outfit. In other words, no girls. What's the best way to make it clear that 'Ironstorm' is an estrogen-free zone without being too obvious?
    a. Say "raw metal warriors only" in your ad, and ask all applicants how heavy a sword they can lift
    b. Require all applicants to send in their codpiece size
    c. Include photo in Craigslist ad that emphasizes location and density of your body hair
    d. Make clear that a background of at least 10 years playing "Gamma World"

09. You've got the chops, you've got the look, you've got the band name, and you've got the willingness to take all the credit for other peoples' work. So what is the most important thing your guitarist should bring to the band's sound?
    a. A decent practice space.
    b. A reliable weed connection.
    c. A mic (for you, and for himself, if needed).
    d. A girlfriend whose commitment to the relationship is questionable.

10. For your new indie-rock/chamber-pop band, you will be handling the lead vocals, because you can't read or write music and you don't know how to play any instruments. Nonetheless, you would like to be credited as the band's primary musical architect. How to get the band to do all the work while still taking all the glory?
    a. Hum the vocal melody into a tape recorder and hand it over to your guitarist. After he writes the rest of the song, come up with some lyrics and say you'll "clean it up".
    b. Tell the band two songs you already like, and ask them to "kinda mix them together and see what happens". Anything original that results? You get a writing credit!
    c. Argue that picking the lion's share of covers makes you the band's primary songwriter.
    d. Hire a guitarist with limited English skills, have the percussion handled by a drum machine, and set up a "Lennon/McCartney-type deal" where you get a writing credit for anything your band produces regardless of how little you had to do with it.

CHAPTER 13

PANCAKE TURNERS & BUTTON MASHERS

DUMBER THAN A RECEDING MULLET. More sorrowful than a bag of dead kittens. Able to crossfade horrible songs in every town. Look! Up on the stage! It's a turd! It's a shame! It's DJ Littaboxxx! Yes, it's DJ Littaboxxx — strange visitor from another planet who came to Earth with powers and abilities far below those of normal men. DJ Littaboxxx — who can contaminate every drink in the building in the blink of an eye, finger blast every hot skirt in a single nap, and who, disguised as Donny Floyd, mild mannered mechanic for a popular tire and service center, fights the never ending battle for Rohypnol distribution, glitter on dudes, and that one house beat. Should you be this guy's sidekick? Take the test and seal your fate.

THE INDIE
CRED TEST

YES/NO

THE INDIE
CRED TEST

COMPLETE THE FOLLOWING QUESTIONS WITH A YES/NO ANSWER OR SUFFER THE CONSEQUENCES.

YES   NO

01. Do you know where all the '80s nights are in your city? ☐ ☐

02. Can you name type, make and year of manufacture of all the various pieces of equipment making random chirping, buzzing and "whomp-whomp" sounds during any given breakdown? ☐ ☐

03. Would you consider dating someone not as "into" DJ culture as you are? ☐ ☐

04. What about fighting someone not as "into" DJ culture as you are? ☐ ☐

05. Have you ever paid good money to go into a club to watch a celebrity "spin records" from their iPod? Exactly how do you define "good money"? ☐ ☐

06. Do you find yourself reminding the chatty people at the bar that this is a DJ set, not a drunken meat market? ☐ ☐

07. Do you then find yourself wondering what that specific difference actually is? ☐ ☐

08. Can you tell the difference between separate DJs from Barcelona based on their smell alone? ☐ ☐

09. Do you try to convince friends that the Winter Music Conference is as relevant as South by Southwest and/or Sean Hannity's Freedom Concerts? ☐ ☐

10. Do you let your Burning Man "friends" crash at your apartment when their tie-dyed, hemp-diesel welfare bus rolls through town? ☐ ☐

11. Are you in touch with the DJ communities of Europe? ☐ ☐

12. Do you have a sneaking suspicion that they secretly make fun of American DJs when you're not around? ☐ ☐

13. Do you plan family vacations according to festivals in foreign countries? ☐ ☐

14. Have you ever recorded your own mash-up mix, or collection of "breaks" from one of your favorite artists? ☐ ☐

YES   NO

15. Have you ever plugged your iPod into the stereo and taken over a house party? ☐ ☐

16. Have you ever made an intentionally terrible mash-up mix (ex.: Celine Dion's "My Heart Will Go On" with Ray Parker Jr's "Ghostbusters") for the sole purpose of sabotaging a house party and spraining people's eardrums? ☐ ☐

17. Are you more likely to go to a record convention at a certain time because your childhood idol DJ Fannyballz is spinning? ☐ ☐

18. Is your favorite night to go out dancing on a weird off-night like the third Wednesday of every month because that's "obscure psychedelic soul night" or "aggro dub night" or some other lousy subsubgenre? ☐ ☐

19. Has your once-happy record player started throwing dishes at you because of all the bullshit you use it for now? ☐ ☐

20. Do club scenes in movies excite you because you're bound to spot a movie DJ, the most renowned of all DJs? ☐ ☐

FILLING THE PANTS

21. Are you a DJ with actual turntables and a mixer, or do you just plug in your iPod/MacBook (iTunes) with a preselected playlist? ☐ ☐

22. Do you work that little iPod wheel dial like a record while fiddling with...wait, what do you fiddle with? ☐ ☐

22A. How the fuck is this a show?

---

23. Do you start your playlist with some slower warm-up songs and then "turn up the tits" when people start showing up at midnight? ☐ ☐

24. Do you consider standing around looking cool while you spin your playlist to be a form of "performance art"? ☐ ☐

25. How many times since 1999 have you been booed right the fuck out of a club? ☐

YES   NO

26. Have you ever not been paid for a set because, let's face it, you're really just a dude forcing people to listen to songs you like? ☐ ☐

27. Have you done a "wrong-speed night"? ☐ ☐

28. Do rappers network with you after your DJ set? ☐ ☐

28A. And you're not a hot chick? ☐ ☐

28B. What about assailants? ☐ ☐

29. Does your cool-down session consist of a 30-minute set of Midnight Star and you and other DJs hooking up with each other's MySpace pages? ☐ ☐

30. Do you consider your mash-ups "an art"? ☐ ☐

30A. Does anyone else? ☐ ☐

31. Do the free watery drinks you get from DJing at shitty bars justify the unreasonable amount of money you spend on records? ☐ ☐

32. Have any of your laptop remixes ever made it to a tribute album? ☐ ☐

32A. Which album, so I know not to buy it? ☐ ☐

33. Do you consider "turntabling" a verb? ☐ ☐

34. Are you working towards a corporate sponsorship? *('cuz DJ Dr. Scholl's has a nice ring to it....)* ☐ ☐

35. Do you consider your mixing a form of musicianship, even though you can't actually play any musical instruments other than air drums? ☐ ☐

36. Do you do anything else unrelated to the task of DJing while you DJ? *(Examples: checking IMs, texting, crop dusting, attempting suicide, etc...)* ☐ ☐

37. Do you work as a waitress/bouncer/janitor in any of the establishments you DJ for? ☐ ☐

38. Are any of your "sets" archived in podcast form for your international audience to download/enjoy? ☐ ☐

39. Are you oblivious to the fact that your peeps call you DUMB JANITOR, DICKLESS JAP, DAS JERK, DAPPER JAN, and DIRTY JEW when you're spinning? ☐ ☐

YES   NO

40. Have you ever thought of killing yourself, but just don't want all that sweet equipment to get split up amongst your family and that one friend you hate? ☐ ☐

41. Do you confuse your mom when you tell her you're going to spinning class, but not the kind she goes to? ☐ ☐

RAVE CULTURE

42. Do you have a garbage bag full of raver pants, green-mesh tank tops and knee-high socks waiting for that particular fashion trend to come around again? ☐ ☐

43. Did you keep any of the VapoRub-coated surgical masks you wore while rolling? ☐ ☐

44. Do you still occasionally use a dash of glitter makeup on your cans or sack before attending a DJ set? ☐ ☐

45. Did you attend a "real" rave back in the day and then lecture people at "fake" raves about it? ☐ ☐

46. Did you ever order a vanity plate that read RAVR4EVR? ☐ ☐

46A. What about DATERAPE? ☐ ☐

47. Did you downgrade from ecstasy and espresso to Adderall and Miller Lite after you violently shit your pants at that Tiësto concert? ☐ ☐

48. Do you still walk into empty warehouses and think, "This would be a totally sick spot for a rave"? ☐ ☐

ARTIST SPECIFIC

49. Did you buy a plane ticket to Colorado just to see Armin van Buuren at Red Rocks Ampitheatre? ☐ ☐

50. Do you feel sorry for contemporary electronic music fans who never saw Moby in his heyday? ☐ ☐

51. Have you ever played Another Bad Creation? ☐ ☐

52. Have you ever been removed from DJ duty at a party for playing Montel Jordan/Jonas Brothers mash-ups? ☐ ☐

ALBUM/SONG SPECIFIC

53. Would you rather listen to the *Grey Album* than *Dark Night of the Soul*? ☐ ☐

54. Do you consider "The Devil Went Up to Michigan" an anthem? ☐ ☐

	YES	NO

55. Do you get excited when you realize that Steely Dan's "Peg" transitions "perfectly" into Haircut 100's "Love Plus One" for an imaginary "ironic dance night" set? ☐ ☐

56. Do you consider "Hey Ya" to be the pinnacle of "songwriting"? ☐ ☐

57. Do you host a weekly '80s dance night where drunk college girls do "The Molly Ringwald" to "Love Will Tear Us Apart" or "The Pee Wee Herman" to "Tequila"? ☐ ☐

58. Does having Clarence Carter's *Strokin'* in your vinyl collection automatically make you a strip club DJ? ☐ ☐

THE INDIE CRED TEST

MULTIPLE CHOICE

THE INDIE CRED TEST

NEVER BEFORE HAS THE POWER OF SELECTION BEEN SO INDISCRIMINATE.

01. Which of the following best describes your dancing style:

A. A mix of the "best" of other dancers you've seen over the years
B. Several thinly veiled variations of your best humping strokes
C. Epilepsy with a hint of drowning-panic
D. The same as my bar-brawling style, "Pants-Shitting Rage"

02. How do you get paid at your DJ gigs?

A. Actual money
B. iTunes gift card
C. Pitchers of house draught
D. Club owner gets you stoned
E. A "thank you" (if lucky)
F. A three frat-boy "courtesy ass kicking" for not playing enough Blues Traveler/Dave Matthews/Stevie Ray Vaughn mash-ups.

03. Which records are you most pissed that Madlib sampled before you did?

A. *Dharmatma OST* by Kalyanji Anandji
B. *Recorded Live* by the Wooden Glass, feat. Billy Wooten
C. *The Third Reich 'N' Roll* by the Residents
D. *Chapter One* by BLO
E. *Zip Zap Rap* by Devastatin' Dave the Turntable Slave

04. What is the greatest untapped source of samples?

A. The Vertigo Records catalogue
B. Scott Walker's solo albums
C. Any pre-1989 Einstürzende Neubauten release
D. Vietnamese poetry slams

THE INDIE CRED TEST

FILL IN THE BLANK

THE INDIE CRED TEST

CRAM IT, DAMMIT!

01. If you're more of a revivalist DJ who plays old, obscure material, what is the most you have ever paid for a "Northern soul" single? And what was it?

_____

_____

_____

_____

02. How much do you hate taking requests?

_____

_____

_____

_____

_____

THE INDIE CRED TEST

Fetishizing African-American culture has been an integral part of establishing cred ever since Jeff Beck invented the blues in 1965. Use the following chart to determine how "worldly," "down," or "totally not racist, I swear" you are compared to your friends.

NOTE: IF YOU ARE ACTUALLY BLACK, CAN WE HANG OUT SOME TIME?

	YOU "TOTALLY FEEL" OR THAT "TRANSCENDS RACE"	YOU DABBLE IN (OR AT LEAST ENJOY WITH THE SAFE, CONDESCENDING IRONIC DISTANCE YOU ESTABLISHED AT YOUR LIBERAL ARTS COLLEGE)	MAKES YOU WANT TO RUN BACK THE COMFORTING EMBRACE OF YOUR OF MONTREAL RECORDS AND SUBSCRIPTIONS TO THE BELIEVER
Recordings of "field hollers"	WORLDLY	DOWN	TOTALLY NOT RACIST (I SWEAR)
Blues records played via your 78 RPM record player	WORLDLY	DOWN	TOTALLY NOT RACIST (I SWEAR)
Any jazz artist under the age of 35	WORLDLY	DOWN	TOTALLY NOT RACIST (I SWEAR)
Alice Coltrane	WORLDLY	DOWN	TOTALLY NOT RACIST (I SWEAR)
Detroit hip-hop producers who aren't Dilla	WORLDLY	DOWN	TOTALLY NOT RACIST (I SWEAR)
Art Ensemble Of Chicago	WORLDLY	DOWN	TOTALLY NOT RACIST (I SWEAR)
The Watts Prophets	WORLDLY	DOWN	TOTALLY NOT RACIST (I SWEAR)
Liking Rufus Thomas before he was on Jon Spencer records	WORLDLY	DOWN	TOTALLY NOT RACIST (I SWEAR)
Obscure regional soul groups that "those fucking jokers at Numero Group should be putting out if they had any brains"	WORLDLY	DOWN	TOTALLY NOT RACIST (I SWEAR)
David Axelrod	WORLDLY	DOWN	TOTALLY NOT RACIST (I SWEAR)
Any primarily black hardcore band that's not Bad Brains	WORLDLY	DOWN	TOTALLY NOT RACIST (I SWEAR)
R. Kelly (pre-Chocolate Factory)	WORLDLY	DOWN	TOTALLY NOT RACIST (I SWEAR)
Circa 1980 "Battle tapes" from Harlem World	WORLDLY	DOWN	TOTALLY NOT RACIST (I SWEAR)
The Funky 4+1	WORLDLY	DOWN	TOTALLY NOT RACIST (I SWEAR)
The Wild Style soundtrack	WORLDLY	DOWN	TOTALLY NOT RACIST (I SWEAR)
Malcolm McLaren and the World Famous Supreme Team	WORLDLY	DOWN	TOTALLY NOT RACIST (I SWEAR)
12"s of rapping ventriloquist dummies from the early '80s	WORLDLY	DOWN	TOTALLY NOT RACIST (I SWEAR)
12"s of rapping actors and/or sitcom characters from the mid '80s	WORLDLY	DOWN	TOTALLY NOT RACIST (I SWEAR)
Second-tier songs from the "Roxanne Wars"	WORLDLY	DOWN	TOTALLY NOT RACIST (I SWEAR)
The Fat Boys when they were "The Disco 3"	WORLDLY	DOWN	TOTALLY NOT RACIST (I SWEAR)
Too $hort (pre-Jive cassette releases only)	WORLDLY	DOWN	TOTALLY NOT RACIST (I SWEAR)
Schoolly D	WORLDLY	DOWN	TOTALLY NOT RACIST (I SWEAR)
Any Miami bass that Luther Campbell wasn't personally involved in	WORLDLY	DOWN	TOTALLY NOT RACIST (I SWEAR)
Ultramagnetic MC's	WORLDLY	DOWN	TOTALLY NOT RACIST (I SWEAR)
The "Stop The Violence All-Stars" and/or "The West Coast All-Stars"	WORLDLY	DOWN	TOTALLY NOT RACIST (I SWEAR)
3rd Bass	WORLDLY	DOWN	TOTALLY NOT RACIST (I SWEAR)
The Geto Boys who aren't Scarface or Bushwick	WORLDLY	DOWN	TOTALLY NOT RACIST (I SWEAR)
Ganksta N-I-P	WORLDLY	DOWN	TOTALLY NOT RACIST (I SWEAR)
Diamond D and the Psychotic Neurotics	WORLDLY	DOWN	TOTALLY NOT RACIST (I SWEAR)
Shaquille O'Neal	WORLDLY	DOWN	TOTALLY NOT RACIST (I SWEAR)
E-40	WORLDLY	DOWN	TOTALLY NOT RACIST (I SWEAR)
Suga Free	WORLDLY	DOWN	TOTALLY NOT RACIST (I SWEAR)
Project Pat	WORLDLY	DOWN	TOTALLY NOT RACIST (I SWEAR)
"jerk music"	WORLDLY	DOWN	TOTALLY NOT RACIST (I SWEAR)
Records from African countries not covered by Sublime Frequencies or Crammed Discs	WORLDLY	DOWN	TOTALLY NOT RACIST (I SWEAR)
Whatever weird colored-vinyl thing Stones Throw put out this week	WORLDLY	DOWN	TOTALLY NOT RACIST (I SWEAR)
Whatever Atlanta "trap-rapper" indie-rock blogs like all of a sudden	WORLDLY	DOWN	TOTALLY NOT RACIST (I SWEAR)
Third most popular MC from whatever regional scene the Fader is covering this month	WORLDLY	DOWN	TOTALLY NOT RACIST (I SWEAR)
Anyone in Brick Squad besides Gucci, Waka or OJ	WORLDLY	DOWN	TOTALLY NOT RACIST (I SWEAR)
Rap-A-Lot or Duck Down rappers currently on their tenth record	WORLDLY	DOWN	TOTALLY NOT RACIST (I SWEAR)
Owning more than 200 Lil B tracks	WORLDLY	DOWN	TOTALLY NOT RACIST (I SWEAR)
Odd Future Wolf Tumblr (or whatever the fuck they're called)	WORLDLY	DOWN	TOTALLY NOT RACIST (I SWEAR)

THE INDIE CRED TEST

CHAPTER 14

THIS IS YOUR LIFE!
CONDENSED INTO COUNTLESS MILK CRATES

HERE IN THE 21ST CENTURY, the greatest status an individual can possibly attain is that of a vinyl fanatic. It's not even debatable. Records sound so much warmer and more genuine than digital media. The jacket is, like, a collectible unto itself. The process of dropping a stylus into a groove and letting that mellifluous sound wave hit your cochlea is a more glorious, intense and praiseworthy sequence of human behavior than reading to blind children. Remember, you can't ever really own the 1's and 0's that make up an MP3, but vinyl is forever.

So, you need to ask yourself: Am I a hero?

YES/NO

COMPLETE THE FOLLOWING QUESTIONS WITH A YES/NO ANSWER OR SUFFER THE CONSEQUENCES.

YES NO

01. Can you define what an "obi" is without any Jedi references? ☐ ☐

02. Do you get irrationally pissy when you hear that a release you want is MP3 only? ☐ ☐

03. When someone says "I'll burn a copy for you," do you tell them not to worry about it? ☐ ☐

04. Do you ever ask if they can press a copy for you instead? ☐ ☐

05. Have you ever used the phrase "Six-Eye" in a casual discussion about records? ☐ ☐

06. Have you ever pushed someone aside in order to ensure a positive acquisition? ☐ ☐

07. Have you ever stolen any of your parents' records only to learn that the sixties/seventies/eighties may not have been all they were cracked up to be? ☐ ☐

08. Do you know random people who have said, "Hey, I have boxes of those giant antique black CD things in my basement, do you want them?" ☐ ☐

09. Have you installed a state-of-the-art suspension system so you can listen to records in your car? ☐ ☐

10. Do you replace vintage inner sleeves with paper/plastic ones, then store the original inner outside the jacket in the plastic LP sleeve to prevent further damage? ☐ ☐

11. If so, have you seen a therapist about this? ☐ ☐

12. What's the biggest order you've placed with Bags Unlimited, or any other place that pretty much sells boxes for your bullshit? ☐ ☐

13. Have you ever worn out a record? ☐ ☐
    Cassette? ☐ ☐
    8-track tape? ☐ ☐
    CD? ☐ ☐
    Music box? ☐ ☐

14. Have you ever bought a record because of the shock appeal of the sleeve art? ☐ ☐

15. Have you ever eaten a record because you loved it so much and wanted it to be a part of you forever? ☐ ☐

16. Have you ever decided against buying a record because it wasn't on candy rainbow carnival colored vinyl? ☐ ☐

YES NO

17. Have you ever tried to pass off an LP slightly melted by heat exposure as a "European remix"? ☐ ☐

18. If a sticker or poster comes with a record, do you wait so long trying to find that perfect spot for it that you wind up losing it before you can ever post it? ☐ ☐

19. Have you seen *Vinyl* by Alan Zweig but dismiss it as sensationalism? ☐ ☐

GEAR

20. Do you own a belt driven or fixed drive record player? ☐ ☐

21. Does your turntable say "Fisher Price" anywhere on it? ☐ ☐

22. Did you spend more on the needle for your cartridge than on the rest of your audio system combined? ☐ ☐

23. Do you own a "Nitty Gritty Dirt Vac" or other high-falutin' home system to keep LPs clean and static-free? ☐ ☐

24. Even though the superiority of vinyl is utterly unquestionable, have you ever used modern technology to "digitize" one of your favorite records for easier mobile listening? ☐ ☐

25. Could you change your stylus if needed? ☐ ☐

26. Do you wonder when Steve Jobs will return from the dead and develop an iTurntable? ☐ ☐

27. Does your turntable have a reverse button? ☐ ☐

27A. If so, do any of your records tell you things, like how you're ruining your needle? ☐ ☐

COLLECTION

28. Do you own any odd sized records (i.e., 8", 4', 4'8", etc.)? ☐ ☐

29. Do you own any die-cut records or records with die-cut packaging? ☐ ☐

30. Do you actually listen to your ten-inch collection? ☐ ☐

31. Is it tedious to have to get up and flip one of a single after the four minutes of music on side one is over? ☐ ☐

32. Have you ever shown your collection off to people who couldn't give a shit? ☐ ☐
    (i.e., grandparents, in-laws, mailman, etc.)

33. When a band stays at your house, is your collection the first thing you show them, or is it your wang? □ □

34. Have you ever gone through your collection and suddenly wanted candy? *(Starburst or Skittles, to be exact.)* □ □

35. Have you ever gone into debt or incurred mafia-inflicted bodily injury for the sake of your record collection? □ □

36. Is your singles collection worth more than the rest of your records and CDs combined? □ □

37. Do you ever buy records just so people can see they're in your collection? □ □

38. Do you prominently display certain records and/or CDs in a place distinct from your collection? □ □

39. Do you own any records that you keep sealed and unplayed? □ □

40. Do you put all of your records in clear plastic bags? □ □

41. Has anyone in your family suggested you sell some of your collection to make improvements on your home? □ □

42. Do you have any records you won't let anybody touch or play? □ □

43. Have you ever physically attacked someone for calling records "vinyls"? □ □

44. If so, did they totally whip your ass because, as everybody knows, record-collecting nerds can't fight for shit? □ □

45. Have you insured your record collection? □ □

46. Has your record collection ever been appraised? □ □

47. Have you ever purchased someone else's entire record collection? □ □

48. Ever bought a record you already own because the sleeve is in better condition? □ □

49. Do you actually play your picture discs? □ □

50. Does your collection have an "untouchable classics" section? □ □

51. Does it also have an "internal debate about whether it qualifies as an untouchable classic" section? □ □

52. Does your "untouchable classics" section include a bunch of shit that nobody's ever heard of? □ □

53. Does the time you devote to listening to your records count as "work" in your brain because of an internal OCD need to properly classify everything? □ □

54. Has a pet ever destroyed any part of your collection and if so, did you then destroy the pet? □ □

55. Do you have a rule regarding how much time needs to pass between listenings of an LP for it to go on the "sell" pile? □ □

56. During tax season, does your accountant tell you that you spend far too much money on music? □ □

57. Do you have the world's largest collection of that "famously obscure" local band's only vinyl release? □ □

58. If you have to move your records, do all of your friends mysteriously disappear? □ □

59. Does the number of jazz, soul, rap and blues albums you own outnumber the number of black people you know by at least a 20:1 ratio? □ □

60. Have you ever spent more than $250 on a single record? □ □
    More than $500? □ □
    $1,000? □ □

61. Have you ever bought a record on colored vinyl and sold the one you owned on black? □ □

STORING/MOVING

62. Do you have to keep part of your record collection at your parents' house due to its size? □ □

63. Do you have so many records that they've spilled over into the bathroom? □ □

64. Are your records stored in some form of condensed shelving units? □ □

65. Have you ever stored records flat because of a lack of space? □ □

66. Do you have a closet dedicated solely to record mailers? □ □

67. Are you repulsed when you find people who leave on the original shrink wrap to "protect" the record cover? □ □

68. Is the furniture that holds your vinyl nicer than the furniture you sit on to listen to your vinyl? □ □

69. Have you raided liquor store back rooms for boxes in order to move your vinyl? □ □

YES NO

70. Have you entrusted your fragile plates and glasses to moving professionals, but opted to move your vinyl on your own? ☐ ☐

FILING

71. Is your collection alphabetized? ☐ ☐

72. Do you alphabetize solo artists by first name and discredit any other alphabetizing style? ☐ ☐

73. Is your collection separated into genres? ☐ ☐

74. If an LP comes with a bonus single, do you file them together? ☐ ☐

75. Have you ever arranged your collection by color because you saw a picture of someone doing that online or in some magazine and almost immediately regretted it because you can't find anything you're looking for anymore? ☐ ☐

RECORD STORE

76. Are record store employees actually nice to you? ☐ ☐

77. Does your skin actually prickle with anticipation when you inhale the musty odor of used records? ☐ ☐

78. Do you buy records and later discover you already have them at home? ☐ ☐

79. Have you ever uttered the phrase "but when's it getting a PHYSICAL release"? ☐ ☐

80. Did you ever decide not to buy a record because you were afraid of what the counter clerk would say? ☐ ☐

81. Do you go out of your way to get colored vinyl or limited editions of records? ☐ ☐

82. Do record store employees keep a stack of stuff for you behind the counter? ☐ ☐

83. Have you ever refused a lucrative job offer because you'd have to move to a city with no good record stores? ☐ ☐

84. Do you have a collection of "ironic" thrift-store records you have never listened to? ☐ ☐

85. Would you consider downloading MP3s in lieu of a trek to your local shop? ☐ ☐

86. Do you get angry when you can't find parking due to some shitty band's in-store? ☐ ☐

87. Do you know what Record Store Day is? ☐ ☐

88. If yes, do you visit more than one store on that day? ☐ ☐

YES NO

89. If yes, do you map out and prioritize which record stores are most likely to have your want list items? ☐ ☐

90. If a terrible band gets better visibility on the rack, will you "accidentally" replace their records with those of a band you like? ☐ ☐

91. Does your local record store allow you access to their back room stash of super-rarities? ☐ ☐

92. Do you hog the store's one listening station? ☐ ☐

93. Ever been in a fist, knife or gun fight with an employee over the store's poor selection? ☐ ☐

94. If yes, did you go home after the fight and vow to open the "perfect store"? ☐ ☐

95. If yes, did you give up halfway through taking copious notes to smoke a bowl? ☐ ☐

96. Ever held up the check-out line to ask ludicrous questions about multiple box sets? ☐ ☐

97. Have you ever purchased a book at a record store? Was it of any remote literary value? ☐ ☐

98. Have you ever purchased a band sticker, button or t-shirt at a shop? ☐ ☐

99. Have you ever tipped into the beer jar on the counter? ☐ ☐

100. Have you ever balked at a store's poor selection of 33 $1/3$ books? ☐ ☐

101. Have you ever demanded they change the trip-hop or electro-pop in favor of something "harder," such as Winger? ☐ ☐

102. Do you pre-order? ☐ ☐

103. Does the word "mono" mean anything to you? ☐ ☐

104. Does your day job merely support your record buying habit? ☐ ☐

105. Have you ever actually waited outside a record store for it to open, for any reason at all? ☐ ☐

106. Does your local shop hold in-stores? ☐ ☐

107. Do you ever buy records for their speculative future value? ☐ ☐

108. Have you had a serious discussion about the superiority of 78s to all other vinyl formats with a record store employee? ☐ ☐

109. Have you ever eaten inside your local record shop? ☐ ☐

THE INDIE CRED TEST

YES　NO

110. Have you ever spent the night at your local record shop?

111. Do you rip the poly wrapping off, or just slit it?

112. Do you have an open tab at your local record store?

113. Does your local record store have a "by appointment only" policy during the week, solely with regards to you?

114. If a trip to a shop looks more and more like a waste of time, do you stay to check the jazz, soul, reggae, hip hop, world, folk, country, spoken word, and/or vocal sections, just in case?

115. Do you ever come home with "what the fuck was I thinking" purchases from those sections?

116. Do you ever end up really enjoying a "what the fuck was I thinking" purchase?

117. Are you well known for getting into heated "screaming and throwing shit" kind of arguments at record stores?

FANATICISM

118. Do you buy remastered editions of recordings you already own?

119. Do you buy albums you already own for bonus tracks?

120. Do you buy Greatest Hits albums for new songs/versions of songs?

121. Do you buy international copies of albums you own?

122. Do you buy vinyl and CD releases of the same album?

123. Are any of your records signed and framed?

124. Did you ever put cash in an envelope to buy a record you saw advertised in *MRR*?

125. Have you followed the career of any musician through more than four of their bands?

126. Have you ever spent more on music in a week than you have on groceries?

127. Do you own more recorded material by an artist than the artist himself owns?

128. Do you wring your hands when reissues come out because you're worried what it'll do to the value of your originals?

129. When talking about any post-vinyl format, do you sound like Abe Simpson?

ARTIST/TITLE/LABEL SPECIFIC

YES　NO

130. Did you buy your first copy of *Appetite for Destruction* on cassette?

131. How about the single by Neil Hamburger's old band?

132. Have you ever played Hum's "Stars" backwards and heard an advertisement for a vehicle?

133. Have you ever bought a Tim Kinsella record on purpose?

134. Do you have that one Lifter Puller record about the kids who take drugs?

135. Do you remember when K just released cassettes and occasional seven inch singles?

136. Do you own *With Sympathy* and *Twitch* so that you can say you have every Ministry album?

137. Did you buy any Pavement records prior to *Slanted and Enchanted* being released?

138. Do the initials "R.V.G." mean anything to you?

139. Do you have a separate, secret box of shameful guilty pleasures, like a collection of Madonna 12"s, or really shady Black Metal albums?

140. Do you only own jazz records that were sampled by hip-hop artists?

141. Does your *Diamond Dogs* have a dick on it?

142. Does your *Body Count* have "Cop Killer"?

143. Does your copy of *12 Golden Country Greats* have the Muhammad Ali quote?

144. Do you put all your Will Oldham music under "O" (for Will Oldham), or do you have his records filed in half a dozen places (Palace, Bonnie Prince Billy, Will Oldham, Arise Therefore, Box of Chocolates, etc.)?

145. Do you file the Marshall Tucker Band under T?

146. Wait, why do you own Marshall Tucker albums?

147. Do you keep Mothers next to Zappa?

148. Do you keep everything Mike Patton's on in one spot?

149. Do you have a "well, I'll be damned, it's worth over $100" late-period mono or early-period stereo Beatles album that you bought for less than a dollar?

ACCEPTABLE REASONS TO SELL
YOUR RECORD COLLECTION

It's 1987 and CDs just came out. *Duh*.

Your "collection" consists solely of Tom Petty's discography.

The Bob Pollard portion of your collection takes up the whole garage.

You own a lot of shitty-but-rare promos, and well, you've heard of that eBay thing.

You want a Bowflex so chicks will stop throwing up when you take your shirt off.

You just know that reel-to-reel is making a comeback.

You finally realized you'll never get into John Zorn and Johnny Paycheck.

All you need is fuckin' *Led Zep 4* anyway, man.

Only two of your records have backwards messages.

You found a dead cat under your picture discs.

Your employer at the record store has started paying in vinyl. It's a wonderfully vicious cycle.

You heard on NPR that it's no longer hip to like music "that much."

You've decided once and for all to not be a loser.

To subsidize a hipper, more cred-worthy record collection.

They sound all poppy and scratchy.

Some French guy wants to give you a house for it.

It's just a buncha fuckin' jazz.

Your wife needs that closet for her shoes.

Your insurance won't cover treatment for SuperEbolaCancerAIDS.

Your wife needs a kidney. And not just any kidney, but a gold kidney with diamond inlay.

Your mail order bride is available via Paypal.

You're 60. I mean, come on. You're not going to live long enough to listen to the whole thing anyway.

Your financial advisor suggested that you move your money to CDs and *you* didn't know what he meant because you majored in bong hits and Super Mario Brothers in college.

You just realized you have a limited edition copy of *ESPN Jock Jams* on marble vinyl, signed by Stuart "Booyah" Scott, and thus no taste at all.

You realized that colored vinyl sounds really racist, and that's not what you're about.

Just because they're vinyl doesn't mean that you can melt some of them down into a sweet pair of pants. Too bad you tried anyway and now you need money to cover the extensive skin grafts.

You just found out you're deathly allergic to vinyl and hazmat suits make you look fat.

How else are you going to pay for that fancy-pants lobotomy?

You move once a month *(to a different friend's couch)*.

We all need to sacrifice in this time of war.

A spiraling descent into honesty allows you to finally admit you can't tell the difference between records and MP3s.

Because last night's episode of *Hoarders* hit a little too close to home.

Because 400 records at ten bucks a pop... that's like 100 bucks!

You're joining a religious cult that reveres 8-track recordings.

By pulling the ultimate cred move, you now refuse to listen to anything not on wax cylinders.

It's beginning to take up valuable space that could be used for a collection of stamps, coins, kidney stones or deer heads.

You need a few hundred million dollars to get this one super-rare record.

You finally realized that over-consumption of collectables for the sheer sake of collecting is a waste of your finite life force.

You don't actually listen to the most valuable ones anyway because they suck…because that's what record collecting is; it's the arbitrary assignment of value to things that are rare, and the rarest and therefore most valuable things are generally rare for one reason: because they suck. Or else they're extremely valuable because they're both rare and very good, in which case you don't listen to them because you don't want to damage them, which means they're essentially useless, which also sucks, and which also means that they're of no actual value. So you might as well sell them. And while you're at it, might as well sell the whole fucking thing, because as much as you enjoy listening to your top 500 favorite albums on vinyl, what are you, a fucking baby? You need to swaddle yourself in a sonic womb for the rest of your life? You can get money for those things and spend it on, like medical attention for starving children in Haiti, you dick bag. Why not sell it? Do you actually think you're exempt from pitching in just because you don't "work for the man" and you have enough "integrity" to "get along just fine" with "only" making like 30 grand a year, and you've "worked really hard" for a long time to compile this massive, useless collection of shit that nobody cares about and, further, doesn't actually help anybody? I dare you to look yourself in the mirror and say you're doing this for any reason other than your own self-obsessed neurotic compulsion to exclude yourself from the rest of human society by spending years of your pointless existence digging through musty crates, reading and talking about this stuff, getting high on drugs that were sold to you by a network of murderers, putting some stupid black (or color or picture) disc on a machine, listening to a bunch of guitars go "woo woo woo" and going "wow, man, I did a great job finding, buying, and subsequently owning and displaying this for the eyes and ears of all whom I elect into my circle of the lucky chosen," like it's some kind of a badge of honor that precludes you from the inescapable existential misery of life and renders you, in some small but important way, immortal. Sell it, you delusional motherfucker, because: **Cha-ching!** *Money!*

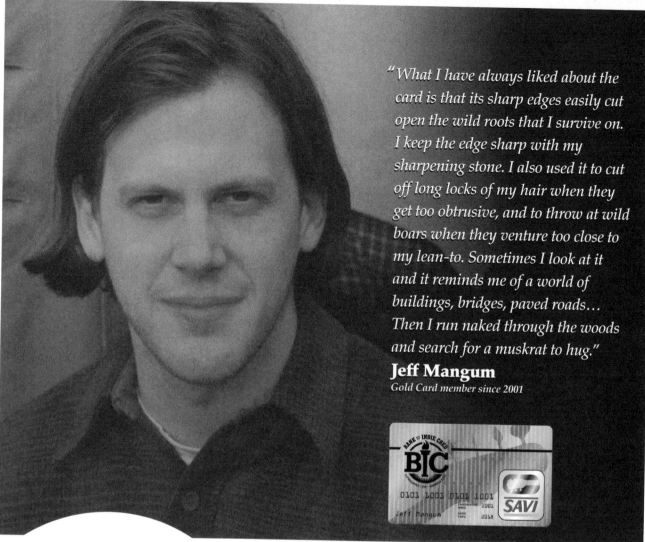

"What I have always liked about the card is that its sharp edges easily cut open the wild roots that I survive on. I keep the edge sharp with my sharpening stone. I also used it to cut off long locks of my hair when they get too obtrusive, and to throw at wild boars when they venture too close to my lean-to. Sometimes I look at it and it reminds me of a world of buildings, bridges, paved roads… Then I run naked through the woods and search for a muskrat to hug."

Jeff Mangum
Gold Card member since 2001

GET BACK TO NATURE, BUT DON'T FORGET YOUR YOU-KNOW-WHAT.

Whether it's your demanding management team, your career pressures, or the relentless chain of bloggers documenting your every breath and fumble, it may finally be time to make good on that sabbatical you've been threatening (until the time is right for that all-important cash grab). Before you go deep into the woods or off the grid, make sure you've packed your Bank of Indie Cred card in that rucksack full of granola bars and bandanas. Even off the beaten path, your cred will come in handy when bartering for a few extra lengths of jute cord or another night in an abandoned Eastern European hovel. And when all else fails, simply use the BIC card's reflective surface to shine a distress signal to the sky and our exclusive Cred Concierge Service will deliver a chauffeur to whisk you back to civilization, adoration, and your fully-restored cred rating.

DON'T PLAY A NOTE WITHOUT IT. ™

Visit **chunklet.com** today to see what **you** can acquire.

	YES	NO

150. Do you own any records on which the band neglected to designate an RPM speed, forcing you to conduct trial and error experiments where the band's sound alternates between the Melvins on Xanax and the Jonas Brothers on meth and helium? ☐ ☐

151. Have you ever bought an album based on its kick-ass cover art only to be severely disappointed when you heard the music? *(i.e., Grim Reaper, Molly Hatchet, High On Fire.)* ☐ ☐

152. Do you own the *Bleeaauurrggh* and *Son of Bleeaauurrggh* comps on Slap-A-Ham? ☐ ☐

	YES	NO

153. Did you buy multiple Big Chief records because you heard that that fat dude from the Necros was in the band? ☐ ☐

153A. If so, did you quickly give away said records? ☐ ☐

Do you own any/all of the seven inches from:
154. All three Sub Pop Single Clubs? ☐ ☐
155. Dope Guns 'n' Fucking in the Streets? ☐ ☐
156. Melvins monthly AmRep series? ☐ ☐
157. Simple Machines Working Holiday series? ☐ ☐
158. Pushead Fan Club? ☐ ☐
159. HoZac Hookup Klub? ☐ ☐

THE INDIE CRED TEST

MULTIPLE CHOICE

THE INDIE CRED TEST

NEVER BEFORE HAS THE POWER OF SELECTION BEEN SO INDISCRIMINATE.

01. Which do you own:
A. 99 Records-released *Liquid Liquid*
B. Grand Royal-released *Liquid Liquid*
C. Mo' Wax-released *Liquid Liquid*
D. Domino-released *Liquid Liquid*
E. Downloaded *Liquid Liquid*
F. No *Liquid Liquid*

02. My local record shop is best described as:
A. A Walmart-sized behemoth.
B. Mid-sized next to the Lazer Tag place.
C. Small and surrounded by taquerias and passed-out hookers.
D. In the basement of a local 65-year-old's guest house *(cash only)*.

03. What term do you use for a record?
A. Vinyl
B. Record
C. CD
D. Gramophone
E. LP
F. Wax
G. Platter

04. Seriously, how often do you clean your records?
A. Every play
B. Once a month
C. Once a year
D. When I buy them, if they're dirty; later if I notice they need it
E. Fucking never ever
F. Only when it can possibly make a huge scratch go away
G. Somewhat obsessively, like every 30 minutes or so

05. How prominent in your home is your turntable(s)?
A. In living room as a component with main entertainment system.
B. In home office/study for personal enjoyment.
C. Displayed in glass case as visual statement of your esoteric streak, not unlike a Jeff Koons vacuum cleaner encased in Plexiglas.
D. You have records, but no record player.

06. Where did you acquire most of your record collection? Was it:
A. At the time they came out, from touring bands, record stores and distro boxes.
B. Via miraculous thrift store "finds."
C. On eBay, two weeks after the bands you previously didn't like became cool.

07. When you find a "great score," who is the first person you tell?
A. Your life partner
B. Your best friend
C. An invite-only web forum

08. Have you ever foregone any of the following after a particularly monumental record binge?
A. Heat
B. Food
C. Shoes

09. Do you file Weird Al under:
A. music
B. comedy
C. mustache
D. annoying

10. How many copies of the *Merzbox* do you own?
A. None
B. 1 to 2
C. 3 to 9
D. 10 or more

11. What term/phrase best describes the majority of your record collection?
A. Foil-stamped
B. Splatter-colored
C. Hand-silkscreened
D. Mother-approved
E. Poly-bagged
F. Irresponsibly large given the current state of the economy

12. In which city have you spent the most money on records?
A. New York City
B. San Francisco
C. London
D. Chicago
E. Los Angeles
F. Noblesville, Indiana

13. How exactly do you organize your massive collection of vinyl?
A. Music type, then by artist alphabetically, then by release order
B. Year of release, regardless of music type
C. Vinyl color
D. Monetary value
E. Alphabetized through and through
F. Alphabetized by artist, then chronologically by album
G. Genre, alphabetized by artist, et. al.
H. Autobiographically (taking the *High Fidelity* route)
I. Organized by label
J. Recorded by Albini and not recorded by Albini
K. Order of importance
L. Order of how many bitches (or bubbas) have been boned while playing

14. You bought *69 Love Songs* on vinyl because:
A. You thought it would sound better than the CD.
B. It was cheaper than the CD.
C. You hoped the gripping cover art would look better in a large format.
D. Stephin Merritt gave you a blow job.

15. Your record collection has lately served as:
A. A conversation/debate starter when friends come over to drink your beer.
B. Something to stare at while the slow march toward death slowly guts your ambition and optimism.
C. A functional way to keep your cat from peeing on the shelves.
D. Collateral for your adopted son.

16. You own Insane Clown Posse's *The Great Milenko* because:
A. It's hilarious if you get stoned enough.
B. The previous occupant left all his crappy music behind and you haven't cleaned it out yet.
C. You sort of liked them when you were younger and can't bring yourself to get rid of it.
D. You were able to trade your autographed copy for one that wasn't.

17. In-store performances at record stores are:
A. Calculated but good-hearted attempts to draw in customers.
B. The only way people can wrap their heads around the notion that music can be made, then sold.
C. Distractions best left in bigger, gayer cities where they belong.
D. A sad reminder of Terence Trent D'Arby's current career.

18. Your relationship with the clerk at your favorite record is best described as:
A. Close and mutually beneficial.
B. Friendly, but rife with passive-aggressive jabs.
C. Boiling with elaborate rape fantasies.
D. Check back when (s)he is released from the hospital.

19. What letter of the alphabet is utilized most if your collection is in order by artist name?
A. M (because of all the Melvins and Morrissey)
B. J (because of all the Joy Division and The Jesus Lizard)
C. P (because of all the Pink Floyd and Portishead)
D. It's even...except you're a fucking liar. It's really S (due to all the Slayer) because you're a metal head and too afraid to be yourself.

20. Your favorite ex-record store clerk who "made it out" is:
A. Matt Groening.
B. Grant Hart.
C. Dave Grohl.
D. Danger Mouse.

21. Which label do you throw around in casual conversation the most, assuming everyone is familiar with it?
A. Thrill Jockey
B. Matador
C. Siltbreeze
D. In The Red
E. Not Not Fun
F. Sublime Frequencies
E. your own "label"

THE INDIE
CRED TEST   THE INDIE
                                             CRED TEST

FILL IN THE BLANK

COMPLETE THE FOLLOWING QUESTIONS BY FILLING IN THE BLANKS, BUT SPARK UP A BIG OL' HOG LEG FIRST.

GENERAL

01. Which record in your collection do you wish you had on the original Edison cylinder?

02. How far did you have to drive to buy your first punk record?

03. What is the one piece of music you couldn't find in the late '80s/early '90s that finally made you break down and buy a CD player?

04. Please list all labels that you buy everything on, regardless of whether you like it.

05. What was the last record you bought simply because it was limited?

06. What is the smallest pressing/edition release you own?

07. What was the first Dischord record you purchased?

08. Which label's releases are worse: post-David Hayes Lookout! Records, or Too Many Records?

09. Are *Purple Rain*, *Under a Cherry Moon*, *Batman*, and *Graffiti Bridge* Prince albums or soundtracks?

MONEY

10. What's the most you've ever dropped in one day on records?

11. How much money have you spent on unfinished pine shelving?

12. What is the *most* you have paid for a valuable record?

13. What is the *least* you have paid for a valuable record?

AMOUNT

14. How many nights a month do you have wet dreams about finding rare records?

15. How many records do you buy in a month?

16. How many of the records do you own that include you on the thanks list?

17. How many records do you own from countries that only recently developed vinyl pressing technology?

18. How many records have you bought with the intent of using the material on them to make other records?

19. How many records did you buy after seeing the band on *120 Minutes*?

20. How many rooms are occupied by your music collection?

21. How many iterations of the *Nuggets* box sets do you own? No, really.

22. In the last 18 months, roughly how many times have you made positive references to the b-side of Agnostic Front's "My War"?

23. How many times have you quoted the whole Neil Young spiel about CDs being the equivalent of "pornography for the ears"?

24. How many Lookout! releases do you own that were released after 1993?

25. How many different recordings of "Louie Louie" do you own?

26. Originals vs. reissues? Which one do you play and why?

How many different singles do you own by:

27. Blues Explosion?............ ☐
28. Boyracer?...................... ☐
29. Braid?........................... ☐
30. Dingleberry Bob and the Underground Apple Orchard? .... ☐
31. Fucked Up?.................... ☐
32. Frankie Goes To Hollywood?................. ☐
33. Chris Gaines?................. ☐
34. Harvey Milk? .... ☐
35. J Church?...................... ☐
36. Julian Lennon? .... ☐

37. Man...or Astro-Man? ..... ☐
38. Melt Banana?................. ☐
39. Melvins?........................ ☐
40. Mr. Big? .... ☐
41. The Wonder Stuff?......... ☐
42. Rocket from the Crypt?.. ☐
43. Shellac? .... ☐
44. Stereolab?..................... ☐
45. Steve Stevens Atomic Playboys? .... ☐
46. Unsane?........................ ☐

How many of the following do you own:

47. Bootleg LPs?............ [ ]
48. Flexi-discs?............. [ ]
49. Cassingles? .... [ ]
50. Digital cassettes?..... [ ]
51. MP3 CDs? .... [ ]
52. Test pressings?......... [ ]

53. "Suitcase" collections? .... [ ]
54. "White label" pressings? *(and have no idea what they are or who they're by)* .. [ ]
55. Ironic '50s era instructional records?...... [ ]
56. Original-pressing LPs released on United Artists?......................... [ ]

PERCENTAGE & RATIO

57. Percentage wise, how much of your music collection consists of NPR recommendations? [ ] %
58. Percentage wise, how much of your music collection consists of drunken, talkative, overly-friendly-dude-by-the-pool-table recommendations? [ ] %
59. Percentage wise, how much of your music collection consists of compilations? [ ] %
60. What is the percentage of your novelty/ironic vinyl purchases? [ ] %
61. What percentage of your records have never met the needle? [ ] %
62. What is your LP to 7" ratio? [ ] :
63. What is your CD to vinyl ratio? [ ] :
64. What is your Indie to Major label ratio? [ ] :
65. How much of your earnings (%) do you blow frivolously on buying music? [ ] %

WHEN

66. When did you first receive an Ajax or Parasol mail order catalog? [MONTH] [YEAR]
67. When did you download your first MP3 (legally or otherwise)? [MONTH] [YEAR]
68. When was the last time you said your local record store sucks? [MONTH] [YEAR]
69. When did you stop your membership with the Sub Pop Singles Club? [MONTH] [YEAR]
70. When did you figure out you were playing your Dazzling Killmen singles at the wrong speed? [MONTH] [YEAR]
71. When was the last time you prowled around eBay looking to score deals on records you don't need? [MONTH] [YEAR]
72. When did you stop buying records that were classified as post-hardcore? [MONTH] [YEAR]
73. When did you stop buying records on Merge? [MONTH] [YEAR]
74. When did you realize you were sitting on enough records (you never listen to) to pay rent for two months? [MONTH] [YEAR]
75. When did your first relationship end because of your music addiction? [MONTH] [YEAR]
76. When did you realize that you take music way too seriously? [MONTH] [YEAR]

CHECK ALL THAT APPLY

01. Do you own:

- [ ] The *Gremlins* storybook/record sets
- [ ] Any of the Skin Graft comic book/record sets
- [ ] Anything by CCR or Bob Seger's old garage rock bands
- [ ] An original 13th Floor Elevators record on International Artists
- [ ] The Chrome six-LP box set
- [ ] Dinosaur records without the "Jr."

- [ ] Any '80s era Jandek records
- [ ] All the Tortoise 12"s
- [ ] That one single by Chunk
- [ ] Boys II Men's "End of the Road" 7"
- [ ] Lou Rawls' *Here Comes Garfield* LP
- [ ] A numbered *White Album*
- [ ] An original copy of *Tigermilk*

- [ ] A copy of Elvis' *Blue Hawaii* that's not on blue vinyl
- [ ] Any Daniel Johnston Stress cassettes
- [ ] A Subterranean Pop compilation tape
- [ ] The single by (the good) L-Seven
- [ ] Anything by (the good) Fuel
- [ ] An original copy of *Propeller* on LP *If yes, will you sell it to me?*

TOTAL MONETARY VALUE OF YOUR COLLECTION

PLEASE ATTACH NOTARIZED APPRAISAL, AFFIDAVIT OR PERSONAL VOUCHER.
ALSO INCLUDE AVERAGE RECORD VALUE AND ANY RELEVANT PHOTOGRAPHS.

SUBMIT WITH FINISHED APPLICATION.

FORM 583-AIJ

SECTION IV

UNLOADING EVEN MORE IRONY UPON THE SHELVES:

ARTS & ENTERTAINMENT

CHAPTER 15

YE OLDE PICTURE SHOWS & WHATNOT

OH, MOTION PICTURES! IS THERE any emotion you *can't* make us experience and then pathetically weep over? Whether you're a comedy buff, a horror nerd, a drama fruit or just one of those sad-sacks who inexplicably buys every DVD offered by K-Mart, movies continue to sap humankind's productivity and intellectual capacity at a *blockbuster* pace. Plus, talkies killed Vaudeville. Think about that the next time you're watching your pirated VHS copy of *Dunston Checks In 2: Statutory Ape.* And pass the popcorn, dammit.

YES/NO

COMPLETE THE FOLLOWING QUESTIONS WITH A YES/NO ANSWER OR SUFFER THE CONSEQUENCES.

YES   NO

01. Have you ever used the word "dénouement" in conversation? Has anybody punched you in the face for that yet? ☐ ☐

02. Have you ever watched a DVD on 1.5x speed so you'd have more time to watch another? ☐ ☐

03. Have you ever hosted a silent movie night? ☐ ☐

04. How about a *Silent Night, Deadly Night* movie night? ☐ ☐

05. On a scale of 1 to 10, how impressive is your Laserdisc collection? *(Trick question! By definition, every Laserdisc collection is unimpressive.)*

    01 02 03 04 05 06 07 08 09 10

06. Do you collect vinyl from horror film soundtracks, other than those of Goblin or John Carpenter? ☐ ☐

07. Has your klezmer-style Foghat cover band ever attempted to compose a silent film score? ☐ ☐

08. Were some members of your band confused because they didn't know how to make silent music? ☐ ☐

09. Can you understand foreign films without subtitles? How about with subtitles? How about without foreigners? ☐ ☐

10. Have you ever participated in a Shakespeare Festival? If yes, give me a minute to finish laughing at you. ☐ ☐

11. Are you more likely to watch a Razzie winner than an Oscar winner because other people's success, secretly, makes you jealous enough to kill? ☐ ☐

12. Have any of your videos gone viral? ☐ ☐

13. Have any of your virals gone video? ☐ ☐

14. Did you protest stark naked in front of your local cable provider, eating your own poop and crying, until they agreed to carry the Independent Film Channel? ☐ ☐

15. Did you really only want it for *The Henry Rollins Show* and to casually make it known in conversations that you have IFC, and that, like, the Sundance Channel is soooo much better? ☐ ☐

YOUR GODAWFUL OPINION

16. Do you cheer when there's a big explosion in a movie? ☐ ☐

17. Do you think the extra scene that sometimes follows credits should come before so you don't have to do all that reading/waiting? ☐ ☐

YES   NO

18. Do you find soundtracks in movies too distracting? What about plot and dialogue? ☐ ☐

19. Do you think movies ruin the book? ☐ ☐

19A. Do you think books should get off their high horse and suck it? ☐ ☐

20. Is the movie sometimes better than the book but you're too scared to admit it? ☐ ☐

21. Do you think zombies in today's horror movies are just too fast? Have you ever argued that they are not actually real zombies because of this? ☐ ☐

22. Has your mom stopped complaining about those black bars taking up the screen? ☐ ☐

23. Do you decry the growth of Landmark Theaters as the corporatization of independent cinema? ☐ ☐

24. Do you decry the success of *Napoleon Dynamite* as the independentization of corporate cinema? ☐ ☐

25. Did you like the Moldy Peaches before *Juno* came out? ☐ ☐

26. Why the hell would you like the Moldy Peaches? ☐ ☐

27. Have you ever killed and eaten another human being because they disrespected William Shatner's acting chops? ☐ ☐

FILM-SPECIFIC

28. Do you refuse to watch *Timecop* unless it is a 70mm print? ☐ ☐

29. Do you only watch *Nosferatu* with a fresh group of people each time so you can provide commentary on what was going on in Klaus Kinski's personal life in each scene, according to Werner Herzog's memoirs? ☐ ☐

30. Do you like to inform people that the *Saving Private Ryan* cinematographer also filmed *Cool as Ice*? ☐ ☐

31. Have you seen all five versions of *Blade Runner*? ☐ ☐

32. Did you coin the term "Fight Club ending"? *Bullshit! We did.* ☐ ☐

33. Do you maintain that Don "the Dragon" Wilson's *Bloodfist III: Forced to Fight* is, in essence, a scathing cinematic critique of the rampant injustices of the US prison system, in the face of the fact that it's really just a poorly choreographed piece-of-shit karate movie? ☐ ☐

		YES	NO
34.	Do you still own a LaserDisc player because it's perfect for the opening scene of *Ernest Saves Christmas*?	☐	☐
35.	How many times did you vomit during *Garden State*?	☐	☐
36.	Do you lie through your fucking teeth and tell people that *Apocalypse Now Redux* is the only way to experience the film?	☐	☐
37.	Do you almost involuntarily blurt *"Blue Velvet* was the perfect allegory for the Reagan years" any time you hear the name of the 40th president of the United States?	☐	☐
38.	Do you ironically collect Jar Jar Binks merchandise?	☐	☐
39.	Do you lie to yourself about liking *The Darjeeling Limited* because you don't want to taint your Wes Anderson collection?	☐	☐
40.	Has *Rocky* come full circle?	☐	☐
41.	Do you still break out the phrase "It'd be a lot cooler if you did"?	☐	☐
42.	Do you sincerely maintain that the 219-minute *Heaven's Gate* is *the* greatest film that will ever be made by virtue of the fact that it was too political for cineplex audiences because "Hel-loooo, it was a narrative of government-sanctioned killing of settlers, in a 'western' format!"?	☐	☐
43.	If somebody had previously professed a fondness for *Forrest Gump, Field of Dreams,* or *Dances with Wolves,* would you piss on them if they were on fire?	☐	☐
44.	Was watching *Twin Peaks: Fire Walk with Me* a low point in your life?	☐	☐
45.	Was watching *Big Top Pee-wee* an even lower point in your life?	☐	☐
46.	Was watching *Ninja III: The Domination* a high point in your life? *Mine too!*	☐	☐
47.	Do images from *Red Sonja* still find their way into your "spank bank"?	☐	☐
48.	Did images from *Mask* ever find their way into your "spank bank"?	☐	☐
49.	Dude, do you realize how *twisted* that is?!	☐	☐
50.	Do you claim that copy of *9 Songs* you own is "only for the music"?	☐	☐
51.	While discussing the best punk rock 'n' roll narrative films at a keg-based soirée, have you uttered this conversation killer? "I was going to say *Salt of the Earth,* with its literal do-it-yourself credo of blacklisted artists enduring draconian peril to tell the all-too-true-story of striking Mexican-American miners (y'know, real life and death stuff), but I guess it wouldn't qualify if there's a soundtrack rubric, since it wasn't until the next year, 1955, that *The Blackboard Jungle* featured your bourgeois electric guitar music."		

So yeah, I'd concur that *Rock 'n' Roll High School, Suburbia,* and *Ladies and Gentlemen, The Fabulous Stains* should make any Top Ten list."

DIRECTOR-SPECIFIC

		YES	NO
52.	Is all of your film cred due to the fact that you made sure your friends noticed the horror movies by Lucio Fulci and Dario Argento on your shelf 20 years ago?	☐	☐
53.	Do you think Darren Aronofsky is ticklish?	☐	☐
54.	When people say Godard, do you sometimes mistake him for Truffaut?	☐	☐
55.	Do you ever think to yourself, "Why, George Romero? Why?"	☐	☐
56.	Did Wes Anderson take a cred hit when he made that American Express commercial?	☐	☐
57.	Have you used the term "Felliniesque" without ever having seen a Fellini movie?	☐	☐
58.	Have you ever dressed up like a Wes Anderson character for Halloween?	☐	☐
59.	And by "Halloween" do you mean "every day of the year"?	☐	☐
60.	Do you show older Woody Allen films to friends just so you can say, "How could anyone not see the Soon-Yi thing coming?"	☐	☐
61.	Are you afraid to say the name "Michael Moore" because others might think you're a commie?	☐	☐
62.	Do you honestly think that if the movies Martin Scorsese made in the second half of his career had been the movies he made in the first half of his career, he'd be a "living legend"?	☐	☐
63.	Do you keep watching Todd Haynes movies even though you really wish you could have those two hours of your life back every time you do?	☐	☐
64.	Do you refuse to believe that Kevin Smith will ever make a movie better than *Chasing Amy*?	☐	☐
65.	Whenever you're at the beach, Hooters, or wherever large breasted women are in abundance, do you jump at the chance to say, "Feels like we're in a Russ Meyer film"?	☐	☐
66.	Have you claimed to love David Lynch and then realize you meant George Lynch?	☐	☐

Have you recommended more than two films by any of the following directors to someone:

		YES	NO
67.	Harmony Korine?	☐	☐
68.	Kelly Reichardt?	☐	☐
69.	Nick Cassavetes?	☐	☐
70.	Ed Wood?	☐	☐
71.	Miranda July?	☐	☐
72.	Larry Clark?	☐	☐
73.	Andrew Bujalski?	☐	☐
74.	Michael Bay?	☐	☐

MULTIPLE CHOICE

THE INDIE
CRED TEST

THE INDIE
CRED TEST

WELL?

01. Bernard Herrmann's best score was:
A. *Citizen Kane.*
B. *Vertigo.*
C. *Psycho.*
D. *Taxi Driver.*
E. *License to Drive.* Wait, did he do that one?

02. The most critically underrated actor of the 20th century was:
A. Yahoo Serious.
B. Whoopi Goldberg.
C. Jean-Claude Van Damme.
D. Keenan Ivory Wayans.

03. My adolescent coming-of-age story is best represented by the film:
A. *Sixteen Candles.*
B. *Leaving Las Vegas.*
C. *Debbie Does Dallas.*
D. *Hotel Rwanda.*

04. Four-hour silent documentaries about gay, French ballet dancers:
A. Got a tissue?
B. Got a pillow?
C. Got a handgun?
D. Gotta get outta here!

05. Finish this Jean-Luc Godard quote, "Cinema is truth _____"
A. and books are liars!
B. at twenty four frames per second.
C. and you can't handle the truth!

06. The real comic genius in *Brewster's Millions* was:
A. Richard Pryor.
B. John Candy.
C. Yakov Smirnoff.
D. the lack of a sequel.

07. Scorsese's best non-*Raging Bull* '80s film was:
A. *The King of Comedy.*
B. *After Hours.*
C. *The Color of Money.*
D. *The Last Temptation of Christ.*
E. *Days of Thunder.*

08. Sneaking *Days of Thunder* onto that list of Scorsese films was:
A. Horrifying until I realized it was just a stupid joke.
B. Funny until I realized that it's basically the same movie as *The Color of Money*, which makes me reconsider how much I like Scorsese.
C. Just plain fucking stupid, like everything else in *Chunklet.*

09. Which film totally didn't deserve a Criterion Collection™ release on DVD?
A. *Bottle Rocket* by Wes Anderson
B. *Two-Lane Blacktop* by Monte Hellman
C. *Gomorrah* by Matteo Garrone
D. *Koko: A Talking Gorilla* by Barbet Schroeder
E. *Godzilla vs. Mechagodzilla* by Jun Fukuda

10. Whose films would be the least fun to have worked on?
A. Alfred Hitchcock
B. Lars von Trier
C. Werner Herzog
D. Darren Aronofsky
E. Steven Seagal

11. After watching the *Twilight* series, I chose:
A. Team Edward.
B. Team Jacob.
C. to breakdance on a land mine.

12. I believe that what's inside the *Pulp Fiction* briefcase is:
A. a treasure map to One-Eyed Willie's.
B. a big stack of *Hustlers.*
C. a dead raver.
D. a big pile of radioactive kangaroo fetuses.
E. that same shit that was in the trunk of that car in *Repo Man.*

13. Which of the following films has not been optioned for a Hollywood remake?
A. *Oldboy* (dir. Chan-wook Park)
B. *Akira* (dir. Katsuhiro Otomo)
C. *The Host* (dir. Bong Joon-ho)
D. *Der Baader Meinhof Komplex* (dir. Uli Edel)
E. *Analnauts 12: Deep Space Probing* (dir. Peter Pullen)

14. Which of the following composers did *not* appear on a Stanley Kubrick soundtrack?
A. Iannis Xenakis
B. Edward Elgar
C. György Ligeti
D. Duke Ellington
E. Rob Zombie

15. Best pick for an ironic movie night:
A. *Plan 9 from Outer Space*
B. *No Holds Barred*
C. *The Karate Kid, Part III*
D. *Xanadu*
E. *The Warriors*
F. *Gigli*
G. *Battlefield Earth*
H. *Cop and a Half*
I. *Rhinestone*

16. Rank these Stanley Kubrick films in order of best to worst:

____ *The Killing*
____ *Paths of Glory*
____ *Spartacus*
____ *Lolita*
____ *Dr. Strangelove*
____ *2001: A Space Odyssey*
____ *A Clockwork Orange*
____ *Barry Lyndon*
____ *The Shining*
____ *Full Metal Jacket*
____ *Eyes Wide Shut*
____ *Teenage Mutant Ninja Turtles 2: The Secret of the Ooze*

FILL IN THE BLANK

YA GOTTA, Y'KNOW, LIKE QUESTION THE ANSWERS, MAN.

01. How many movies are currently in your Netflix queue because you "should" watch them, not because you "want to"?

01A. Why in God's name do you *still* have a Netflix account?

02. How many of the movies that you own are screener copies?

03. How often has this gotten you blown?

04. Which character in *High Fidelity* do you most relate to?

05. Which movie have you jacked off to more, *Porky's* or *Fast Times at Ridgemont High*?

06. Define the term *mise-en-scène* as it relates to the underpinnings of the 1996 masterpiece *Kazaam* and any and all subsequent ramifications it had upon Shaquille O'Neal's ovation-worthy performance therein.

07. Who is a better freestyle rapper, Boris Karloff or Bela Lugosi?

08. Name three Hitchcock cameos in his films. Wait, never mind, don't.

09. Better Frank Stallone soundtrack: *Staying Alive* or *Rocky III*?

10. Name something that Jim J. Bullock worked on that was not *Hollywood Squares* or a cock.

11. Better chest hair: Burt Reynolds or Chewbacca?

12. How many times, while on the pot, have you said, "You know who'd make a real good Gargamel if they ever do a Smurfs movie?"

13. When did you finally admit your man-crush on Brian Dennehy?

14. When was the last time you snuck food/drinks into a theater?

15. When was the last time you snuck a bottle of wine into the theater? Was it inside you? Was it inside your date?

16. When was the last time you snuck a three-foot bong full of hash into a theatre?

17. Thelma or Louise, which one would you bang and why?

18. What book do you wish they'd make into a movie so you won't have to read it?

19. What is Rosebud?

20. What is your favorite line from *The Big Lebowski*?

MOVIE CHECKLIST

I. Fill in the blank grab bag

01. To date, the most unbelievable exclusion from the Criterion Collection is:
_____

02. The exact date that video became an acceptable medium to use was ___/___/_____ .

03. In ten words or less, "mise-en-scène" means what exactly?
_____
_____
_____
_____

04. The *New Yorker* film critic who followed Warren Beatty out to Hollywood (only to return to New York City with tail between legs) was:
_____

05. Which 1975 film that defined "summer blockbuster" was nearly cancelled mid-shoot by the studio cost and schedule overruns?
_____

06. When shooting *Finian's Rainbow* on the Warner lot, Francis Coppola mentored a young film student from USC named:
_____

07. The director who most consistently made acting cameos in his own films was:
_____

08. What Charlie Chaplin film was the *Fahrenheit 911* of its time. *(Hint: pre-WW II Europe.)*
_____

09. Steven Soderberg collaborated with what indie-rock institution on 2004's *Bubble*?
_____

10. In *Sullivan's Travels* (1942), what was the name of the rabble-rousing film the hero sought to make at the start of the picture? *(Hint: The Coen Brothers actually used this as the title of one of their own films.)*
_____

II. Movie Match: Match each work with its director

A. *THX-1138* .... ☐   01. Peckinpah
B. *Mean Streets* ...... ☐   02. Spielberg
C. *Killer's Kiss* ...... ☐   03. Hughes (Howard)
D. *Shadows* .... ☐   04. Bertolucci
E. *Christmas in July* .. ☐   05. De Palma
F. *Triumph of the Will* .. ☐   06. Lucas
G. *Scarface (1983)* .... ☐   07. Cassavetes
H. *The Exorcist* ...... ☐   08. Kubrick
I. *Dogville* .... ☐   09. Tarantino
J. *Rashomon* .... ☐   10. Kurosawa
K. *Hell's Angels* ...... ☐   11. Bigelow
L. *The Breakfast Club* .. ☐   12. Anger
M. *The Sugarland Express* .. ☐   13. Sturges
N. *The Conversation* .... ☐   14. von Trier
O. *Intolerance* ...... ☐   15. Riefenstahl
P. *Modern Times* ...... ☐   16. Friedkin
Q. *The Leopard* ...... ☐   17. Hughes (John)
R. *Last Tango in Paris* .. ☐   18. Coppola
S. *It's A Wonderful Life* .. ☐   19. Griffith
T. *The Magnificent Ambersons* .. ☐   20. Scorsese
U. *The Hurt Locker* .... ☐   21. Chaplin
V. *Kustom Kar Kommandos* .. ☐   22. Visconti
W. *Blue Collar* ...... ☐   23. Mazursky
X. *The Killer Elite* .... ☐   24. Schrader
Y. *Bob & Carol & Ted & Alice* .. ☐   25. Welles
Z. *Reservoir Dogs* .... ☐   26. Capra

Answers:
A-6, B-20, C-8, D-7, E-13, F-15, G-5, H-16, I-14, J-10, K-3,
L-17, M-2, N-18, O-19, P-21, Q-22, R-4, S-26, T-25, U-11,
V-12, W-24, X-1, Y-23, Z-9

III. Please check boxes next to the following items to indicate ownership and/or willingness to trade:

Item	HAVE	LOOKING FOR	WILLING TO TRADE
Flipside video collections 1 and 2	○ HAVE	○ LOOKING FOR	○ WILLING TO TRADE
Butthole Surfers Family Style Barbeque	○ HAVE	○ LOOKING FOR	○ WILLING TO TRADE
The T.A.M.I. Show	○ HAVE	○ LOOKING FOR	○ WILLING TO TRADE
SST: The Tour (1985)	○ HAVE	○ LOOKING FOR	○ WILLING TO TRADE
Minutemen "Corndogs" documentary	○ HAVE	○ LOOKING FOR	○ WILLING TO TRADE
PiL- Tom Snyder Tomorrow interview with Lydon/Levene	○ HAVE	○ LOOKING FOR	○ WILLING TO TRADE
American Bandstand appearance by PiL	○ HAVE	○ LOOKING FOR	○ WILLING TO TRADE
Velvet Underground films *(including early '66 Warhol Factory rehearsal)*	○ HAVE	○ LOOKING FOR	○ WILLING TO TRADE
Sex Pistols on Bill Grundy show	○ HAVE	○ LOOKING FOR	○ WILLING TO TRADE
Bill Hicks: It's Just A Ride	○ HAVE	○ LOOKING FOR	○ WILLING TO TRADE
The Blank Generation	○ HAVE	○ LOOKING FOR	○ WILLING TO TRADE
Fred Armisen's tape from SXSW	○ HAVE	○ LOOKING FOR	○ WILLING TO TRADE
The Decline of Western Civilization III	○ HAVE	○ LOOKING FOR	○ WILLING TO TRADE
Big Black and Sonic Youth, live '85	○ HAVE	○ LOOKING FOR	○ WILLING TO TRADE
Dope, Guns & Fucking Up Your Video Deck (any volume)	○ HAVE	○ LOOKING FOR	○ WILLING TO TRADE
The Frogs "Toy Porno"	○ HAVE	○ LOOKING FOR	○ WILLING TO TRADE
Hüsker Dü/Replacements at 7th St. Entry, Minneapolis, Sept. '81	○ HAVE	○ LOOKING FOR	○ WILLING TO TRADE
Lenny Bruce black and white club performance footage, '65	○ HAVE	○ LOOKING FOR	○ WILLING TO TRADE
"The Stones In The Park" July 1969 Stones in Hyde Park tribute to Brian Jones *(first performance by Mick Taylor with the Stones)*	○ HAVE	○ LOOKING FOR	○ WILLING TO TRADE
"Metallica Drummer"	○ HAVE	○ LOOKING FOR	○ WILLING TO TRADE
Steve Vai "Pussy Candle"	○ HAVE	○ LOOKING FOR	○ WILLING TO TRADE
The Last Waltz	○ HAVE	○ LOOKING FOR	○ WILLING TO TRADE
Suburbia	○ HAVE	○ LOOKING FOR	○ WILLING TO TRADE
Repo Man	○ HAVE	○ LOOKING FOR	○ WILLING TO TRADE
Urgh! A Music War	○ HAVE	○ LOOKING FOR	○ WILLING TO TRADE
Amadeus	○ HAVE	○ LOOKING FOR	○ WILLING TO TRADE
Almost Famous	○ HAVE	○ LOOKING FOR	○ WILLING TO TRADE

IV. Please rate the following movies on a scale of one (not at all) to ten (completely) as to how accurately they portray the subculture each is about:

Movie	01	02	03	04	05	06	07	08	09	10
I Am Trying to Break Your Heart	○	○	○	○	○	○	○	○	○	○
Backbeat	○	○	○	○	○	○	○	○	○	○
Hedwig and the Angry Inch	○	○	○	○	○	○	○	○	○	○
That Thing You Do!	○	○	○	○	○	○	○	○	○	○
This Is Spinal Tap	○	○	○	○	○	○	○	○	○	○
The Rutles: All You Need Is Cash	○	○	○	○	○	○	○	○	○	○
1991: The Year Punk Broke	○	○	○	○	○	○	○	○	○	○
Lovedolls Superstar	○	○	○	○	○	○	○	○	○	○
Rock 'n' Roll High School	○	○	○	○	○	○	○	○	○	○
Making Friends Is Easy	○	○	○	○	○	○	○	○	○	○
The Decline Of Western Civilization (parts one and two)	○	○	○	○	○	○	○	○	○	○
Anvil! The Story Of Anvil	○	○	○	○	○	○	○	○	○	○
The Jazz Singer (1927)	○	○	○	○	○	○	○	○	○	○
A Mighty Wind	○	○	○	○	○	○	○	○	○	○
The Runaways	○	○	○	○	○	○	○	○	○	○
Jesus Christ Superstar	○	○	○	○	○	○	○	○	○	○
8 Mile	○	○	○	○	○	○	○	○	○	○
Walk the Line	○	○	○	○	○	○	○	○	○	○
Crazy Heart	○	○	○	○	○	○	○	○	○	○
A Star Is Born	○	○	○	○	○	○	○	○	○	○
The Last Waltz	○	○	○	○	○	○	○	○	○	○
Suburbia	○	○	○	○	○	○	○	○	○	○
Repo Man	○	○	○	○	○	○	○	○	○	○
Urgh! A Music War	○	○	○	○	○	○	○	○	○	○
Amadeus	○	○	○	○	○	○	○	○	○	○
Almost Famous	○	○	○	○	○	○	○	○	○	○

CHAPTER 16

BIBLIOPHILIACS & READERASTS

LETTERS MAKE WORDS. Words make sentences. Sentences make paragraphs. Paragraphs make chapters. Chapters make books. Books make nerds. Nerds make money. Therefore, books are money. So if you want money, you need to be knowing about the books. Whether you prefer the selected works of Geoffrey Chaucer or the crude scribblings of Larry the Cable Guy, your brain is only as badass as what it reads. Now I know America tends to exercise it's freedom to NOT read books, but surely most of you have read at least part of a book at some point in your life, even if it was by accident. So quick, take this test on books before President Palin makes 'em illegal.

YES/NO

THE INDIE CRED TEST   THE INDIE CRED TEST

COMPLETE THE FOLLOWING QUESTIONS WITH A YES/NO ANSWER. THIS IS SERIOUS.

READING

YES NO

01. Books. Do you read them? *(This one doesn't count.)* ☐ ☐

02. Do you eat them? *(This one does.)* ☐ ☐

03. Have people ever gotten angry with you for reading? ☐ ☐

04. Do you consider hardbacks the "vinyl" of literature? ☐ ☐

05. Does your literary intake mainly consist of content from billboards and medicine labels? ☐ ☐

06. Are you impressed when modern works of fiction have footnotes? ☐ ☐

06A. Conversely, are you frightened and confused when they have endnotes? ☐ ☐

07. Have you ever been mentioned in a book? ☐ ☐

08. Was it for something you were actually proud of? ☐ ☐

09. Do you only own first-edition hardcovers? ☐ ☐

09A. Are you aware of how pretentious this is? ☐ ☐

10. Do books take up more space in your house than furniture? ☐ ☐

11. Is the ratio of books you own to books you've read greater than 3:1? ☐ ☐

11A. Does your ratio improve significantly if you include comic books in this equation? ☐ ☐

12. Do you read literature in languages besides English? ☐ ☐

12A. If yes, do you make sure people see you doing so? ☐ ☐

12B. If yes and you live in Alabama, is Tim "Speak English or Die" James aware of this? ☐ ☐

13. Do you recognize that poetry isn't *writing* any more than shuffling off to the bathroom to take a dump during the commercials is running a marathon? ☐ ☐

14. Have you ever gotten angry with someone for criticizing or misinterpreting a book you only pretend to have read? *(Or did you only get pretend-mad?)* ☐ ☐

15. Are you one of the 273 Americans who still actively frequent libraries? *(University libraries don't count.)* ☐ ☐

YES NO

16. Do you have an MFA? Is that a Master of Fine Arts or Mutha Fuckin' Asshole? ☐ ☐

17. Do you consider yourself and your friends to be well-read intellectual types, even though you secretly only read the sports section and titty mags? ☐ ☐

18. Do you still read your mail order record catalogs from the '80s and '90s? ☐ ☐

19. Do you bemoan the proliferation of Kindles, even though you haven't read a whole book in over a year? ☐ ☐

20. Do you think the Kindle is awesome because it gives you hundreds of books at your fingertips, even though you haven't finished a book in five years? ☐ ☐

21. When reading graphic novels, do you crouch and shield the pages in shame? It's not like you're reading *The Nine Doors to the Kingdom of Shadows* during the Inquisition, y'know. ☐ ☐

22. Do you tease people who like "short fiction"? ☐ ☐

23. Do you own books that discuss music you've never heard, like Djalu Gurruwiwi's *The Didgeridoo Phenomenon*? ☐ ☐

24. Do you have books stashed away in numerous locations, "just in case"? ☐ ☐

24A. Is *Fahrenheit 451* one of them? ☐ ☐

25. Have you ever purchased a hard copy and an audio book of the same release? ☐ ☐

25A. If so, did you at least do it a few minutes apart, wearing a fake mustache? ☐ ☐

26. Do you still resist the thought that graphic novels can be "literature"? ☐ ☐

27. Do you read anything by authors who weren't drunks, junkies, or convicts? ☐ ☐

28. Do you refer to any books as "canonical"? ☐ ☐

29. Have you ever described a book by taking the last name of another author and adding "-esque" as a suffix? ☐ ☐

30. Has a book ever been dedicated to you? ☐ ☐

30A. Did you blow the author or something? ☐ ☐

31. Do you have the scrote to read this book all the way through? ☐ ☐

32. Will that make you feel "connected" to the world of underground music and self-conscious hipster humor? ☐ ☐

YES   NO

33. Is a book something that requires a battery? ☐ ☐

34. Do you think introducing zombies into classic literature is an abomination? ☐ ☐

WRITING

35. Do you claim to be a poet or writer? ☐ ☐

35A. If so, do you know what the word "revision" means? ☐ ☐

36. Seriously, we'll ask this *one more fucking time.* Do you know what the word "revision" means? ☐ ☐

37. Do you refer to yourself as a "writer" because of your blog, Tumblr, or Twitter? ☐ ☐

38. Would you half-heartedly attempt suicide just so someone would read your shitty novel? ☐ ☐

39. Have you ever considered self-publishing a book and planting it in bookstores? ☐ ☐

40. Would you ghostwrite a book if it were for someone you admired? ☐ ☐

40A. How about for someone you wanted to bone? ☐ ☐

40B. How about for Henry Rollins? ☐ ☐

41. Have you ever actually dropped the cash for access to the OED? ☐ ☐

41A. Have you ever masturbated to the updates? *(Fucking liar.)* ☐ ☐

42. Would you describe your writing as "stream of consciousness" even though trying to read anyone else's "stream of consciousness" writing makes you want to pull your brains out through your ears? ☐ ☐

42A. Shouldn't that tell you something? ☐ ☐

43. Do you blog with the misguided intention of getting a book deal? ☐ ☐

43A. How about Twitter? ☐ ☐

PRESENTATION

44. Do you hold books a certain way on the train so people can see the cover and know what you're reading? ☐ ☐

44A. Would you still do that when reading something with a title like *An Oral History of Anal* by Richard Corngood? ☐ ☐

45. Do you take books with you to read at the bar? ☐ ☐

45A. If so, do you choose your books in the same meticulous way you choose a band shirt to wear to a show? ☐ ☐

46. Did you buy a special shelf for all your 33 1/3 Series books? ☐ ☐

YES   NO

46A. Does it fit in one hand? ☐ ☐

47. Do you keep a selection of punk rock books on your shelf to impress the people who come to your house to drink free beer and then make fun of you after they leave? ☐ ☐

48. When you see someone else's book collection, do you perform a mental calculation about how many authors are gay, women, people of color, etc.? ☐ ☐

48A. Why the hell do you do that? ☐ ☐

49. Have you ever looked over someone's book collection and felt more sexually attracted to them? *(No. The answer is no.)* ☐

BUYING/SELLING

50. Do you frown on people who shop for books at Barnes & Noble, etc.? ☐ ☐

51. Do you order from Amazon even though you live next door to a pretty decent bookstore? ☐ ☐

52. Do your local used bookstore employees know you by name, or do they just yell "Stop, thief!"? ☐ ☐

53. Have you considered selling rare or valuable books for drinking/drug money? ☐ ☐

54. Does your local indie bookseller hold stuff for you, without you calling ahead, just knowing that you'll want it? ☐ ☐

55. Do you know the face of "the book guy" at the garage sales and thrift stores in your area? ☐ ☐

55A. Are you "the book guy"? ☐ ☐

55B. Did you bang "the book guy" in an effort to gain some of his literary knowledge through some sort of way-scientific osmosis process? ☐ ☐

56. Do you have a comics "subscription" at the local comic shop? ☐ ☐

56A. Do you still show up every Wednesday, even though you do have a subscription, just in case you missed ordering something *really* important like *Spawn Marries Archie*? ☐ ☐

57. Are there any books that you always buy if you find them used, even though you have numerous copies already? ☐ ☐

57A. Is you crazy? ☐ ☐

58. Did you buy this book you're now holding? ☐ ☐

58A. If not, did you barter for it? ☐ ☐

58B. Was it exchanged for a six-pack of Olympia and/or a DVD of the Fugazi documentary *Instrument*? ☐ ☐

59. Do you use local bookstores like they're showrooms for Amazon? ☐ ☐

YES NO

60. Have you ever decided not to buy a book in a store because you know you can find it for, like, a dollar cheaper online? ☐ ☐

60A. Do you know you're part of the problem? ☐ ☐

AUTHOR-SPECIFIC

61. Have you ever spent time at a party talking to people about the mysteries of J. D. Salinger's or Thomas Pynchon's semi-hidden identities? ☐ ☐

62. Do you know what people are talking about when they say something is Richard Brautigan-esque? ☐ ☐

63. Have you ever read a work by Shakespeare, Melville, or Hawthorne when it wasn't assigned in a college class *(i.e., for "fun")*? ☐ ☐

64. Do you list George Orwell as a "hero"? ☐ ☐

65. Do you list Dan Brown as a "hero"? ☐ ☐

66. Norman Mailer: dillweed? ☐ ☐

67. Do you grudgingly relate to Humbert Humbert? ☐ ☐

68. Would you consider naming your first-born son *Holden*? ☐ ☐

69. Do you hide your J. K. Rowling books when you have guests? ☐ ☐

69A. How about your Stephenie Meyer books? ☐ ☐

70. Have you ever mentioned a Jack Kerouac book to someone as your favorite that was not? ☐ ☐

71. Do you write song lyrics referencing J. G. Ballard? ☐ ☐

72. Do you title your songs after things that involved Ken Kesey? ☐ ☐

73. Can you say "Philip K. Dick" without smirking? ☐ ☐

73A. How about "Michael Moorcock"? ☐ ☐

73B. Do you often think, "What the fuck happened to Gay Head?" ☐ ☐

74. Have you ever publicly berated a Tom Robbins fan? ☐ ☐

75. Are you a white person who enjoys poems by Amiri Baraka? ☐ ☐

76. Are you a straight male who enjoys poems by Adrienne Rich? ☐ ☐

77. Do you have a poster of David Foster Wallace in your home or office? ☐ ☐

78. Have you ever had a heated discussion/brawl in a bar about the "true" identity of the author of Shakespeare's works? ☐ ☐

YES NO

79. Do you read (or claim to read) Harry Crews because you read about him in a Thurston Moore interview? ☐ ☐

80. Do you read (or claim to read) Hubert Selby Jr. because you read about him in a Henry Rollins interview? ☐ ☐

81. Do you read (or claim to read) Amy Hempel because you read about her in a Chuck Palahniuk interview? ☐ ☐

82. Do you keep your Henry Rollins books on a different shelf than the "serious" shelf in your living room? ☐ ☐

Have you recommended more than two books by any of the following authors to someone:

83. Amy Hempel? ☐ ☐
84. John Cheever? ☐ ☐
85. Carson McCullers? ☐ ☐
86. John Kennedy Toole? ☐ ☐
   (Trick question. He only wrote two books.)
87. Gerald Vizenor? ☐ ☐
88. Milan Kundera? ☐ ☐
89. Aeschylus? ☐ ☐
90. Jerzy Kosinski? ☐ ☐
91. Donald Barthelme? ☐ ☐
92. Kurt Vonnegut Jr.? ☐ ☐
93. Harold Pinter? ☐ ☐
94. Nikolai Gogol? ☐ ☐
95. Joseph Heller? ☐ ☐
96. Sean Hannity? ☐ ☐

BUKOWSKI

97. Be honest. While reading Charles Bukowski, have you ever become aroused? ☐ ☐

98. Do you like Bukowski because it's convenient to blame your alcoholism on him? ☐ ☐

99. Does Bukowski's work inspire you to think that because you're a hostile, misogynistic drunk, you can write? ☐ ☐

100. Have you tried the Bukowski diet (nothing but Paydays and booze) for extended lengths of time? ☐ ☐

101. Do you hate Bukowski as much as you hate fans of Bukowski? ☐ ☐

102. Have you ever taken an ice pick to your face to look more Bukowski-esque? ☐ ☐

103. Are you big enough of a dickhead to ever use the term Bukowski-esque? ☐ ☐

104. Do you talk shit about Bukowski's poetry while claiming that his novels are "the real deal"? ☐ ☐

105. This whole time did you think we were talking about bukkake? ☐ ☐

THE INDIE CRED TEST

VONNEGUT

YES   NO

106. Do you think Kurt Vonnegut's tone has been confused entirely?

107. When someone asks you what you like about Vonnegut, is "the satire, man, the satire" your only answer?

108. Did you ever start smoking Pall Malls because they were Vonnegut's cigarette of choice?

109. Would you become granny-punchingly irate if someone were to tell you that Kurt Vonnegut is College 101 reading?

110. Have you ever called Chuck Palahniuk "the new Vonnegut"? If so, did you kill yourself immediately afterward?

BURROUGHS

111. Do you refer to William S. Burroughs as "Billy Burr"?

112. Did the last chapter of *Naked Lunch* tie it all together for you?

113. Have you ever tried heroin to validate your love of William S. Burroughs?

114. Do you read William S. Burroughs books straight through? Whadaya want, a fuckin' cookie or something?

115. Do you give Burroughs credit for "doing it first" even though you've never read a whole book of his?

116. Have you searched on eBay for a typewriter that actually looks like a giant roach?

HEMINGWAY

117. Do you like Ernest Hemingway?

118. Do you claim to fish just so it appears that you're Hemingway-esque?

119. Have you ever tried to find out what Hemingway drank in an effort to write like him?

120. Did you just give up and start drinking a lot and claim to be living the Hemingway lifestyle?

121. Did you nickname your beard Kilimanjaro?

THOMPSON

122. Would Hunter S. Thompson have liked you?

123. Did you propose at the fist memorial?

124. Do you own a vintage typewriter?

125. Have you ever smoked through a TarGard filter?

YES   NO

126. Have you ever referred to your writing as "gonzo journalism" to mask the fact that you didn't do a single bit of research and smoked pot the whole time?

127. Have you ever referred to *anything* as gonzo-whatever?

KING

128. Have you ever used defamation/general shit talk/threats of physical violence towards literary academia to defend Stephen King?

129. Do you feel that Stephen King does his best work when he's too drunk to see what keys he's hitting on his typewriter?

130. Have you ever made a joke about King "retiring" and still continuing to publish books?

131. Did this guy *ever* get writer's block?

DAVIS

132. Is your understanding of suburban angst enhanced after reading the complete works of Jim Davis?

133. Do you feel that *Garfield Tips the Scales* was a pivotal point in Davis's career?

134. Have you ever said "Jim Davis" when you meant Jim Goad?

135. Do you think *Garfield Minus Garfield* is the best thing Davis has ever done, even though it was someone else's idea?

TITLE-SPECIFIC

136. Do you own the RE/Search book *Incredibly Strange Music*?

137. Did you have to look up any words while reading Mötley Crüe's *The Dirt*?

138. Do you own any book whose title ends with "for Dummies"?

139. Have you ever given a copy of Iceberg Slim's *Pimp: The Story of My Life* to a younger relative?

140. Do you own any of the Harry Potter books?

140A. If so, do you consider yourself a grown-up?

140B. Does anyone else?

141. Are you on Team Edward or Team Jacob?

141A. What's wrong with you?

142. Do you cry like a fucking baby when Don Quixote admits defeat, reclaims his name as Alonso Quixano, and dies? Oh shit, did that just ruin the ending for you? My bad. Damn. Sorry.

AUTHOR CHECKLIST

The four columns for each author are: **"UNDERSTAND"**, **HAVE ON SHELF***, **CAN QUOTE**, **THINK IT WOULD BE COOL TO QUOTE**

Author	"UNDERSTAND"	HAVE ON SHELF*	CAN QUOTE	THINK IT WOULD BE COOL TO QUOTE
Aeschylus	○	○	○	○
Anderson	○	○	○	○
Auster	○	○	○	○
Ballard	○	○	○	○
Bangs	○	○	○	○
Barth	○	○	○	○
Barthelme	○	○	○	○
Barthes	○	○	○	○
Bataille	○	○	○	○
Baudrillard	○	○	○	○
Blake	○	○	○	○
Blanchot	○	○	○	○
Bolaño	○	○	○	○
Brautigan	○	○	○	○
Browning	○	○	○	○
Bukowski	○	○	○	○
Burroughs	○	○	○	○
Byron	○	○	○	○
Céline	○	○	○	○
Chaucer	○	○	○	○
Chekhov	○	○	○	○
Chomsky	○	○	○	○
Chusid	○	○	○	○
Clowes	○	○	○	○
Coleridge	○	○	○	○
Corso	○	○	○	○
Crane	○	○	○	○
Crowley	○	○	○	○
Dante	○	○	○	○
Dawkins	○	○	○	○
DeLillo	○	○	○	○
Derrida	○	○	○	○
de Sade	○	○	○	○
Dick	○	○	○	○
Dickens	○	○	○	○
Dong	○	○	○	○
Donne	○	○	○	○
Dostoevsky	○	○	○	○
Eggers	○	○	○	○
Eliot	○	○	○	○
Ellis	○	○	○	○
Ellison	○	○	○	○
Emerson	○	○	○	○
Euripides	○	○	○	○
Fante	○	○	○	○
Faulkner	○	○	○	○
Fitzgerald	○	○	○	○
Forster	○	○	○	○
Foucault	○	○	○	○
Frost	○	○	○	○
Gaddis	○	○	○	○
Gibson	○	○	○	○
Ginsberg	○	○	○	○
Goad	○	○	○	○
Greene	○	○	○	○
Hegel	○	○	○	○
Heidegger	○	○	○	○
Hemingway	○	○	○	○
Homer	○	○	○	○
Hughes	○	○	○	○
Jackov	○	○	○	○
James	○	○	○	○
Jonson	○	○	○	○
Joyce	○	○	○	○
Kant	○	○	○	○
Kerouac	○	○	○	○
LaVey	○	○	○	○
Le Guin	○	○	○	○
Lévi-Strauss	○	○	○	○
Lowell	○	○	○	○
Mamet	○	○	○	○
Marcus	○	○	○	○
Marvell	○	○	○	○
Marx	○	○	○	○
McCullers	○	○	○	○
McKuen	○	○	○	○
McLuhan	○	○	○	○
Melville	○	○	○	○
Meyer	○	○	○	○
Miéville	○	○	○	○
Miller	○	○	○	○
Milton	○	○	○	○
Molière	○	○	○	○
Moorcock	○	○	○	○
Moore	○	○	○	○
Murakami	○	○	○	○
Nietzsche	○	○	○	○
Nimoy	○	○	○	○
Nin	○	○	○	○
O'Casey	○	○	○	○
O'Neill	○	○	○	○
Ovid	○	○	○	○
Plath	○	○	○	○
Poe	○	○	○	○
Pope	○	○	○	○
Postman	○	○	○	○
Pound	○	○	○	○
Pushkin	○	○	○	○
Pynchon	○	○	○	○
Rabelais	○	○	○	○
Rilke	○	○	○	○
Robbins	○	○	○	○
Roth	○	○	○	○
Rousseau	○	○	○	○
Rowling	○	○	○	○
Russell	○	○	○	○
Salinger	○	○	○	○
Sandburg	○	○	○	○
Sappho	○	○	○	○
Schopenhauer	○	○	○	○
Shakespeare	○	○	○	○
Shelley	○	○	○	○
Spenser	○	○	○	○
Stevens	○	○	○	○
Tenniselbow	○	○	○	○
Tennyson	○	○	○	○
That one guy that wrote *Trainspotting*	○	○	○	○
That dude who wrote *High Fidelity*	○	○	○	○
Thompson	○	○	○	○
Tolstoy	○	○	○	○
Vale	○	○	○	○
Vonnegut	○	○	○	○
Wallace	○	○	○	○
Ware	○	○	○	○
Waugh	○	○	○	○
Whitehead	○	○	○	○
Whitman	○	○	○	○
Wilde	○	○	○	○
Williams	○	○	○	○
Wilson	○	○	○	○
Wordsworth	○	○	○	○
Wright	○	○	○	○
Zinn	○	○	○	○

YES NO

143. Do you think people who love Kerouac's *Dharma Bums* should be curb stomped? ☐ ☐

144. Are you frustrated when you see would-be-smarty-pantses carrying around copies of *Infinite Jest?* ☐ ☐

145. Without a second thought, can you recite the last sentence in *Infinite Jest?* ☐ ☐

146. Did you read *The Canterbury Tales?* ☐ ☐

146A. Did you actually like it? If so, are you *sure* you actually read it? ☐ ☐

147. Did you read *Beowulf?* ☐ ☐

148. When reading *Beowulf*, did you think to yourself, "Holy shit, Vikings, mead, and man-eatin' monsters, how much more fucking metal can a book get?" ☐ ☐

149. Did you enjoy *Beowulf?* ☐ ☐

149A. If not, what is your fucking problem? ☐ ☐

149B. If so, did you take the next step and read John Gardner's *Grendel?* ☐ ☐

149C. Did you then feel like a dick for the way you now realize you have been stereotyping large, man-eatin' monsters? ☐ ☐

150. Have you ever gotten around to actually reading that copy of *Fight Club?* ☐ ☐

151. Did you read *Ulysses?* ☐ ☐

151A. Did you "get" *Ulysses?* Honestly? ☐ ☐

152. When it comes to *Ulysses*, do you read Gabler but secretly long for Kidd? ☐ ☐

152A. Part II: Do you feel no shame? ☐ ☐

152B. Part III: Do you understand why there needs to be a Part III question? ☐ ☐

153. Was *The Catcher in the Rye* a life-changing book during your punk rock adolescence, or did you find it "faggy"? ☐ ☐

YES NO

153A. When did you realize that it was actually about you being an adolescent prick? ☐ ☐

154. Did reading Dick Hebdige's *Subculture: The Meaning of Style* enhance your view of punk rock, or do you still make fun of modern hipsters? ☐ ☐

155. Has *Twilight*-mania made you feel ashamed for loving supernatural fiction? ☐ ☐

156. Have you read the Bible, but you know, just as literature, man? ☐ ☐

157. Do you have a $300 original hardback printing of *The Hundredth Monkey* sitting prominently on your ghetto-ass bookshelf made of milk crates? ☐ ☐

158. Do you own a first edition of *The Crying Of Lot 49?* ☐ ☐

159. Speaking of Pynchon, have you ever defended *Vineland?* ☐ ☐

160. Have you ever seen a staged version of Ionesco's *Rhinoceros?* ☐ ☐

160A. It would have been much more effective with real rhinos, yes? ☐ ☐

161. Do you think Shakespeare's *Titus Andronicus* is an underrated part of the Bard's canon? ☐ ☐

161A. If so, was this before the New Jersey punk band of the same name started getting popular? Cuz we're betting it wasn't. ☐ ☐

Have you actually made it all the way through the following books:

162. *Paradise Lost?* ☐ ☐
163. *The Aeneid?* ☐ ☐
164. *The Soft Machine?* ☐ ☐
165. *Naked Lunch?* ☐ ☐
166. *Gravity's Rainbow?* ☐ ☐
167. *Finnegans Wake?* ☐ ☐
168. *How to Live Life with a Huge Penis?* ☐ ☐

THE INDIE CRED TEST

MULTIPLE CHOICE

THE INDIE CRED TEST

CHOOSE THE MOST APPROPRIATE ANSWER BEFITTING YOUR VACUOUS EXISTENCE.

01. Your favorite poet is:
A. Jim Morrison.
B. Patti Smith.
C. Arthur Rimbaud.
D. Space Ghost.
E. yourself.

02. Your favorite rocker-turned-writer is:
A. Richard Hell.
B. Ryan Adams.
C. Henry Rollins.
D. Nick Blinko.
E. Chris Jericho.

03. When penning your own Great American Novel, who do you put on for inspiration?
A. Jawbox.
B. Sore Throat.
C. Smashmouth.
D. Emmet Otter's Jug Band Christmas.

04. Who is the top noir stylist?

A. Raymond Chandler
B. Jim Thompson
C. Harry Crews
D. Tito Ortiz

05. Please check the title NOT written by Henry Rollins.

A. *A Mad Dash*
B. *Black Coffee Blues*
C. *Get in the Van*
D. *Are You There God? It's Me, Henry*

06. Which metal biography makes you most wish you were a headbanger?

A. Mötley Crüe's *The Dirt*
B. Slash's *Slash*
C. *Stryper: Loud and Clear*
D. *Lords of Chaos: The Bloody Rise of the Satanic Metal Underground*

07. My method of place keeping is:

A. dog-earing.
B. Post-it note.
C. a "you're purrrfect!" kitten bookmark.
D. a place-keeping app.
E. a knife.

08. Which author's suicide do you privately think is actually kind of hilarious?

A. Ernest Hemingway
B. Sylvia Plath
C. Hunter S. Thompson
D. David Foster Wallace
E. John Kennedy Toole

09. Of your assigned reading in high school, which most insulted your intelligence?

A. *A Separate Peace* by John Knowles
B. *Pride and Prejudice* by Jane Austen
C. Court summons from an Assistant State's Attorney
D. The Bible

10. Which of the following writers *didn't* endorse, either implicitly or explicitly, terrorism?

A. Chuck Palahniuk
B. George Orwell
C. Don DeLillo
D. Alan Moore
E. Jean-Paul Sartre

11. Which language do you want to learn so you can read which author's work as he intended?

A. French/Albert Camus
B. Russian/Fyodor Dostoevsky
C. German/Immanuel Kant
D. Spanish/Roberto Bolaño
E. Swedish/Stieg Larsson
F. Japanese/Haruki Murakami
G. Scottish/Irvine Welsh

12. Which "writer" should really just stick to music?

A. Steve Earle
B. Lee Ranaldo
C. Nick Cave
D. Leonard Cohen

13. Most of the books on your shelf are written by:

A. dead Germans.
B. music critics.
C. alcoholics who can speak French.
D. comedians.

14. The works of which author have been the most raped by Hollywood?

A. Philip K. Dick
B. J. G. Ballard
C. Jane Austen
D. Lewis Carroll

15. Can graphic novels be considered true literature?

A. What, are you stupid?
B. Two words: tentacle porn
C. Anything with more onomatopoeia than dependent clauses ain't literature.
D. Only if the movie adaptation wasn't as good as the source material

16. Please rank the following authors from least to most dissolute:

A. Dylan Thomas
B. Dorothy Parker
C. Charles Bukowski
D. William Burroughs
E. James Joyce

17. Please rank the following musicians from least to most worthy of literary analysis:

A. Bob Dylan
B. Captain Beefheart
C. Mark E. Smith
D. Blixa Bargeld
E. Rakim

18. Please rank the following philosophers from least to most full of shit:

A. Plato
B. Friedrich Nietzsche
C. Jean-Paul Sartre
D. Jacques Derrida
E. Slavoj Zizek

19. *Infinite Jest* is:

A. a must-read.
B. not your cup of tea.
C. best used on bookshelves and in coffee shop conversations as date-bait.
D. a totally awesome doorstop.

20. Which of the following things have you done?

A. Brought a book to a strip club
B. Arbitrarily picked a writer, poet, or critic to publicly despise
C. Left clothes out of your suitcase to make room for books
D. Claimed to have read a book in galley form
E. Actually read a book in galley form

21. If you are a writer, do you:

A. spend the majority of your advance on copies of your book?
B. bring a box of copies of your book to social functions?
C. sign copies of a book for which you were one of 24 contributors?
D. spend more time telling people about your book than writing your book?
E. tell people you are a "professional author" although you technically have never been paid?

FILL IN THE BLANK

BARREN SPACES SHALL BE SUBSEQUENTLY PLENISHED WITH REMARKS RELATIVE TO YOUR OWN DUMB ASS.

01. On a scale of one to FUCK, how much do you hate other writers?

02. How far along are you with your novel? Really?

03. When did you realize that you were just drinking and not writing or being published?

04. Which drugs inspired the Book of Revelation?

05. How many issues of the *New Yorker* have you trashed?

06. How many rejection letters from publishers/literary magazines are stuffed in your desk drawer?

07. ¿Quién es más macho: writer or musician?

<u>08.</u> Do you have "arty" books that you move to prominent positions in your bookcase when guests come over? If so, what books do they replace?

<u>09.</u> Right now, how much do you owe in overdue fees at the public library?

<u>10.</u> How many books from Dalkey Archive Press do you own/have you read?

<u>11.</u> How many of your books have been converted to hollowed-out weed stashes?

<u>12.</u> Per week, how many of your solipsistic rants end with "fuckin' Eggers"?

<u>13.</u> Do you say "King James Version" or "Kay Jay Vee"?

<u>14.</u> How many books in your library are by people you know?

<u>15.</u> How many books do you read in a day? Week? Month? Year? How many if you exclude self-help books and instruction manuals?

<u>16.</u> What exact percentage have you read of all books ever written?

<u>17.</u> On average how often do you talk about books at parties?

<u>18.</u> Define magical realism without using the words "Harry Potter."

<u>19.</u> True or false: The librarian fetish thing is so played out.

<u>20.</u> How did reading C. S. Lewis post-*Screwtape Letters* affect your opinion of Tooth & Nail Records?

<u>21.</u> How often does a discussion of *The Unbearable Lightness of Being* lead to oral sex?

<u>22.</u> How long before/after reading *On the Road* did you carry it around with you?

<u>23.</u> For hardcover books, do you take the dust jacket off or leave it on?

<u>24.</u> Honestly, did you start loving Cormac McCarthy before or after *No Country for Old Men*? We're talking about the movie.

<u>25.</u> How many times have you started, and not finished, *Infinite Jest*? *Ulysses*? *The Recognitions*?

<u>26.</u> List all the parts of Jon Savage's *England's Dreaming* that you highlighted.

<u>27.</u> List, in reverse-alphabetical order, all microgenres of literature (Restoration literature, 19th century war poetry, etc.) that you consider yourself an expert on.

<u>28.</u> Kilgore Trout is _____ .

<u>29.</u> Bloomsday is _____ .

<u>30.</u> John Barth is more _____ than Donald Barthelme.

<u>31.</u> My beat period lasted _____ months.

<u>32.</u> My Bukowski phase lasted _____ months/years/court appearances.

<u>33.</u> My headache lasted _____ after trying to read *House of Leaves*.

<u>34.</u> How is Gordon Lish like Malcolm McLaren?

<u>35.</u> What's up with John Irving and bears? And wrestling?

<u>36.</u> When was the last time you signed out more books than CDs from your library?

<u>37.</u> When was the last time your late fees at the library were more than your late fees at the video rental place?

<u>38.</u> When was the last time you finished reading a book (magazines, newspapers, and liner notes do not count)?

<u>39.</u> Number of magazines stacked on your toilet tank waiting to be read:

ESSAY

<u>01.</u> Science Fiction versus Fantasy. Go!

<u>02.</u> Richard Meltzer. Groundbreaking journalist or indecipherable asshole?

Would you classify any of the following as a "hack"?   **HACK**

<u>03.</u> Jim DeRogatis .... ☐
<u>04.</u> Nick Sylvester .... ☐
<u>05.</u> Christopher R. Weingarten .... ☐
<u>06.</u> Doug Mosurock .... ☐
<u>07.</u> Mark Ebner .... ☐
<u>08.</u> Robert Greene .... ☐
<u>09.</u> If so, why? *(100 words or less, please.)*

<u>10.</u> Explain *McSweeney's.*

<u>11.</u> What the fuck was Heidegger talking about?

<u>12.</u> Explain in 500 words or more your interpretation of the following quote from John Keats' "Ode On A Grecian Urn": "Beauty is truth, truth beauty—that is all ye know on Earth, and all ye need know."

THE INDIE CRED TEST

SECTION V

WRAPPING IT UP:
HOW TO KNOW A LOT WHILE LEARNING ABSOLUTELY NOTHING

CALCULATING YOUR SCORE

CONGRATULATIONS!

YOU HAVE COMPLETED THE BANK OF INDIE CRED™ INDIE CRED TEST©®™. NOW IT'S TIME TO TABULATE YOUR INDIE CRED SCORE, WHICH WILL SERVE AS A BAROMETER OF YOUR INDIE CREDWORTHINESS FOR ALL BIC INDIE CRED SERVICES INCLUDING BUT NOT LIMITED TO: TOTAL FUCKING CASH-INS, MEMBERSHIP-ADJUSTED LAUREL RESTING RATE, PERSONALIZED LAUGH-IN-YOUR-FACE SERVICE, AND NAÏVE ART SCHOOL STUDENT DATE RAPE POTENTIAL INDEX (NASSDRPI).

THEOREM OF CREDIBILITY

Cred was always believed to be immeasurable. However, you'll see many scores assigned to items throughout *The Indie Cred Test*. This seemingly random score per item is actually calculated using an advanced mathematical algorithm currently being studied in some of the nation's top schools. The theorem of credibility surmises credibility is able to be measured quantitatively and objectively using this simple mathematical equation:

$$C = \sigma \: of \sqrt{(\alpha - |S|)(O)/S - (w + \Delta)}$$

C *(cred)*=The standard deviation(∞) of: The square root (√) of (age(a) minus- the absolute value of (|years in music "scene"*(S)|)") multiplied by (Ownership(O) of entire output of favorite artist in all media) /S(snark) – ("old looking" concert t's or other faux memorabilia (w) purchased at a chain store + cost of concert ticket bought for the purpose of "being seen" at the show and not because you like the artist(Δ)).

> *"scene" as a variable has different standard values, depending upon geographical area and "insider/outsider" status of the person or object being measured. Please refer to the upcoming textbook *The Credibility Quotient* for exact values for your area. As negative numbers are seen in some places and with the "outsider" status, the use of absolute values in this equation is essential.

A WORD ON AGE: The older the person/thing being measure is, the higher its inherent cred. After a certain point, however, this cred level changes to "old school." When "old school" falls into kitsch (K), cred is lost and becomes part of (w). Whence this alteration happens is currently being studied.

Ownership of knitting needles automatically moves the owner into the Hipster Kitsch Theorem that involves grandmothers, stale beef jerky and the need to listen to "power ballads." As this combination is reprehensible, researchers have rightly shied away from actually creating the equation in which to measure this aberration.

CONCLUSION

$$E_1 + \frac{B_n}{1 + n_{the}} + \frac{(O_{tf} + R_{tf} + H_{mo} + L_{sd} + V_{0-})}{(K_{iss} + R_{allen} + S + P_{cp} + I_{cp})}$$

1

Multiply by lifetime ethnicities fucked (E_f) (mixed-ethnicity fucks count as one ethnicity, though multiple independent mixed-ethnicity fucks can each count as long as the ethnicity mixture is unique; European Caucasian varieties like "German" or "Italian" do not count unless the person speaks English only as a second language; add a bonus ethnicity to your lifetime total if you were with somebody who does not speak any English (E_f+1), another extra ethnicity if they didn't speak any English and you only speak English (E_f+1), and add another ethnicity bonus if you got siblings of any ethnicity (E_f+1). Note: imaginary ethnicities (Smurfs, Werewolves, Hot Martian Bitches) do not count.

2

Divide by number of bands you've been in with "The" somewhere in the band's name (B/n_{the}) (add an extra "The" point for every band you've been in with a "Thee" in it (n_{the}+1), ten extra "The" points for band names with "The" in between two other words (n_{the}+10), twenty extra "The" points for all "And The" or "& The" bands (n_{the}+20), and a hundred extra "The" points if you were in The The (n_{the}+100), and a thousand extra "The" points for any band you've been in with a "Crystal," a "Wolf," or a "Laser" in the name (n_{the}+1,000), unless you're in a joke band called "Laserwolf Crystaldick," in which case you get a million extra "The" points (n_{the}+1,000,000)—joke bands are for losers: funny losers). If you have never been in a band with "The" in the name, start one, dumbfuck. Then take the test again.

3

Add the total number of: major label offers you've turned down (O_{tf}), $50+ records in your collection you've given away to somebody because you don't really listen to them (R_{tf}), STDs you've given to Danny Fields (H_{mo}), times the ghost of Robert Johnson has appeared onstage next to you and jammed out a silent accompaniment that only you can hear (L_{sd}), and whether or not you've contracted any known strain of vampirism from any member(s) of Type O Negative (V_{0-})- enter 1 for positive, 0 for negative.

4

Subtract the total number of: times you've changed into a costume or put on make-up before playing a show (K_{iss}), lifetime multicolored shorts worn (R_{allen})(like total obnoxious shorts-wearing occasions), pairs of shoes you own (S), times the ghost of Stevie Ray Vaughn has appeared onstage next to you and jammed out a silent accompaniment that only you can hear (P_{cp}), and times you've tried to make your show seem more lively by verbally encouraging increased mosh pit activity (i.e.: "I wanna see y'all crazy bastards go apeshit in the pit on this next song!!") I_{cp}.

WARNING: BANK OF INDIE CRED IS NOT RESPONSIBLE FOR QUANTUM FLUCTUATIONS OR DIMENSIONAL DRIFT

YOUR FINAL SCORE

NEGATIVE ONE BILLION (-1,000,000,000)
An Indie Cred Score of "Negative One Billion" indicates that you're trying too hard to come up with a funny joke about how little you care about your Indie Cred Score, which actually means that you care too much about your Indie Cred Score and you don't realize that trying to be uncool is as bad or worse than trying to be cool, and you probably love Frank Zappa, but it is highly doubtful that he returns said love.

NEGATIVE 100 (-100)
An Indie Cred Score of negative 100 indicates that you are a formerly smug mutherfucker who works in the industry. Like, "votes on the Grammy Awards" level. You're a dinosaur. Extinct. Good luck with the bankruptcy proceedings. By now we know that the "indie" wing of the recording industry is no longer inherently good, but that doesn't mean that your old top-heavy business infrastructures are no longer inherently bad. That's why we're pissing on your grave right now. Hey, guess what. We're downloading Metallica. Illegally. Right now. And then we're burning illegally downloaded Metallica onto a CD-R full of illegal mp3s, and were splitting it in two and we're shoving the shards into the middle of that stupid smirk on your pimple ridden puss, and as you shriek in slug salted, vampire-in-the-sunlight horror about what we're doing, your only method of distracting us from the unholy nightmare beatdown we're issuing is to beg and plead for mercy and offer us Eagles tickets and try in vain to convince us, via press releases to surviving major newspapers and radio stations, that it's *the* concert event of the summer, which makes us almost pass out from laughing, but not quite, because we know we have to keep an eye out for you, you twisted leprechaun of a child's ear abuser. Although individual results may vary. But yours probably won't. Dick.

"I WONDER HOW I'D DO IF I TOOK THIS TEST" (-99 TO -2)
An Indie Cred Score of "I wonder how I'd do if I took this test" indicates that you're about as "cool" as Brian fucking Setzer. You would not do well if you took this test. Nobody would do well if they took this test. This test is jokes for nerds. If you are a nerd and you like jokes, go ahead and look at the test. If you actually want to know how cool you are from some kind of a cool test, then the answer is "you're exactly as cool as a person who wants to do well at a cool test," which on our arbitrary cool scale falls somewhere between "assistant middle school principal who wears a bow tie and teaches strictly classical oboe to neighborhood kids for $20 a lesson (not ballsy enough to be a rip-off artist, not cool enough to work for free)" and "that one 45-year-old paralegal aunt with a subscription to *Cat Fancy* who's still unmarried even though she's not even a lesbian." You should just go ahead and put this book back on the shelf or son's toilet where you found it.

NEGATIVE ONE (-1)
An Indie Cred Score of negative one means that you're a totally regular normal guy who's maybe just a little too excited for Blues Fest.

ZERO (0)
An Indie Cred Score of zero entitles you to the following life benefits: sustaining a loving relationship between two equals having fun with friends; being well-liked; enjoying time spent with your family; financial, emotional, and spiritual stability; home ownership; and general happiness. It does not entitle you to an insightful, well-informed opinion about Glenn Branca's œuvre that you can impress some yellow-toothed ethnomusicology Ph.D. dropout with, though, so your loss. Good luck with all that happiness. We'll be the ones fucking your girlfriend the next time you have a night with the guys. FYI, we have herpes.

ONE (1)
Congratulations, you have achieved the perfect score!

FIVE (5)
An Indie Cred Score of five indicates that you picked up on enough context clues to know that everybody who contributed to this book thinks Mates of State sucks. But you actually like Mates of State. And other, you know, "underground" "indie" "rock" like Rogue Wave or Kings of Convenience. Good for you. We apologize for the confusion, and suggest that you return this book in exchange for some poetry, or a journal, or a book about "feelings", or whatever hippy tripe you read while we're busy compiling our next book, *The 17 Least-Known Krautrock Bands Of 1974* (Penguin) out next fall. You're fine. Just consider the validity of our argument that Mates of State sucks. Also, if you could, please go to Bonnaroo instead of SXSW. We're trying to keep you people together.

EIGHTEEN TO TWENTY ONE (18 TO 21)
Indicates that you Googled many of the references in this book because you really want to know what's up and you're at a loss now that Lala.com shut down and you can no longer listen to the music while Pitchfork tells you if it's good or not. You fit perfectly the position of trend-jumping, tight-pantsed hipster fuckwad. You always glom on to the latest Internet-buzz, but by the time your hopelessly mundane, single-pierced ears hear about it, you're usually about four to six weeks behind the tastemakers and aggregators that are filtering the flavor of the week towards you, and that ballyhooed "buzz" has metastasized into a full-on, "expose yourself to the boss's underage daughter"-level drunk. You had just gotten your British imports of all of the dubstep and grime records you were so hot about, but the indie press had already moved on the to beard-folk or something else. You aren't particularly politically correct (in fact, you're downright disrespectful to women—even if you are one), but any bad publicity will turn you off from things rather easily. For example, you gave yourself whiplash overreacting to both Wavves and the Wavves tantrum. You tend to talk smack about most of the mainstream popular culture, but you add a caveat like "except for *America's Next Top Model*" because you actually enjoy watching all dumb reality TV and that's the one show that has been deemed "acceptable" by your similarly damaged peer group, all of whom are larval-stage yuppies and afraid to admit it. You like to use phrases like "game-changing episode" and "cascading waterfalls of guitar" in casual conversation. You spend a lot of money and time on clothes and hair in order to look like you don't. And Googling is cheating, so the title "trend-jumping hipster fuckwad" might be generous. You might just be a douchenozzle.

"WORLD MUSIC" (22 TO 31)
An Indie Cred Score of "World Music" means that you desperately need to fuck a nonwhite person (and maybe tell a mildly racist joke). If you are a nonwhite person and your Indie Cred Score is "World Music," you desperately need to stop sleepin' with all them honkeys.

THIRTY TWO TO FORTY FIVE (32 to 45)
An Indie Cred Score between 32 and 45 indicates that you used to have your ear to the ground, but at a certain point, dated within three to six months of acquiring a mortgage, you just gave up. The kids at the record store started giving you the stink-eye, and you started feeling self-conscious about still getting a hard-on for women who looked like they just came back from a Suicide Girls shoot. Your areas of expertise go as far as whatever music, movies, and literature was hip in the decade preceding your 32nd birthday, and no further. You are still cooler than most of the people at your lucrative but highly embarrassing job, even though your sole gesture towards denying that you have become The Man is occasionally wearing a black button-up shirt instead of a white or blue one. Your primary source for music news is now NPR (making you a walking encyclopedia of Wilco and Garrison Keillor knowledge), and every consecutive year you stay alive, you will hate popular music a little bit more. Occasionally you will go to a show if it's at a venue you like, you can score a babysitter, and it's for some kind of Come, Gumball, 11th Dream Day, or Giant Sand reunion, and you will enjoy yourself without really having fun (in exactly the same manner as at your wife's unfun dinner parties) at these shows because they are boring, but that's ok with you because you are also boring. Soon you will stop pretending to give a shit about any of this, and it will make you feel moderately better for the last three or four remaining decades of your life.

FIFTY (50)
An Indie Cred Score of 50 means you're not winning any contests, but you can contribute to the average conversation overheard at a record store without embarrassing yourself by using such techniques as joking and being honest when somebody mentions something you don't know about while quickly understanding the context of the information. Like, you've never heard of Crime, but when somebody says "they were from San Francisco," you say "was that before or after Flipper?" And when they respond by saying "before, like '76" and you say "oh, wow" and mean it, what you don't overtly share is your nearly complete lack of interest in the subject. There's a decent chance that before indie rock appeared on your radar, you put in a long but halfhearted stint in an aboveground, major label subsidiary supported youth subculture, like as a jam band fan, metalhead, goth, skate/pop punk (Pennywise), or maybe (it's a stretch) even a suburban hip hop kid. You look back at that time with a mixture of nostalgia and embarrassment, and you're not much of a joiner anymore. There may be some substantial holes in your credibility, but you are well-versed in the obsessive behavior needed to achieve a higher Indie Cred Score, and you say "no thanks" to it more often than not. Most likely you have been a lifetime scene spectator. You have amassed quite an enviable record collection but are lacking the "on the job" training and experience that yields a higher score. Now may be the time to impose your talents onto the scene. Or it may be the time to keep a cool head and continue doing what you're doing. Because you're right, all this shit is pretty useless.

SIXTY NINE (69)
An Indie Cred Score of 69 indicates that you've probably never participated in a real 69 and hence don't know how pleasant-then-almost-immediately-unpleasant of a sexual thrill it is to be suffocated by somebody while suffocating another person. Or else you're in the 15 to17-year old zone where you can't convince anybody to go all the way with you, and 69 is the best thing going. For us grown ups for whom banging is an option, a 69 is like two minutes of semi-fun, tops. The only thing fun about it is that it's named for a number that you can see by accident on scores and phone numbers and things, and every time you see it you get to think "ha ha, those two numbers are going down on each other." In which case, we are with you and we'll always be with you, it's funny. It's even more funny once you've done it, because now you know that at least one of those numbers can't wait to switch to 66 or at least a 6a.

"I STUCK TO MY GUNS AND NOW I WIN" (73 TO 84)
We've got to hand it to you. This is the only place where liking Led Zeppelin in kindergarten pays off. Yes, you were shunned out of cliques and friends because you weren't into the latest pop trend and damn if you didn't cry...in front of them. But it was a defiant rage cry. You knew they would all envy you one day. It wasn't easy, we know, but you did it. You stuck to your guns when metal was dying. You called Cobain a pussy even when everyone was trying to be like him and, best of all, you never danced. Not even to Prince. You always knew that, as Robert Plant said, "Your time is gonna come." Well, guess what, big guy? It's here. Kudos. Now, can I please get a refill on this water? This is an awesome brunch place. Thanks.

ONE HUNDRED (100)
An Indie Cred Score of 100 indicates that you work at a record store and/or indie label, and your chronic, insatiable desire for validation that you never got from your awkward, unloving parents has found its ultimate expression through your knowing everything there is to know about music. You genuinely enjoy both music and the process of learning everything there is to know about it. You have formed a rigorously enforced, unimpeachable, genuinely impressive set of aesthetic values that you feel indicates exactly who you are as a person, and you are able to communicate this through your musical preferences in a way that other people immediately understand even if they don't agree with. You don't proselytize, though, and you don't judge. In other words, you have perfect taste. But the amount of time and money and effort that's gone into having perfect taste is ridiculous. It's offputting, even. Have you ever noticed how people always want to play gotcha with you to trap you into saying something stupid or undiplomatic? That's only natural, even if you're basically a nice guy, because who the fuck do you think you are, spending all that time and money and effort on having perfect taste in music? It's just music. You know, la la la la la. Music. So what. It's great, sure, but it's not worth being the only thing in the world you care about. Nothing is. And for you to have staked out your "perfect taste" territory so unwaveringly, you'd have to be antisocial unhealthy-level obsessed over it, to the point where if you had a kid, you would be as awkward and unloving towards it as your parents were to you. Oh, and if you're trying to sidestep the significance of that fact by including "hating children" in your strenuous set of aesthetic values, then that's just dumb. And nobody believes that you actually hate children, by the way. There's no point in it. It's like saying *"I hate raccoons"* because they toppled over your garbage that one time, and then instead of just letting it be an observation you made in an angry-at-raccoons moment, you decided to make raccoon hate into your own personal credo in order to avoid ever having said anything you don't believe, which is like expecting to one day be handed a Nobel Prize for consistency and avant-garde thought over your inability to think beyond the inconvenience of toppled garbage. Or else maybe you have not ever considered the whole "I'm as bad as my parents were" angle because you're one of these mousy types who doesn't shower or talk to people. Or maybe, probably, you're just a dickhead and you know it and you hate yourself and that's why you won't ever have kids.
Regardless, congratulations on acing this test. Unfortunately, you fail the test of life.

ONE HUNDRED AND ONE (101)
An Indie Cred Score of 101 indicates that you treat the bands you've decided to like as if you're a marine and they're a man left behind. You don't give your trust to just anybody, but once they earn it, you give them unwavering loyalty. You never budge even after your favorite band experiments with reggae and starts to blow. You have both Shot and Blue on vinyl. Why? Because a fan is a fan, no matter what. You're not some bandwagon-jumping hipster. No, if a band you've decided to like is doing something shitty, you stick through it, hoping for a light on the other side. And let's face it, there's a lot of darkness.... But you were cut from a different cloth. From a breed of cool that dies liking what they like, for better or worse, even if changing said tastes would allow them to live. You even invented a whole theory about it and wrote a blog and a book. That, my friend, is ballsy. We just hope you don't become president and arbitrarily invade a Muslim country or else we'll be there forever.

ONE HUNDRED AND TEN (110)
An Indie Cred Score of 110 indicates that you picked a genre, you know everything about that genre, and you're staying in it even though everything in that genre is going through some very lean times. Like, you got really into emocore in high school and instead of jumping off the bandwagon once they dropped the "core" and Jade Tree exploded, you kept on the good fight with Man Is The Bastard and Swing Kids until the world rewarded you with Japandroids, and now you're back to being a punchline again. But you're not gonna stop, are you? You won't even be tempted to deviate into shoegaze. No, you're gonna stick with this specific set of rules. These things are cyclical, and you're gonna be semi-awesome in another 15 years, probably. Hopefully. In the meantime, you've got to build up that cred by sticking to your guns. Your stupid, stupid guns.

FOUR HUNDRED NINETEEN (419)
An Indie Cred Score of 419 indicates that you crank one off to Boris. And if you don't, you totally should, man. It's, like, incredible, like getting a high five from God, except you're not, so it's like you're in touch with the God that lives inside of you and everything, AND you're getting a high five too! Oh wow, man. Hey, let's get some snacks. And bring that Bongzilla bootleg...

"OH, I GET IT, IT'S LIKE A JOKE BOOK FOR ROCK KIDS, LIKE *CREEM* MAGAZINE OR SOMETHING, THAT'S PRETTY COOL, I GUESS" (500 TO 540)
An Indie Cred Score of "Oh, I get it, it's like a joke book for rock kids, like *Creem* Magazine or something, that's pretty cool, I guess" means that you're old. But good old. Like the kind of old guy who has hilarious stories about how one time you and your ex-wife dropped acid and went out wearing capes because you were going to fight crime, but then you fucked a tree instead. At least you think it was a tree. Just know that you're a bit of a bummer when you get going about rock, like "I saw Hendrix solo on a 12-string" and all that stuff. It's not that it's not hip to talk about Jimi as reverent-tone God of Guitar Penis (it's very much not hip but who cares), it's just the nostalgia factor, you know, like it's a bummer to think that some day we're going to talk like that about how David Yow stagedived his sweaty ass directly onto our face once in '93. That bummer is not your fault, though. Now tell us about how you spent the entire '80s doing maintenance for a hotel in Jackson Hole, Wyoming, and ended up fucking a ton of recent divorcées who came up there to clear their minds but instead got horny and desperate enough to consider you an option.

"THERE WAS NOTHING ABOUT JAPANESE MUSIC, SO I LOST INTEREST" (553 TO 554)
An Indie Cred Score of "There was nothing about Japanese music, so I lost interest" indicates that you need to understand something: The Japanese do not like you. You know how they pixel out the genitals in Japanese porn? (Of course you do!) That's what they see when they look at you: an indistinct blob of tan-colored blocks in a Badtz-Maru t-shirt. They're happy to take all your money in exchange for manga and various 12" remixes of Kahimi Karie and Pizzicato Five. However, that's where the cultural exchange ends. Music made by girls in knee socks with squeaky voices isn't "pop," "j-pop," or "Lolita pop"; it's music for perverts. As anyone in the merchant marine will tell you, Japan is expert and alarmingly efficient at exploiting those more talented than they are. You'd know this if your court-mandated GPS tag allowed you to travel outside of the country.

SIX SIX SIX (666)
We get it. You like metal. Just watch where you swing that stupid fucking battleaxe. Okay, Wülf?

ELEVEN HUNDRED (1,100)
An Indie Cred Score of 1,100 indicates that you're a 40+-year-old guy whose mom drops you off at the record store, and you stay there all day talking everybody's ear off (until you grow those spit foams on the corners of your mouth) about stuff that's so obscure, it sounds made up, but then upon checking it out later (most of what you say has not even made it onto the internet—in any form—yet) it turns out you're dead-on right about everything you said, except maybe for the creepy over-devotion to all-girl bands. Everybody thinks you're borderline autistic, but you're really just a simple, harmless guy who knows everything about music and used to do a ton of drugs. Uniform: Bratmobile t-shirt, cargo pants, Payless sneakers, matted side-parted hair, B.O. You do not realize that this book is a joke, but you aced it anyway, no sweat. We recommend you continue being exactly who you are, because A. you're great and B. you probably just are going to anyway.

"OH YEAH, THAT'S HENRY'S THING. CUTE." (43,542)
An Indie Cred Score of "Oh yeah, that's Henry's thing. Cute." indicates that you are a test question.

"MY CRED IS SO INDIE, I'M TECHNICALLY RETARDED"
An Indie Cred Score of "My cred is so indie, I'm technically retarded" means that you've never even heard of Kanye West because you've spent the last 10 years exclusively listening to Lexie Mountain Boys cassette-only bootlegs. You should maybe leave the house.

"YOU BOYS ARE STUPID" (ABOVE 1,000,000)
An Indie Cred Score of "You boys are stupid" indicates that we're totally gonna take the trash out as soon as we get home because we love you, and also it's totally cool if Pam comes over on Thursday, we can just go to Matty's house. You win the test, by the way. Thank you for letting us sleep with you sometimes. And sorry I forgot to flush the toilet this morning.

TERMS OF AGREEMENT

☐ **YES!** I filled out the Indie Credit Application so I can get all of the benefits that membership with the Bank of Indie Cred provides, as well as the members-only seven-inch single. I understand that the band slated for its release has not yet been decided, but given the Bank of Indie Credit's esteemed standing, I trust that it will be of the highest quality, and I won't complain or post to some newsgroup about the Bank's inability to get things done in a timely manner if I don't get the goods in six months.

☐ **I REQUEST THE BANK OF INDIE CRED CARD(S):** I hereby vouch that I am certifiably filled with cred, and that I have read and agreed to all the terms, authorizations, and disclosures contained within this form, and that everything I have stated in this application is true and correct. I understand that my new cred status will be with the Bank of Indie Credit, located in Athens, Georgia. I understand that the use of any card issued in connection with this offer will constitute my acceptance of and will be subject to the terms and conditions of the Bank of Indie Cred Credit Agreement and Disclosure Statement, printed in full below. I agree to be responsible for all charges incurred and/or levied against me in accordance with the Cardmember Agreement. I understand that the terms of my account are subject to change as provided in the Cardmember Agreement and that, whether or not I am aware of the changes, I know they were done with my best interests at heart. I rock with the best.

DISCLOSURE STATEMENT

I. GENERAL TERMS AND DEFINITIONS

1. In this agreement, the words "you," "your band," and/or "your screenplay" refer to the applicant named on the application and the words "we," "us," "BIC," and "H2O" refer to Bank of Indie Cred, LLC, Geo., N.A., located at Box 2814, Athens, Georgia 30612, U.S.A. If your application is approved, "applicant" will be promoted to "Hipster" for purposes of this agreement.
2. If we accept your application to open an account, you agree that you will promote only those goods, services, and general manners of conduct befitting and/or further anchoring your hipster status including but not limited to the following:
   A. pursuit of cred-boosting publicity for yourself or your band;
   B. purchase of vinyl records (mint, limited edition, colored, hand-numbered, silkscreened, 7", 10", 12", flexi, "good," etc., all fall under this umbrella);
   C. subscription to, collection of, lording over, submission of original material to, and/or loitering around the local drop-off point for (whether or not you have any real intention of buying) periodical materials (such as magazines,comics, newspapers, journals *[eww]*, quarterlies, and fanzines...unless you're still reading *Cometbus*, in which case you really need to grow the fuck up, especially if you're still dumpster-diving or covering your stamps in glue so that you can wipe off the cancellation marks);
   D. choice/pursuit of a career path that emphasizes "awesome" over monetary gain and/or stability, sobriety, sustainability, or healthy interpersonal relationships;
   E. collection or stockpiling of impressive sums of, but not necessarily the reading of or assimilation of knowledge from, books;
   F. clothing, makeovers, or other methods of social circle enhancement via fashion, for personal, family, and household purposes, from merchants that are considered Chunklet-approved.

II. ACCEPTANCE OF AGREEMENT

1. By signing and submitting (via print, electronically, telephonically [text message not applicable], via facsimile, or by means of a tattoo on the appendage(s) of some raver kid you found passed out on your stoop) the application, you agree to the following terms and conditions of this Credit Agreement and Disclosure Statement, including but not limited to:
   A. use of any materials, counseling, or other advice provided herein is restricted only insofar as to make better-informed lifestyle choices and purchases;
   B. resisting the urge to flaunt, brandish, flash about, or vouchsafe upon others your Cred;
   C. deigning to allow others to make music, write books, film movies, or create anything by any other means;
   D. submission in triplicate of Form 943-6b (06-07) Binding Statement of Nü-Metal Disassociation;
   E. agreement to always have at least one of the following involved in every meal: two (2) cups organic lima beans; one (1) link cruelty-free Andouille sausage; eight (8) oz. tofu; one (1) piece of any Morningstar Farms® product; or one (1) 24 oz. box of Dots® candy.
2. Omission of any information requested on the application may be reason for denial of account or a pink-belly.

III. PROMISE TO PAY

1. You agree to pay or repay all amounts charged to your BIC account, whether incurred by you or any of the following parties:
   A. members of your band,
   B. your bookie, or
   C. that kid who stole your library card while you were hitting on that hot librarian.
2. You are jointly and individually responsible for all cred, regardless of middle-agedness, parenthood, band dissolution, magazine folding, new musical direction taking, label sucking, or drunk-dialing. Any lapse in fulfilling your responsibility to pay or repay BIC requires notification to the BIC in writing and in quadruplicate (because we mean fucking business) with a full explanation of the following:
   A. what you did wrong,
   B. why you did it,
   C. what you're going to do to make up for it, and
   D. why in Ronnie James Dio's name you would ever have agreed to go see a community theater production of *Rent* in the first place.
3. Any attempt to disclaim liability for any such wrongdoing provides the BIC express license to pursue any or all of the following against you:
   A. account closure,
   B. levying of fines and/or penalties,
   C. merciless multimedia bashing,
   D. forfeiture of any and all accumulated Cred,
   E. personal floggings at the hand of the 40 Watt Clubber, Athens's own Basement-League professional wrassler.
4. In any event, you will continue to pay the outstanding balance under the terms of this agreement; however, the BIC will never forgive such infractions and you will herein be regarded as "poser" or "posers." After all we tried to do for you, this is how you repay us? Do you feel no shame, hipster?

IV. ABILITY TO REPRESENT

1. When you use your BIC cred, you represent the ability and the intention to back all claims of hipness, including but not limited to:
   A. record collection size;
   B. musical/literary talents;
   C. drug tolerance;
   D. jaunty-hat wearing, and
   E. free merch-acquiring abilities.
2. Proof of your Cred-worthiness may be solicited by BIC in as many instances and at any times deemed appropriate by the BIC in their sole and infinite, unquestionable wisdom. We may require written citations of your Cred-worthiness in the form of:
   A. interview quotes;
   B. cover appearances on noteworthy publications (not including *Nylon, Alternative Press, SPIN, Blender,* or *Family Circle*);
   C. hotness of significant other(s) in photographic form (camera phone shots are undesirable and will generally detract from Cred, unless used in the form of a "sext" and only if you and your partner can stimulate unfluffed boner);
   D. appearances on "thank you" lists in the liner notes of number one hit records;
   E. tattoos of you, your image, or some facsimile of your work (e.g., lyrics to your songs, passages from your books, ingredient lists from your recipes, etc.);
   F. any others as determined appropriate by the BIC.
3. Written recommendations from other senior-level BIC Cred holders may be accepted in some instances, provided such Cred holders have not submitted similar recommendations for others within the past six (6) months. That's just sloppy, and nobody respects an easy lay.

V. BILLING STATEMENT

1. A monthly Statement of Cred will be forwarded to you for each billing cycle, the end of which will indicate your Cred surplus or deficit. In the case of a deficit, a Finance Charge may also be imposed. The billing statement will provide an itemized chronological listing of all Cred-related activity posted to your account during the billing cycle, including:
   A. all purchases;
   B. show attendances;
   C. name drops;
   D. Chunklet references;
   E. any charges or fees for Cred insurance, Cred maintenance, Cred buoyancy, Cred confluence, or Cred cancellation (if applicable); and
   F. all payments made to BIC.
2. The total amount owed will be indicated on the statement as "Your New Balance." "Your New Balance" is subject to our whims and may or may not mathematically reflect the balance of your indicated activity for the billing month. It may just be indicative of how much money we need to round out our collection of rare Bollywood soundtracks. Tough titties, baby; nobody said Cred was fair.
3. If you think there is an error in your Billing Statement, please contact:

   Bank of Indie Credit
   P.O. Box 2814
   Athens, Georgia 30612-0814 U.S. of A.

   or visit any seedy check-cashing place that has the three (3) inch thick bulletproof glass wrapping around its employees. If you survive, you've probably earned the right to dispute.
   A. After We Receive Your Complaint in Writing
      a. Within thirty (30) days of receipt, we must tell you we received the letter. If our nosy live-in brother-in-law accidentally spills bong water on your claim, we may request a facsimile.
      b. Within ninety (90) days of receiving your letter, we must either correct the error or explain. While waiting to hear a response we suggest the following activities:
   1. learn all the lyrics to *69 Love Songs*
   2. ponder if you would really join a club that would have you as a member
   3. consider opening a line of credit at a less reputable, local branch
   4. learn to cook successfully with tofu
      c. When ninety (90) days have passed, you will be responsible for all disputed charges regardless of your claim. If you still want to dispute the claim please call 1-800-555-CRED and we will be happy to connect you with a surly hipster who will surely rack your brain with obscure questions, forcing you to hang up in frustration.
   B. You may have noticed that these rules are set up to favor us after ninety (90) days. At least we're being upfront about it.

VI. CREDIT LIMIT

You agree not to exceed the credit limit established for you by us. We do not have to honor any use of your Cred, and furthermore reserve the right to decrease your Cred if and when you begin to suck. Yeah, we know...it's definitely when you begin to suck.

VII. CREDIT AUTHORIZATIONS

1. Some purchases/actions will require prior authorization by the BIC, at which time you may be asked to provide proper identification in the form of:
   A. tour passes,
   B. seven (7) inch record collections, and/or
   C. contact lists/Facebook friends.
2. We may not be able to authorize a purchase or career choice, even if you feel you have sufficient Cred at times when we lose interest in you. In the event that this occurs, BIC is absolved of all liability with regard to its effect on your Cred. You should've stayed more relevant. Whose fault is that, hmmm?

VIII. LIABILITY OF UNAUTHORIZED USE

1. You will be liable for the unauthorized use of your Cred (defined as "any use of Cred that was conducted without either your express consent or the express consent of BIC, or occurred without promise of return of appropriate levels of Cred enhancement, as defined in Section A.I.iv ["Return On Cred"] of the BIC Cred Maintenance Manual").
2. You agree to notify us promptly (or immediately after the ecstasy wears off) upon learning of the possible breach or misuse of your Cred, limited to the following:
   A. your music, self, or visage appearing on SNL;
   B. appearing in a *BUST* magazine fashion shoot;
   C. having any visual art (e.g., logos, iconography, photography, etc.) co-opted by Nike; or
   D. sharing your "views" on anything except yourself, your hygiene, cooking tips, or your music, in any venue except your journal.

IX. LOST OR STOLEN CRED

1. You agree to notify us immediately if you think your Cred has been lost or stolen, or if you think someone is using your Cred without your permission. It was probably those damn kids; nothing is sacred to them...
2. You will still be liable for unauthorized use that occurs through theft or loss, which is the only way you'll learn.

X. RATES AND FEES

1. As required by law, the rates, fees, and other costs of this credit offer are disclosed below. The Cardmember Agreement sets forth all account terms and will be sent with the card. Account terms may change. We know change is hard for you. You'll have to learn to embrace it.
2. We have the right to change your APR, fee schedule, and any other terms at any time for reasons including but not limited to lack of support of local music scene, purchasing clothing at national chains, poor tipping practices, purchasing non-cage-free eggs, and other general misuses.
3. We may impose on your BIC account the following fees, which will be added to your account and indicated on your Statement of Cred when assessed. Your account will be assessed often. Fees may include, but definitely are not limited to:
   A. Bad Hair Tax: $250 for each occurrence of faux hawk, nu-mullet, über-sidesweep, or crazy side shave. $500 for each occurrence of eyebrow shaving/waxing or shaving of shapes, phrases, and/or initials into any part of your hair. Additional fees may be assessed for any usage of Manic Panic beyond thirty five (35) years of age.
   B. Questionable Career Move Fee: a fee (commensurate with the degree of laughability and determined at the time of your next billing cycle) and/or corporal punishment for any and all of the following:
      i. contribution to a teen drama soundtrack,
      ii. be-bop Target commercial music making,
      iii. model/acting (this includes whole band sexy makeovers),
      iv. PETA ad appearances,
      v. Sirius radio hosting,
      vi. medium-hopping (e.g., becoming a comedian when your music career is deep-sixed),
      vii. any non-music-related writing (additional fees will be incurred for any memoir writing).

      Punishments may include but are not limited to:
      i. relentless, front-row megaphone heckling,
      ii. random genital punches or "sack-tapping,"
      iii. being the subject of a prominently-featured bumper sticker on Ed Begley Jr.'s Prius, or
      iv. renaming you or your band by adding "gaylord" or "pussy," (i.e., "Gaylords of Leon" or "Grizzly Pussies" (although it must be admitted that both of those are an improvement)).
   C. Skinny Jeans on Unskinny Man Fee: up to $500.01 fine for each occurrence.
   D. Going Solo/Solo Album Fee: This may also apply to any "moonlighting" you do from your main band/account, i.e., guest appearances on and/or production of other bands' records, or side bands formed "for fun." Any attempts to go it alone will be regarded as a default on your Cred and will be subject to limitless scrutiny and fees. Much like your shamelessness, the Going Solo fee has no limits.
4. Rate and Fee Schedule:
   A. Annual Percentage Rate (APR) for purchases: Variable Purchase APR — 19.99%.
   B. Other APRs:
      i. Variable Balance Transfer APR: If you have to ask I wouldn't recommend this.
      ii. Variable Cash APR: 20.90%.
      iii. Variable Penalty: Ticketmaster surcharges imposed at all independent venues for life.
      iv. Variable Rate Information: Your APRs may vary each month based on changes to the Prime Rate and your spending practices (described below). Purchase APR: 16.74% ("Spread") + Prime Rate + number of visits per month to local pornographer.
      v. Balance Transfer APR: 12.45% ("Spread") + gallons of premium gasoline purchased/number of miles traveled by fixed-gear bicycle.
      vi. Cash APR: Dependent on proximity and frequency of visits to local watering holes who still refuse to take plastic. Note: If you encounter this frequently please fill out ADDENDUM 12 ("Solicitation of Indie Card to Local Businesses") and return to drinking establishment. Power in numbers, my friend, DIY and all that shit.
      vii. Penalty APR: Henry Rollins (for remainder of this document referred to as "ENFORCER") will break your kneecaps with a lead pipe.
   C. Grace Period for Repayment of Balance for Purchases: Number of days passed since last Robert Pollard release multiplied by three (3). NOTE: For each billing cycle, the Prime Rate is determined in the month prior to the beginning of your billing cycle. In that prior month, the highest (U.S.) prime rate published in the Money Rates table of Billboard is selected.
   D. Annual Fee: $25 + $7.50 convenience fee + $3 venue fee + $2 historical preservation fee + $3.50 tip + $6 beers (domestic light only).
   E. Foreign Transaction Fee: 3% of the U.S. dollar amount will apply to transactions made in a foreign currency.
5. How To Avoid Paying Interest on Purchases (Grace Period on Credit Card Purchase): In the event you are unable to pay within the thirty (30) day period, please submit your most valuable signed collectible (record, poster, etc.) to our mailing address listed above.

XI. MUSIC CAPITALIZATION

1. No artist once deemed credible shall capitalize unduly upon the intellectual property produced by artist.
2. "Intellectual property" shall take the form of artist's
   A. compositions,
   B. recordings,
   C. lyrics,
   D. heckler comebacks,
   E. insightful podcast anecdotes,
   F. performances, and
   G. personal appearances or likenesses.
3. "Undue Capitalization" of works falling under classification of "intellectual property" as in 2. shall solely vest in the apprehending party or parties at the time of apprehension, such apprehension notwithstanding critical or cultural evaluation of the work in its unduly capitalized context.
   A. "Undue capitalization" may manifest in any of the following exploitations of artist's work:
      a. feature or background appearance in a mainstream television show,
      b. feature or background appearance in a mainstream film or initially independent film that later obtains national distribution,
      c. nonironic appearance in a television commercial including promos for television shows, or
      d. nonironic appearance in a radio commercial, appearances numbering more than once each 168 hours on terrestrial commercial radio station playlists.
   B. Any windfalls reaped in the pursuit of "Undue capitalization" must immediately be tendered to the BIC for disposal at its discretion, which means "don't get your panties in a kink if you see us driving around in that Escalade your label gave you wayyyyyy after you faded from relevance."
4. Determination of undue artist capitalization shall in no case result from eyewitness apprehension of fiduciary details surrounding exploitation of artist's work; in each instance, determination shall be preceded solely by adjudication resulting from eyewitness apprehension, primary or secondary notification of the undue capitalization to be followed by reflexive and presumptive speculation concerning fiduciary details between artist and capital source, such speculation to quantitatively exceed actual or likely capitalization sums by a factor of no less than six (6).
5. Determinations of undue artist capitalization resulting in subsequent credibility revocation shall result in a permanent Cred diminishment, such quantity(ies) not to be less than accrued Cred in the greater sum of
   A. that accrued during the time period intervening apprehender's earliest sexual awakening and dissolution of apprehender's earliest consensual sexual relationship,
   B. that accrued during college, or
   C. that accrued during the time between the earliest exposure of the apprehender to unduly capitalizing artist and the seventh (7th) mix tape or digital playlist assembled by apprehender containing either the work of unduly capitalizing artist or derivative works by other artists owing an objectively quantifiable aesthetic debt to the unduly capitalizing artist.

XII. DEFAULT

1. You will be in default under this agreement upon:
   A. your failure to age in an a semi-attractive way, which includes:
      i. excessive obesity or skinniness,
      ii. plastic surgery disasters,
      iii. ironic mustaches, and
      iv. any adoption of the "earth mother" or "urban farmer" look.
   B. your new "heavy" band becoming the subject of an article in *Decibel* magazine,
   C. your band covering any song by any pop diva,
   D. any infraction listed in *Chunklet* issue 20 (see pages 36 or 37),
   E. not owning *Chunklet* issue 20.

XIII. COLLECTION COSTS

If, in the event of a Cred account default, we refer your account to a collection agency, we may charge you our collection costs inclusive of any and/or all of the following:
   A. smear campaign fees,
   B. reimbursement of past ticket/merchandise costs, or
   C. brainwashing/deprogramming costs.

XIV. CRED CANCELLATION

Termination and/or reduction of your Cred is subject to the published, unpublished, real, and/or imagined requirements and applicable laws set forth by Chunklet and the Bank of Indie Cred, and can occur at any time and for any reason, but will absolutely happen on purchase of anything by a band that was featured as background music on *Grey's Anatomy*.

XV. CLOSING YOUR ACCOUNT

1. You can cancel or close your account, without penalty, by writing the BIC and simply admitting your irrelevance. If you manage that, you may even get a little residual respect for being proactive. On close of your account, you are responsible for all outstanding Cred owed to us according to this agreement. Holders of closed accounts are subject to the following normalizing actions:
   A. personal record collections are subject to inspection and partial/full relinquishment;
   B. hard drives will be erased, with particular attention paid to music (whether legally acquired or pirated), creative output (regardless of medium), contact lists and/or "little black books" and cached porn;
   C. further creative output will be mercilessly debased in an effort to overcome any illusion of residual Cred;
   D. all past accomplishments will be reduced to "Overrated" status; and
   E. and your BIC card will be relinquished to us.
2. Pending a Full Cred Conduct Audit, further penalties may be enacted on closure of your account, up to and including becoming a BIC Cautionary Tale/Punch Line and being featured in BIC promotional content/breakroom educational materials. If you are fortunate, we will forget all about you.

XVI. ADDITIONAL TERMS AND MISCELLANY

1. Platinum services are only available to BIC members who bought their first record before 1977. BIC reserves the right to change the benefit features associated with your card at any time.
2. This offer is available only to applicants who reside in the United States. Cards cannot be issued to applicants residing in the states of Iowa and Wisconsin, because seriously — have you ever been there? It's not like there's Cred hiding in the cornfields or dairy farms. We've got our own rep to worry about.
3. The credit disclosures given above were printed October 1997 and were accurate as of that date. The credit information is subject to change after the printing date. You should contact us for any change after the printing date by writing us at Bank of Indie Credit, P.O. Box 2814, Athens, GA 30612-0814.

XVII. YOUR BILLING RIGHTS

This notice tells you about your rights and our responsibilities under the Fair Indie Credit Billing Act.

You agree that the Bank of Indie Credit has the right to obtain a current Cred Report in connection with any of the following triggering events:
1. BIC's review of your initial application,
2. in connection with any reviewed charge to your account,
3. annual renewal review of your account,
4. change to your credit line,
5. pending any cover article about you to be published in *Razorcake*,
6. any time the BIC has had too much to drink and needs something to do while on the internet.

The BIC has the right to report to others its Cred experience with you. Upon your request, we will tell you the name and address of each consumer reporting agency from which we obtained information about you, as well as three (3) that we did not. It's up to you to figure out which is which.

XVIII. CREDIBLE RESPONSE TO ROCK-INDUCED ANNOYANCE

1. Probable Causes

   The pursuit of Cred can lead applicants to overexpose themselves to the elements, often resulting in adverse reactions. Rock-Induced Annoyance (RIA) is a covert mental process with both acoustic and nonacoustic determinants, preying on an uninitiated Hipster's untrained Irony and Apathy responses. RIA is entirely free of cognitive or emotional influences, so it is not a simple behavior such as a complaint (which may or may not be motivated by annoyance) nor a simple and immediate sensation like loudness. Whereas loudness may cause a slightly more violent-than-normal startle response or the use of makeshift toilet paper "earplugs," RIA's symptoms are much more pronounced and potentially Cred-damaging.
2. General Symptoms
   A. Defense and muscle tension reflex, including but not limited to:
      i. eye-rolling
      ii. shoulder-drooping
      iii. slow head-shaking
      iv. arm-folding
      v. cradling of head or face in hands
      vi. flipping of "the bird"
      vii. cupping of hands around mouth to offer "advice" to the stage
   B. Involuntary nervous system response, including but not limited to:
      i. heart palpitations
      ii. blood pressure increase
      iii. pupil dilation
      iv. vestibular system response

   Symptoms are known to intensify under these circumstances:
   A. use of timed and sequenced light shows, with or without "flashpots,"
   B. any use of musical sequencing devices,
   C. on-stage costuming involving clown makeup, or
   D. perception of the phrase "this next one's a cover" emitting from the stage.
3. Special Notice

   Extended exposure to RIA has been known to result in direct changes of stool frequency and weight. Healthy, credible subjects exposed to RIA (having an A-weighted sound level of 105dB for fifty (50) minutes after a standardized meal of a KFC six-piece Extra Crispy meal [all white meat] and approx. 8 oz. of Johnny Walker Black) showed a significantly delayed, but prolonged, increase of postprandial sigmoid colon motility. Documented cases have produced expressive fecal shapes bearing resemblance to Steinberger bass guitars, thoracic musculature of Iggy Pop, and the state of Idaho.
4. What You Should Do If You Think You're Experiencing RIA

   If you think you're experiencing any of the symptoms of RIA, you are advised to remove yourself from the environment in question (preferably prior to the initiation of the first encore) and find the nearest BIC-sponsored Cred-'N'-Med 24-Hour Clinic. The BIC cannot guarantee the efficacy of any non-sanctioned Cred preservation and/or medical facility.

ENCLOSURES

I have included: ☐ Photographs ☐ Photocopies ☐ Cancelled checks ☐ Concealed cash ☐ Newspaper clippings ☐ Otherwise pertinent information

...that will assist the Bank of Indie Credit in the expeditious processing of my application. I understand that none of the enclosed material will be returned to me, and I forfeit any and all rights to ownership thereof.

Name (First, Middle, Last)

Signature

Date (Month/Day/Year)